MW01205745

Culture and Customs of Australia

INDONESIA
PAPUA NEW GUINEA
Aratura Sea
Timor Sea
Indian Ocean
Coral Sea
Great Barrier Reef
Darwin
Cairns
Townsville
Mackay
Alice Springs
Brisbane
Perth
Fremantle
Great Australian Bight
Adelaide
Sydney
CANBERRA
Melbourne
Tasman Sea
Devonport
Hobart
Tasmania
Indian Ocean
0 500 km
0 500 mi
Lord Howe Island and Macquarie Island not shown

Culture and Customs of Australia

LAURIE CLANCY

GREENWOOD PRESS
Westport, Connecticut • London

Library of Congress Cataloging-in-Publication Data

Clancy, Laurie, 1942–
Culture and customs of Australia / Laurie Clancy.
p. cm.
Includes bibliographical references and index.
ISBN 0–313–32169–8 (alk. paper)
1. Australia—Social life and customs. I. Title.
DU107.C545 2004
306'.0994—dc22 2003027515

British Library Cataloguing in Publication Data is available.

Library of Congress Catalog Card Number: 2003027515
ISBN: 0–313–32169–8

First published in 2004

Greenwood Press, 88 Post Road West, Westport, CT 06881
An imprint of Greenwood Publishing Group, Inc.
www.greenwood.com

Printed in the United States of America

The paper used in this book complies with the Permanent Paper Standard issued by the National Information Standards Organization (Z39.48–1984).

10 9 8 7 6 5 4 3 2 1

To Neelam

Contents

Preface

MOST AMERICANS HAVE heard of Australia, but very few could say much about it. There is a joke in the American film *Dumb and Dumber* where a woman says she is Austrian and one of the heroes says, "Throw another prawn on the barbie," in homage to the Australian tourist advertisements featuring Aussie actor Paul Hogan of "Crocodile Dundee" fame. A similar mistake occurred in Japan some years ago when antifreeze was discovered in some Austrian wines and sales of Australian wines plummeted.

Kangaroos, tennis players, and perhaps more recently wine, film actors, and the idea of Australia as an excellent tourist destination would sum up the extent of many Americans' knowledge of the country. In the 1970s I spent two very pleasant years in the United States on a Harkness Fellowship. During that period, on only one occasion did Australia make the front page of the newspaper with a big story and that was when a girder on the Westgate bridge, then being constructed in Melbourne, collapsed, and 32 men fell to their deaths. Many people I met were surprised at how fluently I spoke English. Some, on the other hand, found my accent incomprehensible.

To some extent, of course, the situation has improved, but Australians, saturated as they are by American culture, still know far more about Americans than vice versa. Even when Australia became only one of two Forces of the Willing prepared to commit troops to the war against Saddam Hussein, its tiny contribution received very little attention from the international press, which was totally focused on Great Britain's role.

And yet Americans would be surprised if they understood how much their country preoccupies the consciousness of Australians, even if in deeply ambivalent ways. Ever since Prime Minister John Curtin made his famous World War II declaration that Australia would now look to the United States for protection and assistance rather than Britain, there has been a seismic change in the attitudes of Australians toward the United States. Beginning with Prime Minister Harold Holt's famous "All the way with LBJ" in the 1960s to Prime Minister John Howard's support of the war against Iraq, eliciting President George W. Bush's eulogy of him as a "man of steel," successive Australian governments have bent over backward (with varying degrees of flexibility) to demonstrate their allegiance to the United States.

The ambivalence is there among some politicians from the left side of Labor. It is to be seen in the huge marches against the Vietnam War in the early 1970s and even in the very considerable protests that accompanied the Australian government's commitment to the invasion of Iraq. It is there to be seen also among Australian writers. In their studies of the presence of American troops in Australia during World War II, novelists such as Xavier Herbert (*Soldiers' Women*, 1961) and Dymphna Cusack and Florence James (*Come in Spinner*, 1951) endorsed the then widely held view of the American troops as "over-paid, over-sexed and over here."

Younger writers, however, such as Michael Wilding, Peter Carey, and Frank Moorhouse, have a much more complex view. While disapproving of Australian participation in the Vietnam War, they are deeply drawn to the dynamic force of American culture, and the conflict is vividly present in the title of Moorhouse's collection *The Americans, Baby* (1972), and Carey's unusually elegiac short story "American Dreams" (1968).

Australia's isolation from the rest of the world, something many Australians don't fully comprehend until they step onto a plane on an international flight for the first time and discover the length of the trip to the nearest destination, has had both its good points (a sense of security, a freedom from invasion) and its bad (parochialism, complacency), but it is an isolation that the new technologies are rapidly bringing to an end, or at least radically qualifying. The title of a book by one of Australia's most distinguished historians, Geoffrey Blainey, was *The Tyranny of Distance* (1968), a phrase that has passed into the language, but it is a tyranny that has been largely overthrown.

In the post–World War II years and especially through the 1950s the image persisted of Australia as a kind of benign Sleepy Hollow, free from the fears and dangers that beset countries to its immediate north or in Europe, for example. No invasions by foreign powers, no civil wars, no fierce battles with the original occupiers of the land (though there is now general recognition that Aboriginal resistance to white aggression was considerably greater than originally thought), virtually full employment until the 1960s—all these are thought to have created a kind of benign, vacuous never-never land. But as with the Eisenhower years in the United States, the Menzies years (1949–1966) in Australia papered over a number of divisions that would reveal themselves only later. They were, after all, the years of attempts to ban the Communist Party, the years of the Stolen Generation, with Aboriginal parents forcibly dispossessed of their children by official government policy, and of mass immigration with its enormous consequences.

Since the 1960s and 1970s or so, in fact, Australia has been a country in a state of almost continual reinvention of itself. There has probably been no country in the world that has been so fascinated with the question of its own identity. As one academic pointed out, Ulysses on his long journey around the world did not constantly put in at each harbor and seek to assure himself of his own Greekness. Australian writers' and intellectuals' obsessive reexamination of the country's past combined with international movements and events to produce a series of crises and transformations. In 1967 Australians voted in a referendum to grant Aborigines full citizenship. This was followed eventually by High Court decisions granting land rights to Aborigines and rejecting the concept that Aborigines had no previous possession of the land because they did not, in the conventional Western sense, settle on it—the so-called *terra nullius* concept.

Australian feminist Germaine Greer's *The Female Eunuch* (1971) began a debate in Australia about the rights and roles of women in society that is still raging. Absurdly anachronistic censorship laws were abolished. The concept of New Australians gave way to the much more complex one of multiculturalism, the idea that immigrants to Australia could become members of the mainstream society while still retaining and valuing the most important elements in their own culture.

The conservative Coalition's Senate's rejection of the Supply Bill in 1975 and the Governor-General's subsequent dismissal of a democratically elected prime minister set in train the debate about Australia becoming a republic and culminated in the unsuccessful referendum of 1999. It is a debate and a movement that shows no signs of dying. In the late 1980s the Labor government implemented a series of policies that would lead to quite radical changes in the economy (the floating of the dollar, the reduction or abolition of tariffs) and in education. And finally, with the turning away of the *Tampa* (September, 2001) and its hundreds of refugees on board, came the debate about people attempting to enter Australia unlawfully and the use of detention camps.

It could be argued, then, that Australia is a country whose profile is changing almost constantly. This book attempts, as objectively as is possible, to document these changes, as well as to look back at the country's past, and place them in some kind of historical context. It is written primarily for an audience of non-Australians, but I hope it will be useful to the citizens of my own country as well.

Acknowledgments

A number of people have assisted me in the preparation of this book. I should like to thank in particular Professor Roy Boland of La Trobe University, Alun Chapman, Emeritus Professor Jack Clancy, formerly of the Royal Melbourne Institute of Technology, John Leonard, Bridget McDonnell, Craig McGregor, Professor Stuart McIntyre of the University of Melbourne, Emeritus Professor John McLaren, formerly of the Victoria University of Technology, Murray and Judy McLeod, Dr. Glenn Mulligan, Tim Shannon, and John Timlin. All of these read at least one chapter and in some cases the entire manuscript, and made useful suggestions and criticisms. Any errors, of course, are my own. My son Jacob helped me considerably with research and my nephew Bill gave me valuable computer instruction. Luna Shepherd proved a wonderfully able research assistant and was largely responsible for the selection of illustrations. My thanks are due to the following people who supplied excellent photographs at short notice and considerable inconvenience: Anna Clemann, Michael Hanrahan, Alice and Jennifer Macklin, Graham McCarter and Craig McGregor. I am also especially indebted to Wendi Schaufer, of Greenwood Publishing Group, who was an extremely efficient and patient editor, and to Impressions Book and Journal Services. As always, I am indebted to the patience and intelligence of my partner Neelam Maharaj.

Chronology

60,000 B.C.?	Arrival of the first Aborigines on the mainland of Australia
1770	English explorer James Cook's discovery of the east coast of Australia
1788	Arrival of the First Fleet from England
1790	Arrival of the Second Fleet
1803	First British settlement of Tasmania
1808	The rum rebellion
1810	Governor Lachlan Macquarie takes office
1813	The Blue Mountains crossed by Gregory Blaxland, William Lawson, and William Wentworth
1825	Van Diemen's Land becomes a separate colony
1829	Settlement established at Swan River, Western Australia
1835	John Batman and J. P. Fawkner settle independently at Port Phillip
1840	Transportation of convicts to New South Wales abolished (later rescinded)
1851	Port Phillip District of New South Wales becomes the Colony of Victoria; discovery of gold in Australia

1852	Act passed to found University of Sydney; British Government abolishes transportation to the eastern colonies
1854	Eureka Stockade, Ballarat, Victoria
1855	Responsible government proclaimed in New South Wales, Victoria, and Tasmania; Van Diemen's land officially renamed
1856	Responsible government proclaimed in South Australia
1859	Queensland formed as separate state
1861	Death of Robert O'Hara Burke and William John Wills
1866	Sir Henry Parkes's Public Schools Act passed
1868	Last group of convicts transported to Western Australia
1875	Ernest Giles leads expedition from Overland Telegraph Line to Perth
1880	Ned Kelly hanged, Melbourne jail, November 11
1885	Gold found in Kimberleys and first Western Australia rush starts
1889	First art exhibition of the Heidelberg School
1890	The Maritime Strike, almost a general strike; responsible government established in Western Australia; University of Tasmania founded
1891	Shearers' Strike, Queensland; First Labor Party formed, New South Wales
1893	Gold found at Kalgoorlie, Western Australia
1899	Draft Constitution Bill accepted by all colonies except Western Australia; Australian troops sent to Boer War; Australia's first Labor government (lasting six days) formed in Queensland
1901	Federation
1902	Women enfranchised for Federal elections
1907	The first basic wage declared by Commonwealth of Conciliation and Arbitration
1909	Explorer Douglas Mawson and his party reach Antarctica; University of Queensland founded
1911	University of Western Australia established

1915	The Gallipoli invasion, April 15, celebrated every year as Anzac Day
1917	W. M. Hughes forms the Nationalist Party out of the Liberal Party and his own group of disaffected Labor members
1918	Sir John Monash takes command of Australian troops in France, not long before the war ends on November 11
1920	Australian Country Party and Communist Party of Australia formed
1922	QUANTAS Airlines brings in first regular air service
1925	Acts to provide widows' pensions and 44-hour workweek passed in New South Wales
1931	Appointment of first Australian Governor General, Sir Isaac Isaacs; establishment of the Statute of Westminster, ensuring the legislative independence of the dominions
1933	Antarctic region of about 4 million square miles becomes an Australian territory
1941	Labor takes office under John Curtin and announces a change of policy
1944	Court case over award of Archibald Prize to William Dobell
1945	Howard Florey becomes first Australian to win Nobel Prize—for medicine
1947	Immigration program begins; 40-hour workweek introduced
1949	Snowy Mountains hydroelectric project launched
1950	Colombo plan to encourage Asian students to travel to Australia and study there with financial assistance from the Federal government adopted
1951	Referendum to ban Communist Party defeated
1952	Victories by Australian women athletes at the Olympic Games; Jimmy Carruthers becomes first Australian to win a world boxing title (bantamweight)
1956	Olympic Games held in Melbourne
1958	Entry permit replaces dictation test as a mean of controlling immigration

1962	Sydney and Melbourne linked by standard-gauge railway; right to vote in Commonwealth elections extended to all Aborigines; Rod Laver becomes the first Australian to win the Grand Slam of major tennis titles
1965	Roma Mitchell appointed Australia's first woman judge; Australian troops including conscripts committed to Vietnam
1966	Decimal currency adopted
1969	Commonwealth Arbitration Court accepts principle of equal pay for women
1972	Australian Labor Party elected to power for the first time in 23 years
1973	Sydney Opera House opened by Queen Elizabeth II
1975	Dismissal of the Whitlam government by the Governor General; Liberal-National coalition easily wins the subsequent election
1992	Mabo judgment, acknowledging land rights to Aborigines
1993	Federal legislation passed, recognizing Native Title
1996	The Wik case, refuting the concept of *terra nullius*
1999	Australians vote "no" to becoming a republic
2000	Olympic Games held in Sydney
2001	The *Tampa,* carrying hundreds of would-be migrants to Australia claiming refugee status, is turned away from the mainland; 10 days later the government creates the so-called Pacific solution by which countries are paid to detain illegal immigrants
2002	The Bali bombing by terrorists occurs; 202 people including 88 Australians die

1

The Land, People, and History

Early History

Australia 120 million years ago was a startlingly different country from the one that now exists, partly because the world was a much cooler place and far less of it was under water than is now the case. Geographically it would have born little resemblance to the country and landscape that now exist. New Zealand and New Caledonia were still firmly attached to the eastern coast of Australia. New Guinea was merely a couple of islands lying near the north coast of Australia. To the south, Antarctica was still attached to Australia, but there were signs of the developing split that was to set Australia moving northward around 80 million years later. Most of the countries now surrounding Australia lay well to the south of their present position, with part of Australia, all of New Zealand, and possibly New Caledonia, lying within the Antarctic Circle.

Even 80 million years ago, Australia had been connected to Antarctica, New Guinea, the eastern part of the Indonesian island of Sulawesi, and a few other smaller islands. The first Aborigines came to Australia from Southeast Asia at least as long as 40,000 years ago and probably longer. At that time, Tasmania was still joined to the Australian continent. The gap between the land of Australia and Indonesia was far shorter than it is now.

The first settlers in Australia were nomads who hoarded little food, ignored husbandry, were not concerned with building houses or fences, wore few clothes, and carried few possessions. Estimates of their numbers range between 250,000 and one million, many living on land that white settlers would later find arid and virtually uninhabitable, although others occupied verdant pastures, which were quickly taken away from them when the white settlements began to spread. The Aborigines spoke as many as 250 languages. They were a hunter-gatherer society who held as firmly to the principle of communal property as the whites who came after them held to the sanctity of private property.

The slow but inexorable rising of the seas as the world's climate warmed 10 thousand years ago eventually made Australia an island, separating it from New Guinea and Tasmania and making Timor far less accessible. The Aborigines were almost completely cut off from the rest of the world.

Australia had existed for many years as an idea in the minds of Europeans before it became a reality. Portuguese and Dutch ships observed the west coast of Australia in the early part of the sixteenth century. William Dampier recorded observations of Aborigines on the northwest coast of Western Australia in 1688. English Explorer James Cook discovered the eastern coast of Australia in 1770, while on a voyage to observe the transit of Venus and hence perhaps to calculate the distance of the sun from the earth. After his favorable report on the promise of Botany Bay, and the rebellion of the North American colonies made the deportation of convicts to America no longer possible, Australia assumed a new status in the eyes of the British leaders. In addition—and the relative importance of these two motives has been much debated—Australia was also seen as the possible source of commercial benefit, in such areas as timber and flax.

THE EUROPEAN INVASION

Optimistic about the promise of the new land, the First Fleet sailed from England on May 13, 1787, under the leadership of Captain Arthur Phillip (who was to become governor), and arrived some eight months later. What they confronted was a landscape and a climate so alien that they might as well have been on another planet. For many years poets and painters struggled and failed to do justice to the unfamiliarity of the spectacle with which they were confronted—brown grass; twisted, stunted gum trees; strange creatures like the kangaroo, platypus, and flying fox; seasons that were the reverse of those in the hemisphere from which they had come.

The early years of white settlement hardly lived up to Cook's vision. The land proved to be less abundant in natural riches than expected and, despite Governor Phillip's relatively enlightened policies in regard to the Aborigines, the gulf between the two cultures was so vast that it could not be breached. Inevitably, misunderstandings led to violence.

Kangaroo. Photo by Alice Macklin.

As well as the Aborigines, there was a second source of misunderstanding and tension. A remarkably high percentage of the convicts were Irish—perhaps as many as 30 percent—and inevitably argument has centered around how many of these were political prisoners as against common criminals. Of the 2,086 convicts transported from Ireland between 1791 and 1803, about 600 were convicted for riot and sedition. There has been similar debate about the gravity of their crimes, with some historians questioning the traditional view that petty misdemeanors led to long sentences in exile.

In the wake of the Irish rebellion of 1798 against British rule, between January 1800 and June 1802, 565 Irish convicts arrived, and there was always going to be tension between Catholics and the Protestant ascendancy. A feeble Catholic rebellion was brutally put down in 1804 and its leaders executed. However, by then, Governor Philip King had accepted Catholics' right to practice their religion and to hear Mass, unlike the situation in England itself, though they did not have their own priests until 1820.

Changes in the Population

Although there were many calls for the end of transporting convicts from quite early in the history of the community, its value as a source of cheap labor made it too attractive at first to be resisted. Between 1821 and 1830, 21,780 convicts were transported to New South Wales and 10,000 to the then Van Diemen's Land (later renamed Tasmania). Men outnumbered women 7 to 1. When transportation finally ceased in Western Australia in 1868, about 162,000 convicts had been transported, of whom about 25,000 were women.

The government began to encourage free settlers to migrate, with promises of land in proportion to whatever capital they could bring with them, with the additional lure of free convict labor. Some came to make or expand their fortunes in a land that seemed to offer greater opportunity to the talented and the daring than did England. Others came to be reunited with loved ones. In 1833, for instance, 8,000 people arrived, of whom 2,500 were free.

Calls for the end of convictism became more strident, though they had a variety of sometimes totally opposed justifications. The transportation of convicts to New South Wales finally ended in 1840, though it continued in Van Diemen's Land until 1853. It was after it ended that the name of the state was changed to Tasmania, as if to indicate symbolically a new beginning.

At the same time, especially under the rule of Governor Lachlan Macquarie (1810–21), those convicts who had shown genuine ability to reform were encouraged to take their place as free citizens and became known as *emancipists*, as against the *exclusivists*—those who saw themselves as gentry and refused to associate with ex-convicts. Emancipists could be granted land and even hold office, although Macquarie's reforms were fiercely resisted by the established classes, such as the colony's principal chaplain, the Reverend Samuel Marsden (1765–1838), or the landed proprietors of the colony such as (most notably) John Macarthur (1767–1834).

Macarthur himself left a mixed legacy. Arriving as a lieutenant in the New South Wales Corps in 1790, he organized a group of officers to purchase rum from ships arriving from overseas. As rum (a generic term for all spirits) was virtually currency in the colony at that time, the monopoly that the Corps commanded—even paying convict employees in rum at exorbitant prices—gave the officers immense power. Two early governors, John Hunter and Philip King, tried and failed to break the "Rum Corps," and when a new governor, William Bligh, who had famously survived the mutiny on the ship *Bounty*, also attempted to end the trafficking, Macarthur took advantage of the widespread dislike Bligh's arrogance had aroused to have him arrested and deposed—the so-called Rum Rebellion of 1808. Not until Governor Macquarie arrived with his own regiment of troops was the monopolistic power of the Rum Corps finally broken.

Yet Macarthur was also in many respects a man of vision who was one of the first to realize the immense possibilities of the colony. Given generous grants of land, he saw potential wealth in raising merino sheep with finer wool than that currently imported into England. With his wife Elizabeth, he was heavily instrumental in establishing what was to become for more than a century Australia's major export industry. Macarthur's legacy was that by 1850 wool amounted to more than 90 percent of Australian exports. Not for nothing was the cliché "Australia rode to prosperity on the sheep's back" coined.

Macquarie, with Phillip, one of Australia's most enlightened governors, commissioned many of Sydney's then finest buildings under the brilliant design of convict architect Francis Greenway, and encouraged diversification of exports into such areas as whale oil, seals, and later cedar felling. These economic developments were complemented by the establishment of schooling designed to further the efforts of the colonials to adapt to a new environment and train young workers and artisans accordingly.

THE STATES

In time Van Diemen's Land, the Port Phillip District, and Moreton Bay were all separated from New South Wales, while Western Australia and South Australia were distinctive as separate and free settlements, the latter learning—sometimes—from the troubles of the former. Western Australia did, however, find itself suffering from the lack of laborers, and between 1850 and 1869, years after transportation had ended in the east, imported 10,000 convicts. But it was the discovery of gold in the 1890s that truly transformed the state. It was persuaded to join the rest of the country in Federation, partly through the promise of a rail connection with the east. This was finally completed in 1917, with one section, at 300 miles across the Nullarbor Plains, forming the longest straight stretch of rail track in the world.

In 1835 John Batman, the son of convicts, joined with a number of other men in forming the Port Phillip Association and was duly sent by them to negotiate the purchase of land from the Aborigines. After amicable dealings, the chiefs of the Dutigallar tribe handed over 100,000 acres in exchange for 20 pairs of scissors, 50 handkerchiefs, 12 red shirts, 4 flannel jackets, 4 suits of clothes, 50 pounds of flour, and a yearly tribute of 50 pairs of blankets, 50 knives, 50 tomahawks, 50 pairs of scissors, 50 looking-glasses, 20 suits of clothing, and 2 tons of flour. Later Batman took possession of another 500,000 acres in the vicinity of the Yarra River. Thus was the settlement of Port Phillip (later the state of Victoria) founded. Upon hearing of this transaction, however, Sir Richard Bourke, the governor of New South Wales, immediately declared it null and void.

The newly named city of Melbourne, rough and violent at first, steadily grew, until by the end of 1840 its population was over 10,000. But as conditions in Melbourne rapidly improved, the necessity of new settlers having to move further out rendered them more vulnerable to the Aborigines, who had become increasingly hostile as they saw their lands and wildlife breeding grounds taken from them.

Meanwhile the district of Port Phillip grew until in 1850 the Imperial Parliament passed the Australian Colonies Government Act, which made the District the separate colony of Victoria. The Act also gave to Victoria, Van Diemen's Land, and South Australia their own Legislative Councils on the New South Wales model and invited all the colonies except Western Australia to submit their own proposals for self-government.

Settlers had also moved into the northern part of New South Wales, later to be christened Queensland. In 1822 a new penal colony had been established near the mouth of the Brisbane River in Moreton Bay, under the command of Captain Patrick Logan, one of the most brutal figures in Australian history. But isolation proved to be insufficient to deter settlers. By 1840 squatters had brought their flocks overland to the rich Darling Downs district on the western slopes of the Great Dividing Range from Moreton Bay. Inevitably, as the population grew, there were demands for separation from New South Wales and, under the leadership of the Presbyterian minister the Reverend Dr. John Dunmore Lang, who had also been influential in helping to secure independence for Victoria, Queensland was proclaimed a colony in 1859.

In 1836 another settlement was established under the guidance of Colonel William Light, with Adelaide named as the capital of the state of South Australia. Under the governorship of Lieutenant-Colonel George Gawler and later Captain George Grey, the settlement steadily pushed out, encroaching onto the most fertile areas of the Aborigines. Once again, the pattern of initial good will toward the Aborigines and attempts to inculcate the rudiments of Christian culture in them gave way, when they resisted, to sorties of revenge and retribution.

Explorers

A common theme throughout the nineteenth century is the attempts of explorers to open up a land that proved extremely resistant to their efforts. In fact, however, the earliest explorers were maritime ones. In 1799 a young naval officer named George Bass (1771–1803) had explored the eastern coastline south of Sydney in some detail, discovered Western Port on the southern coast and circumnavigated Van Diemen's Land, en route examining the estuaries of the Tamar and Derwent rivers. In 1803 he disappeared on a voyage to South America, but the strait of water that divides Tasmania from the mainland is named after him.

Dales Gorge lookout, Western Australia. Photo by Jennifer Macklin.

He had been accompanied on several of these exploratory voyagers by another young officer named Matthew Flinders (1774–1814), and it was he who explored the coast of Nuyts Land at the head of the Great Australian Bight as well as the Victorian coast and much of the South Australian coast. He followed Tasman in making the first circumnavigation of Australia, mapping the coast in detail.

On land, Sydney had been initially hemmed in by the Great Dividing Range until a path was finally found in 1813 by three men who sound like a firm of lawyers, Gregory Blaxland, William Wentworth, and William Lawson—though little mention is ever made of the four convicts who accompanied them. This opened the way for pastoralists to follow with sheep and cattle.

John Oxley (1783–1828) and an assistant followed the rivers downstream south, west, and northwest from the Bathurst district, coming by 1820 to believe that there was an inland sea into which the western rivers flowed. In 1824, Hamilton Hume (1797–1873) and W. H. Hovell (1786–1875), responded to Governor Brisbane's request that they ascertain whether any large and navigable rivers flowed over the territory to the south of the Goulburn Plains. After they crossed what was later to be christened the Murray River they found rich and abundant land and pushed further south.

In 1829 an English army officer, Charles Sturt (1795–1869), and his party headed out on an expedition to the Murrumbidgee River to see whether it flowed into the Darling River, or emptied itself into the sea on the southern coast of the colony. Although the south and east parts of Australia were fairly quickly mapped, heading westward was a different proposition. In 1844 Sturt made the last of several expeditions in search of the inland sea he felt sure existed but was once again unsuccessful. Thomas Mitchell (1791–1855) led four expeditions into the interior, two of which resulted in the discovery of rich land in what is now known as the Western District of Victoria and in south central Queensland, the country around the Warrego, Belyando, and Maranoa rivers. So impressed was Mitchell by the country between the Murray River and the Victorian coast west of Port Phillip that he famously called it "Australia Felix."

E(dward) J(ohn) Eyre (1815–1901) became an experienced bushman after arriving in Sydney in 1833 and soon took on the role of overlander—a man who moved stock from the east coast to the west. He delivered stock to the new Adelaide market, explored the dry north where he discovered Lake Torrens and Lake Eyre and became obsessed with finding a stock route that would lead from Adelaide to Western Australia. Even after incredible hardships and near miraculous escapes he never gave up the idea and was finally successful.

In 1848 Ludwig Leichhardt (1813–48?), who four years earlier had led an expedition from Moreton Bay to Port Essington, set out again with the aim of crossing to the west coast of Australia. He and his party were never heard from again. In 1860 Robert O'Hara Burke (1821–61) and William John Wills (1834–61) set out from Melbourne on an expedition to travel north to the Gulf of Carpentaria. They died on the return journey in the cruelest and most ironic of circumstances, ignoring the efforts of friendly natives to save them. In July 1862, some 18 months after Burke's party had reached the Gulf, McDouall Stuart (1815–66) and a small party reached the Arafura sea, not far from the present site of Darwin. He had discovered a route from Port Augusta to Darwin that had waterholes all along it, and a few years later it formed the basis for the Overland Telegraph line that would eventually connect Australia to the rest of the world.

The final explorations were carried out in 1874 by John Forrest (1847–1918), later premier of Western Australia, who successfully led an expedition from west to east, and Ernest Giles (1835–97), who crossed the central deserts in both directions. The vast, arid inland had finally been mapped.

The latter-day equivalents of these men would be the airmen—Ross and Keith Smith, Charles Kingsford-Smith, Bert Hinkler—who constantly established new records for intercontinental and international flights and as frequently broke them. But there was also the remarkable trek of Douglas Mawson (1882–1958), who led the Australasian Antarctic Expedition in 1911 with Belgrave Ninnis and Xavier Mertz. When Ninnis and his dog team broke though the ice and disappeared after they had progressed 500 kilometers from their base, Mertz and Mawson set about returning. They ate the dogs as they progressed, not knowing their livers were rich in Vitamin A and potentially toxic. Mertz died after 25 days but Mawson miraculously survived, allowing Australia to lay claim to large areas of the Antarctic. He returned on further expeditions in 1929 and 1931.

The geologist Cecil Madigan (1889–1947), who accompanied Mawson on the 1911 expedition, much later, in 1929, made the first aerial surveys of central Australia, including Lake Eyre and the edge of the Simpson Desert. In 1930, he traveled by camel through the MacDonnell, James, and Waterhouse ranges (near Alice Springs). In 1939 he led a party of 9 men and 19 camels across the Simpson from Andado Station in the Northern Territory to Birdsville in Queensland.

Bushrangers

Explorers form an important part of nineteenth-century Australian mythology, along with—on the other side of the fence—outlaws and bushrangers. Of these, unquestionably the most famous was Ned Kelly, whose life, deeds. and character have been recorded over and over again, in films, plays, biographies, dance, folk songs and ballads, many times in novels, and perhaps most famously, in a series of paintings by Sidney Nolan. Born in 1855, Kelly was the eldest son of an Irish ex-convict, John "Red" Kelly, who was transported to Van Diemen's Land in 1842, went to the mainland upon release, and married Ellen Quinn in 1850. After his death, Ellen moved with her children to a small selection in northeastern Victoria. There, as rural Irish poor and small-time cattle duffers (rustlers), a practice more or less widely accepted, they were frequently subjected to harassment by the police and Ned served several short terms of imprisonment.

Accused (almost certainly falsely) of shooting a policeman, Ned went into hiding with his brother Dan and two other men, Joe Byrne and Steve Hart, while his mother received a sentence of three years in jail for her role in the alleged attempted murder. Shortly afterward the gang came unexpectedly upon four policemen, and in the ensuing engagement shot and killed three of them. The fourth survived to give evidence at Kelly's trial.

Now outlaws and inevitably doomed, the Kelly gang survived for nearly two years, robbing banks, carousing with sympathetic locals, and in the end attempting to set off a revolution through a bizarre scheme to derail a special police train, sent up from Melbourne to catch them, and murder the occupants. It was foiled by the local schoolteacher who escaped and warned the police. Kelly appeared at the end in a self-fashioned suit of steel, which became the central motif for Sir Sydney Nolan's famous two series of paintings on the outlaw, perhaps the best known Australian paintings in existence. He was captured, sentenced to death, and executed on November 11, 1880.

The huge mass of material on the Kellys suggests something of the hold they developed on the Australian imagination, though attitudes range from condemnation through a deep-seated ambivalence to near idolatry. Ned's own state of mind in the final days is revealed in the so-called Jerilderie Letter, named after a small town in the district. Composed over two months and comprising 56 pages, it reveals a tormented, if not deranged, state of mind. Kelly defended his shooting of the police on the grounds that "this cannot be called willful murder, for I was compelled to shoot them in my own defence or lie down like a cur and die."

From all accounts Ned died bravely, his last words allegedly being "Such is life," which later became the title for a famous Australian novel by Joseph Furphy. After the sentencing, Judge Sir Redmond Barry having condemned him to death by hanging, Kelly said calmly, "Yes, I will meet you there." A fortnight later Barry died, collapsing from a heart attack. The legend of Ned Kelly lives on; a well-known Australian colloquialism is "as game [brave] as Ned Kelly." Most recently it has been celebrated in Peter Carey's Booker Prize–winning *The True History of the Kelly Gang* (2000) and a film based on Robert Drewe's novel *Our Sunshine* (2001).

THE 1850s AND THE EFFECTS OF THE GOLD RUSH

The 1850s was one of the most turbulent decades Australia had known. It began with one of the worst of what would subsequently prove to be many hugely destructive bush fires—on "Black Thursday," the sixth day of February, 1851. Less than three months later, gold was discovered in Victoria and the country would never be the same again.

The population rapidly expanded as immigrants arrived to work on the fields. From 405,000 in 1850 it grew to exceed one million people in 1858. In Victoria, where most gold was discovered, the figures were especially astonishing; during the 1850s it jumped from 76,000 to 540,000 by 1860, making it for a time the most populous colony in Australia with one of the highest standards of living in the world. Gold became the second largest industry, after wool.

The mania for gold brought men from all walks of life together, working indistinguishably side by side with no chance that worth would win over luck. It ended any possibility that transportation of convicts could be resumed (punish a criminal by sending him to a goldfield!) and confirmed conservatives' worst fears as to the leveling nature of Australian society. To the workers it acted as a catalyst for the coming of what they envisaged as a genuinely democratic society in which every man was as good as his master. It rekindled ambitions of nationhood.

When Governor Charles La Trobe of Victoria announced that a license fee of 30 shillings a month would be imposed, miners reacted with indignation. Unheard of amounts of gold were being exported out of the colony but the average "digger" (or miner) seemed to see little of it, and surface mining especially soon began to yield less. Machinery had to be imported and many of the diggers were forced to give up their independence and work for large companies. The license was beginning to be seen increasingly as an imposition, especially when it was brutally enforced by police.

Eventually, after government vacillation, tensions among the miners ran hot and the Australian flag, the flag of the Southern Cross, was hoisted for the first time. On December 3, 1854, 500 men gathered at Eureka in the Victorian country town of Ballarat, arming themselves as best they could and building a stockade. When troops finally stormed the stockade, only 150 men, all poorly armed, remained. The rebellion lasted a mere quarter of an hour and left 5 soldiers and 24 diggers dead and 12 soldiers and about 20 diggers wounded. So ended the only civil, nonconvict rebellion in Australian history. In June of the following year the miner's license was replaced by the miner's right, one pound per year.

Eureka is regarded, in characteristically Australian fashion, as a failure that led ultimately toward some kind of victory—much as Gallipoli would be some 60 years later. No jury would convict the defendants and most of their demands were soon conceded. But another battle, which took place on the goldfields shortly afterward, is rarely mentioned. One of the largest groups of foreign gold miners were the Chinese; by the middle of 1854 they were estimated to number 40,000. Though from all accounts the most law-abiding of citizens, who mostly worked claims that had already been abandoned by Europeans, they were also the most conspicuous in their appearance, dress, language, and customs, and this made them the targets of hostility and fear on the part of the Australians.

In June, 1861, diggers gathered at Lambing Flat in New South Wales and, to the playing of music and waving of English, Irish, and American flags, marched on the Chinese area, brutally assaulted the miners and their families, seized and destroyed their goods, and in many cases, cut off their pigtails. Very few of the offenders were put on trial.

The whole history of Australian attitudes toward the Chinese is a miserable one of prejudice and vilification, with stereotyped images of opium-addicted, obese, cigar-smoking men who preyed on white Australian virgins and sold them into slavery. Even into the twentieth century, *The Bulletin* magazine luxuriated in these clichés in both its cartoons and short stories, making mockery of their names (Oo Flung Dung). However, behind the fear of the alien or "Other" was a more rational, economic worry that they would work harder for less pay than the Australians and thus undermine their jobs. Many of the Chinese who stayed on after the gold rush ended did, in fact, take up quite menial jobs such as market gardening and laundering and make a success of them.

Even as distinguished a figure as Attorney General (later Prime Minister) Alfred Deakin acknowledged this by saying openly in parliament in a debate on the Immigration Restriction Bill, September 12, 1901: "Unity of race is an absolute essential to the unity of Australia. It is more, actually in the last resort, than any other unity. After all, when the period of confused local loyalties and temporary political divisions was swept aside it was this real unity that made the commonwealth possible" and adding magnanimously of the Chinese and Japanese that, "It is not the bad qualities, but the good qualities of these alien races that make them dangerous to us... It is their inexhaustible energy, their power of applying themselves to new tasks, their endurance, and low standard of living that make them such competitors."

Twenty years after gold had come to Australia, the population had increased immeasurably but the proportion of native-born had also increased. By the 1870s they numbered 60 percent, in 1891, 75 percent, and in the year of Federation the proportion was 82 percent. The growth of a sense of nationalism was an inevitable by-product of this change, even though feeling toward the "mother" country (England) and the British Empire was still strong and few people felt a sense of contradiction between the two allegiances.

The Coming of Steam

In addition to the discovery of gold, the coming of steam was to have equally revolutionary and longer-lasting effects. The journey to and from England was reduced to 70 days, and eventually less than that. Railways began to appear all over the country from the 1850s onward, revolutionizing communication and spelling out the last threat to the well-being of the indigenous man and woman. In the 1870s, steam power replaced the use of animals, such as horses, dogs, and camels as sources of energy and power. It encouraged the growth of railways as well. Between 1871 and 1891 the length of railways opened in Australia multiplied by nine.

At the same time mobility steadily increased over the vast continent in other ways. Two enterprising Americans, Freeman Cobb and James Ruth-

Australian outback. Photo by Craig McGregor.

erford, formed the coaching service of Cobb and Co. and within only a few years had come to dominate inland travel completely with their fast, efficient four-wheeled coaches, the Greyhound Buses of their day. Navigation of the Murray-Darling river system was also a crucial factor, with hundreds of paddle-steamers plying the Murray River.

The Sheep Industry

Up until well into the twentieth century, wool and later mutton was Australia's major export to Europe. Introduced into Australia in the First Fleet, sheep almost immediately proved to be ideally suited to the warmer, more temperate climate of Australia, and their number quickly proliferated. Fencing played a large part in this. "Between 1861 and 1894," reports one historian, "the number of cattle in New South Wales remained approximately constant at about 2,300,000. During the same period the sheep population of the colony increased from about 6,000,000 to 57,000,000."[1] Shearers became significant figures, taking pride in their work, fiercely competitive with one another, and in some cases building up considerable reputations in the areas in which they worked. Much of this is captured beautifully in the film *Sunday Too Far Away* (1975).

But even before fencing the wool industry had grown at an astonishing rate. Sheep raisers went west and sometimes north and south with their herds and simply squatted—claimed the land they occupied without any legal right. Governor Darling's attempts in 1829 to draw a roughly semicircular line on the map at about 250 miles from Sydney were ignored.

Like other European-introduced species, the environmental effect of the sheep was eventually disastrous, especially to the Aborigines, whose land and sources of water were taken and whose feeding grounds were destroyed. Attempts at resistance were brutally put down. Massacres and the rape of Aboriginal women were common. The mistreatment of Aborigines was justified on the ideological grounds of their innate inferiority and savagery, their cannibalism, their inability to become "civilized" or to settle in one place, and their habitual "treachery." Such arguments are still being put forward today.[2]

Disease was an even greater killer than direct violence, such as shooting or the poisoning of flour. Aboriginal people had never been exposed to influenza, measles, smallpox, or venereal disease and their immune systems proved to be vulnerable. Alcohol, too, proved to have destructive effects upon a people who had never previously indulged in it. They were deprived of their land and forced onto small preserves. Not until 1992 did the High Court of Australia recognize the inherent right of Aboriginal people to their own land.

Even in rural industries, technological advances forced constant change. During the 30 years from the end of World War II, 45,000 working horses disappeared from the nation's farms to be replaced by machinery—tractors, ploughs, cultivators, and threshing machines. No doubt spurred on by the absence of labor, the availability of milking machines quickly increased, permanently displacing workers.

The growth of the wheat industry was similarly stimulated by new technologies. Between 1860 and 1890 the total area sown with wheat increased from 1.25 million acres to a still modest 5.5 million. But improved rail and road communications, the breeding of rust and drought-resistant wheat by William Farrar (1845–1906), and the introduction of improved farming machinery, superphosphate manures, and scientific dry-farming techniques led to a rapid growth, so that by 1920 some 15 million acres were under cultivation.

Over the last two decades, ever more rapid technological and economic change has placed further stress on rural areas. Such developments as the reduction of rail transport and the closing of many banks have decimated rural communities and generated a huge backlash, leading to the rise of maverick populist parties such as Pauline Hanson's One Nation.

THE 1890S AND FEDERATION

The last decade of the nineteenth century was tumultuous. It began with the worst Depression the country had ever experienced. Victoria, in particular, suffered. It was the end of "Marvelous Melbourne," as the city had come to be known for its wealth and extravagance, and the number of its inhabitants went into decline, giving way permanently to Sydney as a more populous and famous city. National strikes led by seamen, miners, and shearers were brutally and successfully put down by police under the direction of governments. The end of the decade was marked by Australia's longest and most destructive drought to date, driving many farmers out of business. The Labor Party was formed during this time and was eventually successful in winning seats in parliament. In 1899 the first Labor government in the world came into office in Queensland, though only for a few days. But the decade was also marked by the rise of the Federation movement, culminating in a national Commonwealth being proclaimed in 1901.

Only in retrospect can we see what an extraordinary achievement this was and how near it came to failure, as the movement for a Republic was to do almost a century later. The six colonies had always been fiercely competitive and antagonistic toward one another, as the fiascos of different rail gauges for each state showed, and in many respects remain so today. Until Federation, the colonies were almost like discrete countries, even to issuing separate stamps and controlling their own defense forces, and much of this mentality has survived.

Although the Commonwealth of Australia prided itself on its profoundly democratic nature, its democracy, like that of ancient Greece, had its limitations. The 75 members of the first House of Representatives and the 36 senators were all white and male. They were older than the people they represented and substantially less likely to be Australian-born or Catholic. Only in South Australia and Western Australia did women have the vote, and while Aborigines in theory could vote in four of the states, there was no encouragement for them to do so. The following year, in any case, the Commonwealth Franchise Act removed their eligibility but the vote was extended to women. However, not until 1921 did Edith Cowan win the state seat of West Perth as a conservative. Her most prominent contribution in her sole term was to initiate a bill to allow women to become lawyers. In 1943 Enid Lyons and Senator Dorothy Tangney became the first women elected to federal parliament.

Voting was also voluntary and only 57 percent of the population actually cast their ballot. In 1924 voting became compulsory. Even today, only 25 percent of politicians are female, and the first Aboriginal to be elected to parliament was Senator Neville Bonner in 1971.

WORKERS' RIGHTS

Coinciding with Federation came the first in a complex series of steps toward building a fairer set of relationships between employers and workers. The widespread strikes of the 1890s had dispelled the illusion that such relations could be allowed to continue in an ad hoc way. Between 1894 and 1898 the average weekly wages of those working in the textile industry declined by almost 50 percent. There were exposés in the newspapers of *sweating*—women and children being employed over long hours for a pittance. In 1896 both New South Wales and Victoria passed Factories Acts that dictated the safety conditions and limits of working hours in factories and workshops. When the New South Wales government introduced compulsory arbitration, even the workers were suspicious, fearing that it was a plot to tie their hands in negotiations with their employers.

In 1903 Alfred Deakin went further, introducing a Conciliation and Arbitration Bill, which ran into difficulties over the division of powers between the States and the Commonwealth. However, the Bill became law in May and progress was slowly being made. In 1907 Justice Henry Higgins announced a basic wage, or "living wage," of seven shillings (70 cents) a day, and in 1922 automatic quarterly cost-of-living adjustments were introduced. When in 1929, under pressure of declining exports of wheat and wool and massive overseas debt, the Bruce-Page conservative government attempted to pass a bill to repeal the federal arbitration legislation, retaining for the Commonwealth control only over the shipping and waterfront industries, it dug its own grave. In the ensuing election there was a massive swing to Labor with even the Prime Minister, Stanley Bruce, losing his seat.

Since then further reforms have taken place, though there have also been setbacks. In 1930 the Court introduced the 44-hour workweek and 17 years later the 40-hour week. In 1965 Aboriginal stockmen were granted equal pay, though many station owners responded by firing their Aboriginal employees. In 1968 equal pay for women was phased in over three years, though female earnings still remain well below those of men on average. As recently as 2001, casual workers won the right to parental leave, a belated recognition of the rapidly changing nature of the workforce in recent decades.

"The Australian conciliation and arbitration system," wrote the biographer of Sir Richard Kirby, one of its most distinguished presidents, "was held up as a unique, vital and successful antipodean product worthy of study by the rest of the world."[3] Recent developments toward facilitating workplace agreements, however, have diluted much of its authority and the Industrial Relations Commission, as it is now called, is a far less influential body.

Summing up the pros and cons of Australian economic history, the economy is far bigger and stronger today than in 1901. The population has grown fivefold, from 3.7 million to more than 20 million, and the average standard of living—GDP per person—is four or five times higher. Then, economic activity was still relying to a considerable extent on raw materials though the manufacturing industries were growing. Now there is a huge services and tourism sector and exports are concentrated on rural goods, minerals, and manufactured goods and services.

In 1901, however, Australia had the highest standard of living in the developed world. Today, it is in the middle of the pack. Then, income was equally shared to a remarkable degree and Australia was regarded by many as the workingman's paradise. Today, income is much more unevenly divided and the disparities are continuing to increase.

Australians at War: Relationship with the Mother Country

Although some feelings toward England were often ambivalent, and the Sydney weekly magazine, *The Bulletin*, viewed it satirically, the ties between England and Australia were still very close for the most part. The British Army (Garrison) had left Australia in 1870 but rifle volunteer groups had been formed as early as 1860 and mounted rifle regiments were raised from the mid-1880s. Australia sent 16,000 horsemen to the Boer War between 1899 and 1902 and did not question its justice, at least until near the end when Australia's then most famous poet A. B. ("Banjo") Paterson (1864–1941) was sickened by the mass shootings of civilians and burning down of their houses. A decade after Federation it was clear that war was likely and that Australia had too few soldiers. In 1911 cadet training was made compulsory for boys and in 1912 a militia was formed and thousands of young men were virtually forced to join.

When war finally did break out, however, young Australian men, some below the legal age, some married with children, rushed to enlist. Family and cultural ties aside, Australia was indissolubly attached to England, economically and militarily, and anything that would reinforce those ties was seen favorably. It was a situation that would last until the early 1940s when Japan entered the war, Australian troops were called home from Europe to protect their own country, and Australia attached itself to the United States.

On April 25, 1915, Australian and New Zealand troops with French and English soldiers stormed a beach at Gallipoli on the Turkish coast. Although

In Melbourne, Shrine of Remembrance, built in honor of the men and women of Victoria who served and died in World War I. Photo by Michael Hanrahan.

they fought heroically, they met with unexpected resistance from the tough and well-entrenched Turkish soldiers and suffered heavy casualties in what is now generally construed to have been a deeply misguided operation. By the time they left eight months later Australia had suffered massive (proportionately) losses of some 7,000 lives. It was a day of enormous significance for the young nation, however, and Anzac Day (ANZAC is an acronym for Australian and New Zealand Army Corps) is now celebrated every year throughout the nation as a public holiday.

As the war continued and losses mounted, enthusiasm for it waned. In 1916 the Labor Prime Minister Billy Hughes advocated a compulsory call-up of young men as soldiers. Even members of his own party were lukewarm toward the idea, so he decided to call a referendum on the issue. It was finally and narrowly defeated, partly because of the influence of the Irish Catholic Archbishop, Daniel Mannix, who had arrived in Australia four years before. Hughes and 24 of his colleagues left the Labor Party and clung on to government by forming a coalition with the conservatives. A second referendum in 1917 to introduce conscription again failed.

Although dislocating and in some respects damaging to the economy, the war proved a watershed in other ways for Australians. Their widely acknowledged courage and prowess in battle gave Australian men a sense of maturity and confidence in themselves that perhaps they had not had before. Soldiers like Albert Jacka won one Victoria Cross, the highest decoration for courage, and according to his men, he should have won more. A Melbourne Jewish engineer (Sir) John Monash (1865–1931), became one of the most distinguished generals in the war and later had a brilliant career in civilian life.

Between the Wars

The immediate effects of the war—in terms of the massive losses, with 60,000 men killed—are easy enough to measure, but the more indirect and long-term consequences are far more difficult to assess. Many of the returned soldiers who had been wounded but treated as fully recovered lived far shorter and more troubled lives than they otherwise would have. Jacka, for instance, was only 38 when he died.

Splits in the Labor Party opened up by Billy Hughes's two divisive conscription campaigns spread through the country and Labor was to govern for only two years between the wars, and these in the depth of a Depression it was able to do little about. The end of the war saw Australia deeply in debt, a burden increased by its obligation to pay pensions to war widows and veterans.

Under the soldier settlement scheme, many of the returned soldiers were supplied with small plots of land and encouraged to become self-sufficient. However, the limited size of the blocks (usually a pitiful 320 or 640 acres), their often poor land, and the soldiers' ignorance of farming meant that few of them succeeded. The government's attempts to encourage rural industry were by and large unsuccessful and there was a steady drift of country people to the cities, exacerbating urban problems.

Australia in the 1920s retreated from the ideas and movements that preoccupied the rest of the world but could not insulate itself entirely. The fledgling Communist party of Australia emerged at the same time as disgruntled ex-servicemen formed right-wing groups designed to protect the country from what they saw as the forces of anarchy. Australia felt the force of the Depression more than most countries, partly because of its debts (which the government refused to repudiate) and partly because its income from exports was still heavily dependent on primary produce, for which there was a falling demand. When Premier Jack Lang tried to repudiate New South Wales's public debt, he was dismissed by the Governor, Sir Philip Game. Unemployment went as high as 28 percent in 1931 and there was hardly a family that was not affected. Farmers were forced off their land, city dwellers were evicted from their homes and often took to the road in search of subsistence, and shanty towns grew up, with police constantly moving vagrants on. Although economic recovery slowly began to rise, unemployment remained high and the country had still not recovered completely by the time war was declared in 1939.

World War II and Beyond

Australia's closeness to England finally began to weaken, only through the possibility of direct attack on Australia itself, something it had never experienced. At the beginning of World War II the conservative Prime Minister and fervent Anglophile, Robert Menzies, dispatched the second Australian Imperial Force (AIF) to the Middle East, Africa, and Europe where it fought Germans, Vichy French, and Italians. But when Japan entered the war, posing a direct threat to the Australian mainland, Australia under the new Labor Prime Minister John Curtin withdrew its forces from Europe and turned for assistance to the United States. In a famous speech of December 27, 1941, Curtin said, "Without any inhibitions of any kind I make it quite clear that Australia looks to America free of any pangs as to our traditional links or kinships with the United Kingdom." Such was the uproar the speech provoked, even though it was no more than a recognition of changing realities, that Curtin felt obliged to assert in a speech made just two days later but far less often quoted, "There is no part of the empire more steadfast in loyalty to the British way of living and British institutions than Australia."

The collapse of the English base of Singapore, with 16,000 Australians trapped inside it, completed the transfer of allegiance and, with whatever reservations, the Prime Minister ceded military control to the American commander, General Douglas MacArthur, who had made Australia the base for the U.S. presence in Southeast Asia. Many of the prisoners died under brutal treatment by their Japanese captors, and of those who returned home, most were permanently affected by their experiences.

Although relations with the Mother Country remained close and were strengthened by the postwar immigration program that concentrated initially on British settlers, a process had been set in train that involved a weakening of ties with England, the formation of the ANZUS alliance with the United

In Melbourne, Statue of Sir Edward "Weary" Dunlop, a surgeon in the Australian Army during World War II. He is known for the care he gave soldiers in Japanese prisoner of war camps. Photo by Michael Hanrahan.

States, and eventually a looking toward the Asian nations as, among other things, the country's most important markets. In addition, over the next 50 years, Australia would accept nearly six million immigrants from 140 countries and rapidly redefine and reinvent itself.

As the racist pieties of the Federation era slowly disappeared, Australia found itself under the Labor Chifley government actually supporting Indonesian independence against the Dutch, and in the 1950s formulating the Columbo plan, by which Asian countries were assisted in practical form with Australian aid. As Great Britain moved away from Australia with the rise of the Common Market, Australia moved closer toward its erstwhile enemy, negotiating the Australia-Japan Commerce Treaty in 1957. More recently, Australia has begun to show some independence in foreign policy, leading the group of United Nations forces that guaranteed the independence of East Timor from Indonesia. Most recently, the conservative government of Prime Minister John Howard has followed the George W. Bush line against Iraq unquestioningly, but polls have shown that a significant majority of Australians opposed invading Iraq, except under the auspices of the United Nations. In February 2003 more than one-half million Australians marched in protest against the war.

Participation in war—much of it arguably unnecessary—has been expensive for Australia in human terms; 606 of the 16,463 soldiers who served in the Boer War were killed in action. In the four years of the Korean War 399 Australians were killed, while more than 500 of the 8,000 Australian troops sent to Vietnam were killed.

The Postwar Period: "Populate or Perish"

After World War II, Australia set about restructuring itself. With the experience of near-Japanese invasion fresh in people's minds, the Labor government under Ben Chifley initiated an ambitious program of immigration. As a nation of only seven million people, with huge areas of vacant land, Australians now felt distinctly vulnerable. Labor's Minister of Immigration, Arthur Calwell, borrowed the term "Populate or perish," first employed by Billy Hughes, and preached the need for rapid expansion of the population. He set about encouraging British immigrants in particular, with the lure of a fare to Australia for only 10 pounds ($20), provided they stayed at least two years. However, although the elements of racism in the program had not disappeared, with Calwell arguing in Parliament that "Two Wongs don't make a White," he was forced to cast his net wider to include Italians, Greeks, Jewish survivors of the concentration camps, Poles, and people from the Baltic countries. Non-English migrants were often known, with varying degrees of derision or tolerance, as "Balts" or "DPs" (displaced persons) and were encouraged to assimilate into the community as quickly as possible. The term Calwell coined this time for the migrants was the "New Australians."

He could not have seen the profound implications of his plan, which eventually helped to turn Australia into one of the most diverse countries ethnically anywhere in the world. At first life must have been difficult for the new migrants from non-English-speaking lands. The entrenched prejudices of a deeply isolated, parochial society were hard to overcome. In many cases, their European professional qualifications were not accepted. Many of them found work in factories, on car production lines, or on distant projects like the huge Snowy River hydroelectric scheme. But they did find work, and they succeeded in changing the Anglo-Saxon culture as much as they themselves were changed.

As the White Australia policy slowly crumbled, the original migrants were succeeded by people from even more exotic countries—Lebanese, Hungarians, South Americans, Vietnamese. Many of the victims of authoritarian regimes or invasions tended to appear in Australia not very long afterward. In the 1960s a shortage of schoolteachers, academics for Australia's rapidly expanding universities, and later, businessmen, led to the arrival of visitors from the United States, many of whom stayed on; and just as the term *New Australian* dropped from use in favor of *ethnic*, so the idea of *assimilation* gave way to that of *multiculturalism*, with migrants being actively encouraged to maintain their ties to their old country and its culture, rather than abandon them, even as they were still urged to embrace the values of Australia as well.

The cultural changes that this influx produced in Australia over the second half of the twentieth century were quite profound. They affected eating and drinking habits, art, fashion, language, and in fact, every facet of Australian life. Migrants became artists and writers, football players, restauranteurs, chefs, business leaders, and politicians.

THE 1970S AND 1980S

Sir Robert Menzies retired in 1966, having become with 17 years' rule the longest-reigning prime minister Australia is ever likely to have. An old man, increasingly out of touch with his electorate, he had survived by a combination of shrewd instinct and good fortune; as one commentator put it, he presided over events in such a way as to make it look as if he caused them to happen. The good fortune came in the disastrous split in the Labor Party in which anti-Communist groups defected to form the new Democratic Labor Party that, by giving second preferences under Australia's complex system of voting, ensured that the ALP had little hope of election. It came closest in 1961 when it lost by a handful of votes when unemployment was then at a record high of 3 percent but was later thrashed at the 1966 election when the Liberals, as they had done consistently under Menzies, played on fears of Communism, this time sparked by Australia's growing participation in the Vietnam War.

But three incompetent prime ministers later, Labor was returned to power in 1972 under the reformist government of Gough Whitlam and the slogan "It's time." It signaled a new period of hope and optimism for many groups in society who had felt neglected and abandoned. The energy and optimism the Whitlam government demonstrated seemed to breathe new life into a moribund and provincial society—immediate amnesties to draft resisters, grants to writers and artists, free university education, the emergence of feminist movements, sparked off particularly by expatriate Australian writer Germaine Greer's *The Female Eunuch* and marked by the appointment of the first adviser on women's issues to the prime minister. A radical transformation seemed to be taking place in Australia.

Three years later it was over, in circumstances that will remain forever controversial and the source of lasting bitterness. International events such as the OPEC oil embargo, combined with the Whitlam government's overambitious spending program, drove the economy into a situation of crisis, with high inflation and rising unemployment. In this atmosphere, exacerbated by Labor's attempt to negotiate a $4 billion loan from doubtful sources to build a gas pipeline from the west, the opposition-controlled Senate refused supply—that is, they refused to pass the bills ensuring that public servants were paid and that the government could function normally. The government held out for 27 days. Advised by the deeply reactionary chief justice, Sir Garfield Barwick, the Governor-General Sir John Kerr, a Labor appointee turned conservative, dismissed Whitlam and commissioned the Liberal leader Malcolm Fraser to become caretaker prime minister and call an immediate election.

Fraser won the election in a landslide, but though he governed for eight years before being ousted by a Labor Party led by union leader Bob Hawke, his leadership was always tainted by the circumstances in which he assumed it, while Kerr became a derided, laughable figure until the day he died. The Labor Party recovered office in 1983 and held it until 1996 before it was defeated by John Howard, who has remained in power since.

The Situation of the Aborigines

If multiculturalism remains a remarkable, if ever fragile achievement, little has been done to resolve the situation of Aborigines in Australia and this (along with the treatment of illegal immigrants) remains the greatest contemporary stain on Australian society. Suggestions have ranged from encouraging Aborigines to form their own communities inland, self-governed and isolated from white society with a return to old, prewhite laws and customs ("apartheid," say its detractors), to the argument that indigenous people need to be absorbed back into the community and taught the same skills, given the same opportunities, as whites.

A culture of welfare and dependency, some argue, can be just as destructive for Aboriginal people as earlier, more overt forms of violence. It is an argument that can and has been easily taken up by conservative commentators and politicians as intellectual justification for their position, although recently, even some Aboriginal leaders have supported it, with reservations. What could be called malign neglect here goes even further to become "creative destruction," the assimilation of the representatives of the New Stone Age into the technologically superior society of the West. Prime Minister Howard has consistently refused to make a national apology to indigenous people on the grounds that the wrongs done to them were not done by himself or his contemporaries. This was despite the fact that hundreds of thousands of Australians marched on "Sorry" days in every capital city.

The same commentators have sought to play down or even deny the significance of a report on the so-called Stolen Generation, *Bringing Them Home,* which showed conclusively that even up until the 1950s indigenous people of lighter skin color were taken by force from their parents and merged into white society. They argued that half-caste children who were forcibly removed from their parents had not been stolen but "rescued" from a traditional society in which, if they survived the threat of infanticide at birth, they became abused outcasts—this, despite the torment that many witnesses who testified to the report revealed they had suffered at the forced deprivation.

Whatever the truth, things have certainly not improved for indigenous people in the last few years, despite the fact that the Australian High Court made several significant and controversial decisions in their favor. In 1992, in what became known as the Mabo decision, the High Court established that the Meriam people held native title over the Murray Islands. Four years later, in the so-called Wik case, the Court held that the native title of the Wik and Thayorre people of Cape York had survived the granting of pastoral leases, effectively refuting the doctrine of *terra nullius,* or unsettled territory, on which whites had relied to justify their occupation. The famous landmark of Ayers Rock was rechristened Uluru, and in 1985 returned to its traditional landowners, the Mutijulu people, who leased it back to the Australian government for a 99-year period. None of the dire predictions that followed each of these developments has come true. In addition, a 1991 Royal Commission into Aboriginal Deaths in Custody between 1980 and 1989 (which saw the deaths of 99 Aboriginal and Torres Strait Islander men and women) made scathing comments on police and custodial practices and recommended many reforms. On December 22, 1993, the Labor Prime Minister Paul Keating celebrated the passing of legislation recognizing the legality of native title in Australia.

Ayers Rock (Uluru), a sacred site for the Aborigines. Photo by Jennifer Macklin.

Unlucky Australians

Aborigines are not the only group to be classed, in writer Frank Hardy's term, as "the unlucky Australians." The radical economic initiatives begun by the Labor Party during the 1980s and carried on by the Liberal Party once it assumed power—moves such as the abolition of tariff protection and deregulation of the financial system—have had some unintended side effects. In a comparison of the degree of economic inequality among 21 wealthy countries recently, Australia came in fourth. Almost one-fifth of working-age citizens—over 2.5 million people—receive some form of social security payment. More importantly, though there is no work available, with official figures of more than 6 percent unemployed, but the probability that it is much higher than that, there is increasing hostility toward recipients as undeserving "dole-bludgers." Many people, some with the best intentions, some not, are arguing for a welfare system that is less generous, more conditional, more moralistic.

More recently, strains and stresses have shown up with the issue of the arrival of refugees—or, as the government insists on wrongly calling them, "illegals." The stance of the government—with the timid acquiescence of the Labor opposition and the general approval of a majority of citizens—was shown up in the incident of the *Tampa* in 2001. After first permitting the Norwegian vessel to enter Australian waters with the 433 refugees it had picked up from a leaking boat, the government changed its mind and forced the vessel to wait outside Australian waters. They and the following boat people, who had arrived on a perilous journey from various troubled and war-torn countries such as Afghanistan and Pakistan, were consigned to various Pacific Islands such as Fiji, Nauru, and New Guinea, which were heavily bribed to take them in, thus forming what some commentators have called a "ring of human misery" around Australia.

Also criticized were the conditions of the detention camps already built in Australia and the terms under which refugees can be held, with even children incarcerated behind barbed wire in isolated areas for up to two years. The Howard government's policies won widespread support, however, and its insistence on deciding who could land on Australian soil, together with the sense of crisis created by the bombing of the World Trade Center, saw its reelection by a comfortable margin at the end of the year.

Australia's insistence on immigrants of British stock, and especially ones who would be willing to go to the country areas, still seen as the repository of both virtue and wealth, even by many who live in the cities, meant that it fell behind such common rivals as Canada and Argentina in acquiring imported labor. The "populate or perish" slogan actually went back through Billy Hughes (1937) to as early as 1913. One critic, discussing Australia in the period 1913 to 1939, saw an absolute dichotomy between quarantine and contagion.[4] Racist ideas abounded and there was almost total agreement on the undesirability of taking in people of a color other than white. Such was the superiority of British stock that comparisons could even be drawn with other white nations.

At the same time, and contradictorily, Australia was envisaged as a country that could take in innumerable immigrants, thus becoming a second United States. Estimates of its potential population took wildly optimistic and fanciful forms, from Sir Rider Haggard's 40 or 50 millions of white people through war historian C.E.W. Bean's estimate in 1907 that New South Wales alone could bear at least 40 million people through cooperative irrigation and mixed farming (this despite an estimate that 32 percent of Australia is arid land and 32 percent semi-arid) to Foster Fraser's "restrained calculation" in 1910 that the population could reach 200 million people.

Economic Changes

Certainly there have been huge changes over the past 30 years. In 1901, Australia's exports to Great Britain comprised 57 percent of its total exports;

in 2000, just 4 percent. Conversely, where exports to Japan were 0.3 percent, they now total 17 percent, making Japan by far Australia's biggest customer, almost twice as large as the United States, next with 9 percent. As early as 1959, Japan had become Australia's largest importer of Australian coal and second largest importer of its wool. As Australia by necessity turned away to some extent from Great Britain and toward the United States during the Second World War, so it is slowly being drawn away from the United States and into the vortex of the Asian economies in the postwar period.

The almost schizophrenic nature of Australian society at this time can be seen in the fact that in these same years the conservative Menzies government permitted British nuclear tests during the mid-1950s without even informing the Aborigines on whose lands the tests were being conducted. When they had finished, the British were allowed to bury the toxic waste on those lands. This was in stark contrast to the impassioned protests that greeted French nuclear tests in the Pacific nearly 40 years later. Australia was also virtually alone in supporting England during the Suez Canal crisis of 1956.

Although (the conflict with the Aborigines excepted) no war has been fought on Australian soil, Australians have been constantly engaged in combat overseas. The Boer War and two world wars aside, Australians have also been involved, in varying numbers, in suppressing the Boxer rebellion, in Korea, and in Vietnam, when in controversial circumstances, males too young to vote were conscripted to fight under a lottery system. When Britain faced a Communist-led insurgency in Malaya in 1948, Australia responded by sending military forces in 1950.

Since Vietnam, most Australian expeditions have been in support of UN efforts to end conflicts in other countries, most important in its support of the Gulf War and in acting as international peace keepers in Bougainville and East Timor. Despite its nominal independence in foreign policy, Australia has still linked itself closely to the United States. It has responded enthusiastically to any U.S. calls for assistance, and the alliance extends even to relatively small details, as was seen in 2002 when the government awarded a contract for repairs of its new Collins-class submarines to the United States over the German bid, which a committee had recommended as superior. It was felt that the sharing of knowledge and systems with the United States outweighed purely military criteria.

Notes

1. Cited in Russel Ward, *The Australian Legend* (Melbourne: Oxford University Press, 1985), p. 185.

2. See, for instance, Keith Windschuttle, *The Fabrication of Aboriginal History* (Sydney: Macleay Press, 2002).

3. Blanche d'Alpuget, *Mediator: A Biography of Sir Richard Kirby* (Melbourne: Melbourne University Press, 1977), p. 170.

4. John F. Williams, *The Quarantined Culture: Australian Reactions to Modernism 1913–1939* (Cambridge: Cambridge University Press, 1995), p. 44.

2

Thought and Religion

Catholics and Protestants

Irish Catholicism has always been a prominent element in Australian thought and religion. Between 1791 and 1803, 2,086 convicts were transported from Ireland. More significantly, about 600 of these were convicted for riot and sedition; they were in effect political prisoners, not the wretches of the London slums that had dominated the cargo of the First Fleet, and their number included three priests.

However, the predominant faith was Protestantism, though of many varieties —Anglican, Presbyterian, Methodist, and the various dissenting sects—and Protestantism of a kind that was sometimes fairly enlightened, sometimes evangelical. Protestantism could embrace the fanaticism of Samuel Marsden, but in its milder forms it did not enshrine an absolute belief in the existence of God or survival after death, and there is nothing like the frequent invocation of God that there is, for instance, in the United States. In a study of the Federalist movement and the adoption of the Australian constitution, one historian has noted the secular characteristics of Australian life and their deliberate encouragement even by individuals who were themselves devout practitioners of religion. "They rejected the organized attempts by the churches to have the constitution explicitly recognize Australia as a Christian nation and instead allowed a gesture toward God only in the preamble, while the operative clause prohibited the Commonwealth from establishing or favoring any specific religion."[1] A noted contemporary observer said bluntly, "Puritanism is no longer a force in art or letters or statesmanship; and the Puritan tradition of family life is dead and can never be revived.... Instead of this we have got a new family life, which is infinitely genial, and charming, and natural."[2]

Sectarian tensions, however, would always run deep in Australian society, until the last decades of the twentieth century when the rush of new religions and cultural groups from many new lands placed such squabbles in a wider dimension, which rendered them faintly absurd. Catholics believed, often with considerable justification, that they were discriminated against by the governing classes. The latter feared the Irish, with their egalitarian tendencies and resentment of authority, and associated Ireland and its citizens with various forms of superstition, rebellious tendencies, and anti-monarchical stances; they could even be seen unequivocally as agents of the Devil.

Every so often an event would occur that justified the position of one class or the other. The Eureka Stockade was one, with Irish Catholics such as Peter Lalor prominent in opposing what they saw as oppressive and discriminating laws. Australia's outlaws from the anonymous Wild Colonial Boy to Ned Kelly were mostly of Irish origin and attracted many sympathizers among the poorer people in the areas in which they lived. However, there is some suggestion that, at least later and mainly in the Outback, Australian bushmen were more united in their opposition to squatters and police than they were divided by religious belief. One of Australia's leading writers around the turn of the twentieth century, Henry Lawson, expresses this when he writes

> They tramp in mateship side by side—
> The Protestant and Roman—
> They call no biped lord or sir,
> And touch their hat to no-man!

The early conditions of Australian life gave little opportunity for religious belief and practice to flourish. The first Anglican clergymen were chaplains to convict establishments and therefore, in the eyes of the convicts, indissolubly tied to the establishment and its brutalities. They could offer comfort to men about to be hanged or flogged, but there is little evidence that they actually tried to prevent the event. The novelist Henry Kingsley has one of his characters in his best-selling *The Recollections of Geoffrey Hamlyn* (1859) say

> These prisoners hate the sight of a parson above all mortal men. And for why? Because when they're in prison, all their indulgences, and half their hopes of liberty, depend on how far they can manage to humbug the chaplain with false piety. And so, when they are free again, they hate him worse than any man.

The Rev. Samuel Marsden was a magistrate as well as priest and was renowned for the savagery of his sentences, including flogging men after the Irish rebellion of 1804 in order to induce confessions out of them. The clear conflict of interest here, between the representative of the God who forgiveth all sinners and the representative of the law who dispensed punishment with a severity generally thought to be unmatched by lay magistrates, was far from lost on the convicts. Only among the Catholics, whose priests were outside the establishment, was there some genuine adherence to religion.

For the same reason there seemed to newcomers to be quite different attitudes toward the Sabbath in Sydney and in convict-free, much more Irish, Melbourne. Clergymen were largely absent in the Outback apart from the occasional itinerant. Anti-clericalism died hard. As late as 1905, "Banjo" Paterson published in *The Bulletin* a poem from a contributor that was titled "My Religion." The tenor of it is fairly caught in a few lines:

> I will go to no Church and to no house of Prayer,
> To see a white shirt on a preacher.

And:

> But let man unto man like brethren act,
> My doctrine that suits to a T,
> The heart that can feel for the woes of another,
> Oh, that's the religion for me.

Henry Lawson's deeply satirical portrait of a clergyman in his famous short story, "The Union Buries Its Dead" is not unrepresentative, and many cartoons in *The Bulletin* portray similar feelings.

The inextricable links as well as tensions between church and state, as embodied in a figure like Marsden, spilled over into the realm of education, with the abandonment of the assistance colonial governments gave for religion and education to the larger denominations and its replacement of the ideal formulated by New South Wales Premier Henry Parkes, arguably the most influential politician of the second half of the nineteenth century in Australia, that education be "free, secular, and compulsory."

EDUCATION AND RELIGION

In 1868 Henry James O'Farrell attempted to assassinate the visiting Prince Alfred, second son of Queen Victoria, and after being arrested, claimed he was acting upon the instructions of the Melbourne branch of the Fenians, an Irish organization pledged to drive the English out of Ireland. The accusation was immediately and vehemently denied but Parkes seized the opportunity to rouse fears of a rebellion and to put through a bill for "the better suppression and punishment of seditious practices and attempts." Wild allegations and rumors flourished in an atmosphere of hysteria.

Nowhere did sectarian feelings manifest themselves more than in the various forms of education that were proposed. In order to redress an educational system that was transparently inadequate, the states acted. In 1872 the Victorian government introduced legislation that would provide a system of education that was free, compulsory, and secular. South Australia followed in 1875, as did Queensland. Parkes, who had been the most ardent proponent of these principles, put forward the Public Education Act of 1880, which declared that all aid from the consolidated revenue would be withdrawn from denominational schools in New South Wales. By 1895 the principle had been fairly widely accepted throughout all the colonies.

Initially it had been vehemently opposed by both the Anglican and the Catholic Churches. The Celtic clergy refused to accept the system, and a long and bitter fight ensued as to whether denominational schools should be subsidized by the states. Bishops and teachers were recruited from overseas—especially Ireland—and a diocesan structure set up in the major cities of the country, beginning as early as 1842. The most famous and controversial archbishop was to be Melbourne's Daniel Mannix, who was prominent in leading the fight against conscription during World War I, and much later in the 1950s with his fierce opposition to Communism, as well as being a vociferous proponent of state aid for Catholic schools.

When the Australian Catholic school system was set up in the 1870s, it was specifically seen as a reaction to and refuge from the secular humanism of state schools, which were seen by many clergymen as seedbeds of immorality. As the schools expanded throughout the 1950s, the recruitment of religious orders of teachers from overseas, especially Ireland, as well as locally, was unable to keep up with the demand. Laypeople increasingly bore the brunt of education and this, plus the relaxation of bans on government aid to religious schools, drew the schools into the wider societal system, to the point where even coeducation was countenanced. Today's Catholic schools look far more like state schools than they used to do, with no apparent contamination of the morals of the students in either group.

However, religious—and specifically Christian—feeling has progressively weakened in Australia. In the late nineteenth century approximately 45 percent of Christians were estimated to be fairly regular church attenders. By the 1990s more than one in every five Australians declared that they were not Christian, and the fastest growing religions were, in fact, Buddhism and Islam, while attendance at church continued to decline. The number of regular attenders was estimated to be less than 20 percent. The Protestant faiths were the biggest sufferers, with the Catholic Church being insulated to some extent by the large influx of European migrants as well as stricter injunctions.

Although Australia remains a nominally Christian society, and although state aid to religious schools was restored in 1974, there is little evidence of any strong ideological hold religion has over the people. It would be hard to imagine the kind of influence the Catholic Church had on its faithful in the 1950s, when, in its desperate fear of Communism, the Church effectively destroyed the Australian Labor Party for nearly two decades with its instructions to Catholics to vote for the breakaway, fanatically anti-Communist Democratic Labor Party. Similarly, the 1968 Papal decree forbidding contraception has been largely, if tacitly, ignored by Catholics.

Slowly the various taboos that existed on Sundays and days of Christian celebration—pubs being closed, sports banned from being played, theatres closed, newspapers silent—have broken down. While even today, 77 percent of Australians declare themselves Christians—almost a third of the population is Catholic and a quarter is Anglican—the practice of Christianity is by no means fervent and to the one in five Australians who frankly admit to having no religious allegiance could be added an unknown number whose belief is hardly more than an act of lip service at census time, or who decline to answer the question at all.

Early works of religious history, such as Patrick Francis Moran's *History of the Catholic Church in Australasia* (1894) tended to be polemical, if not outright bigoted in tone, but the rise of a new, more scholarly conception of religious history, which really began only in the 1930s, pays more attention to the multifaceted nature of both Protestantism and Catholicism, refuting the notion that they were and are monolithic movements. There are subtle studies of the conflicts in religious thinking and practice—between those of the faithful who concentrated on the spiritual life as against those who engaged in worldly activities, between the leaders of the major denominations and the often unnoticed practice of the faith at a local, parish level. The contribution of women and even Aboriginal people has finally begun to be assessed.

If the intensity of religious belief has declined, the Churches can still be the cause of considerable controversy. Among the current issues that are raging hotly are that of female clergy (the Catholic Church is firmly against, the Anglicans divided), whether clergy can be married (with again the Catholic Church firmly opposed), and the rights of homosexuals to participate in Church rituals. There have also been a number of accusations of pedophilia against members of clergy, as well as claims that senior clergymen buried the claims and protected the offenders. Archbishop Roger Hollingworth, for instance, was recently forced to resign as governor-general of Australia after retrospective accusations that he had been "soft" on pedophile priests during his rule as spiritual leader of Queensland. Clergymen have also taken the high moral ground on many occasions, to the anger of whichever government is in power. They have called on the government to apologize to the Aboriginal people and have themselves apologized for their own mistreatment of indigenous people in the past; they have criticized official policy on refugees and detainees; and most recently have attacked the current government's willingness to join the United States and Great Britain in the invasion of Iraq.

Australian Identity

The question of Australian identity is a vexing one and has prompted the most extreme reactions from different commentators. Very early in the nineteenth century observers began to note the appearance of a new generation of Australians who, living in a good climate with plenty of fresh air and wholesome food and not under constant scrutiny from the forces of law and order, grew up healthier, taller, more independent-minded than the generation that preceded it. Professor Russel Ward, in his classic work *The Australian Legend* (1958) was partly responsible for creating the stereotype of the *real* Australian. Living in the Outback, the Bush Australians, so it is said, grew up independent, self-sufficient, with a love of freedom and eventually an attachment to the often harsh land they worked. Distrustful of intellect and articulacy, they were intensely devoted to their "mates" and the bond of male mateship became a core element in the myth. Their attitudes toward women are respectful, even chivalrous, but there is an accompanying discomfort, perhaps even distrust of them—or, as some feminists would have it, outright misogymy.

Commissioner John Thomas Bigge, who arrived in 1819 with instructions to inquire into conditions in the colony and the effectiveness of transportation as a form of punishment, was deeply influenced by Macarthur's views that the emancipist classes should not be admitted into polite society. Nevertheless, even he wrote in his *Report on Agriculture and Trade* (1823) of a separate generation that were growing up in Australia very different from their disreputable parents:

> The class of inhabitants that have been born in the colony affords a remarkable exception to the moral and physical character of their parents: they are generally tall in person, and slender in their limbs, of fair complexion and small features. They are capable of undergoing more fatigue, and are less

> exhausted by labor than native Europeans; they are active in their habits but remarkably awkward in their movements. In their tempers they are quick and irascible, but not vindictive; and I only repeat the testimony of persons who have had many opportunities of observing them, that they neither inherit the vices nor feelings of their parents.

Such stereotypes make their way into colonial fiction very early and culminate in the stories of Henry Lawson, Australia's greatest writer of the nineteenth century. In Alexander Harris's *The Emigrant Family* (1849), for instance, the most idealized of the novel's several heroes, Reuben Kable, is referred to constantly as "the Australian," as if that were a sufficient distinguishing feature in itself, and the physical description of him establishes the archetype of the Australian male that will persist for many years. Rolf Boldrewood's most famous novel, *Robbery Under Arms* (1883), has as its hero an Australian who speaks in his own distinctive vernacular: "My name's Dick Marston, Sydney-side native...I don't want to blow—not here, any road, but it takes a good man to put me on my back, or stand up to me with the gloves, or the naked mauleys." The eponymous hero of Henry Kingsley's *The Recollections of Geoffry Hamlyn* (1859) goes so far as to speak of a new class of people emerging in Australia, even though the author and his protagonists remain firmly committed to English imperialist ideals. He writes of the new free class as "a lazy independent class, certainly, with exaggerated notions of their own importance in this new phase of their life, but without the worse vices of the convicts." Even "Banjo" Paterson was surprised to make the same discovery when he covered the Boer War.

A distinguished feminist historian, on the other hand, argues that the taint of convictism plus the dearth of women had a pervasive effect on the moral climate of Australia and links it to what she sees as the central themes of Australian fiction in the period she studied, 1830 to 1930. These are cruelty and isolation.[3] Oddly, she still talks of convictism in the 1870s and even 1890s when at least two generations of postconvict Australians had grown up. She regards the notion of mateship in a quite literal way ("*le vice anglais*" [the English vice]) and sees it, in its ignoring of women, as a wholly destructive phenomenon.

Some critics have even questioned whether the notion of the *Bush*, so mythologized in poetry, fiction, and pictorial art and perpetuated today even in television advertisements, had any reality at all. The social commentator Donald Horne has gone so far as to call it a "political construct" or even an "urban myth." "Tourist industry," he writes, "is now a rural industry—in which the bush becomes a theme park....A new art gallery can gain some of the economic importance once given to a new abattoir."[4]

Nevertheless, the legend persists. It reaches a further apotheosis at Gallipoli and during the Second World War with the heroism of Australian soldiers on the Kokoda trail in New Guinea and fighting in the Middle East where the self-styled "Rats of Tobruk" held out Rommel's army. This war service added elements of "larrikinism"—that is, irreverence toward authority—to those that were previously perceived to be there.

Ward's thesis has been subject to intense scrutiny and revision since it first appeared in 1958 but it is questionable whether it was ever more than a perception or image, rather than something based on fact. Even in the nineteenth century most Australians lived in cities, hugging the (mainly) eastern coast, rather than the inhospitable inland, and in the twentieth century, Australia became the most urbanized country in the world. As poet A. D. Hope puts it in "Australia":

> And her five cities, like five teeming sores,
> Each drains her: a vast parasite robber-state
> Where second-hand Europeans pullulate
> Timidly on the edge of alien shores.

But myths have a way of outlasting facts, and the survival of the Australian legend can be seen in such phenomena as the Crocodile Dundee persona of comedian turned film star Paul Hogan.

In recent times the question of identity has assumed a new urgency and universality in Australian life. It has been argued that so-called multiculturalism has been Australian society's greatest single achievement of the past half century.

Despite its limitations, which have been shown up in the refugees' crisis and in hostility toward Muslim people after the destruction of the World Trade Center in the United States, Australia has still emerged over the past half century as having one of the most ethnically diverse labor forces in the world. It still has surprisingly low levels of interethnic conflict and high levels of cooperation. A large number of languages are spoken and individual secondary schools often include representatives of more than 30 cultures. There are laws explicitly banning racist abuse, and even the leading sports have developed programs that provide educational instruction and lay down very heavy penalties for sportsmen who racially slur opponents. Welfare programs aimed at righting inequalities suffered by vulnerable ethnic minorities (especially women) have been developed. The government funds (some would say underfunds) a television channel, SBS, which is devoted almost solely to ethnic and multi-cultural affairs.

Intermarriage rates between different ethnic groups are surprisingly high and extend even to indigenous and nonindigenous people. In comparison to the United States, for example, the 1994 U.S. Bureau of the Census data shows that black Americans are partnered with black spouses in 91 percent of cases. By contrast, 65 percent of all partnerships involving indigenous Australians are made up of one indigenous and one nonindigenous partner. Australian birth data for 1998 shows that less than one-third of indigenous children born that year had two indigenous parents. The rate of intermarriage in Australia is probably the biggest element in the relative success of multiculturalism as a policy.

Nevertheless, successive events over the last few years have revealed how fragile Australia's much-prized consensus is, how many fears and fantasies it papers over. The meteoric, if brief, rise of Pauline Hanson's One Nation party, which won 11 seats in the 1998 Queensland election, with 23 percent of the vote, is a good example of this. In her maiden speech in Parliament, Hanson said bluntly, "I believe we are in danger of being swamped by Asians." Asked if she were xenophobic, she replied, "Please explain." She also castigated Aboriginal people who lived on government subsidies and, while insisting she was not racist, demanded that whites be given comparable treatment with blacks.

Within a few years One Nation had virtually disintegrated, and early in 2002 Hanson resigned from the party, with a series of charges hanging over her head relating to electoral fraud and alleged false claims. But her legacy has lingered on in a number of ways, and in fact much of it has been adopted by the current Liberal government under the leadership of John Howard. It was Hanson who revealed for the first time the deep disaffection of country people with all the major parties, including their own Country Party, their sense that city and urban dwellers had been privileged by the major parties in comparison to themselves, and their deep-seated fear and sense of helplessness at the rapidity of changes forced upon them—globalization, removal of tariffs, decreasing security of employment, and the closing down of facilities in country towns, as the banks, for example, moved toward automation.

Moreover, she forced the governing Liberal Country Party to move sharply to the right, especially on issues involving Asia and immigration, and the Labor Party to follow them. Her boast about the prime minister after the *Tampa* affair arose—"A lot of people are actually saying I'm John Howard's adviser because he's picking up a lot of the policies and issues I have raised and spoken about over the years"—was not without justification.

Religion and the Intellectuals

One point of view has it that "Happy is the country that has no heroes," especially war heroes, perhaps. Although it has participated in overseas wars, Australia has been fortunate never to have had an invader set foot on its land. The nearest it came was during World War II when Japanese aircraft bombed the northern towns of Broome and Darwin and submarines were observed entering Sydney and Newcastle. Because of this absence of conflict (again with the exception of the Aboriginal people), Australians are often accused of having no inner life, no intellectual passions of sufficient intensity that would drive them to war in defense of their convictions—as if that were some kind of desideratum. Visiting writers like Sir Arthur Conan Doyle in 1921 and especially D. H. Lawrence the following year castigated Australians along these grounds. The nation's physical emptiness, so the argument went, was a moral one as well.

Many historians have indignantly refuted this accusation, pointing to the constant presence of intellectual conflict and division in what is a far from seamless history—the debates over the desirability of convicts, white Australia, the form education should take in Australia, protection versus free trade, federation, land rights, and the labor movement and unions in the nineteenth century alone.

In the twentieth century there have been Billy Hughes's rancorous referenda on conscription, the sacking of a state premier and later a prime minister by the Queen's representative, the shift in foreign policy away from England toward the United States, the frequent debates over Australia's proper relationship with Asia, especially Indonesia (as its closest neighbor of consequence) and Japan (as its biggest trading partner), the anti-Communist referendum, and the questioning of Australian involvement in the Vietnam and Iraq wars. Over the last decade alone there have been major arguments and debates over the Republic; the treatment of Aborigines and questions of land rights and an apology; the treatment of the environment, which is becoming a major concern, specifically issues concerning greenhouse emissions and salinity; globalization; attitudes toward the United Nations, and the present government's stance toward asylum seekers. That these have not led to civil war is hardly a result to be regretted but they remain unresolved issues that arouse fierce debate.

Nevertheless, the perception remains that ideas and issues are not taken seriously enough in Australia, that intellectuals remain marginalized figures, and one reason for this that has been proposed is the lack of religious thought and feeling in Australia, the subjection of any spiritual sense to utilitarian considerations. A contributor to *The Oxford Companion to Australian His-*

tory has asked whether Australian culture tends to play down religious ideas, whether Australian intellectuals feel they have to "conform to the mythology of Australians as a utilitarian, realistic, pragmatic people."[5]

Some years ago the social commentator, John Docker, in his book, *In a Critical Condition* (1984), accused Australian intellectuals and especially poets in the 1950s of attempting to create what he called a "metaphysical ascendancy," the treatment of literature, and especially poetry, as above the material world, in a purely spiritual dimension of its own. Concentrating on the key Cold War figure James McAuley, who edited the CIA-subsidized magazine *Quadrant* in the 1950s, he discusses McAuley's assaults on liberalism and humanism as a "belief in a merely human rationality, which must be inadequate," his aspiration for the untouched, pristine Australia to become a vanguard in the war against communism, and gives in his poetry his idea of submission to the religious order of the world.[6]

A decade later, however, the oratory element in McAuley's poetry is gone, and in poems like "Because" and "Australia" he is writing much bleaker (as well as much finer) poems. The spiritual ideals of which he spoke have fallen into silence since his work, and the work of Vincent Buckley, and perhaps Francis Webb, and later Robert Gray and Kevin Hart. There is a sense of what has been called "the flat imaginary," the space that many intellectuals feel is there instead of the vibrant contesting of moral issues that should be taking place.

Among several writers Miriam Dixson quotes is the leading historian of Catholicism in Australia, Patrick O'Farrell, who speaks in his personal memoir *Vanished Kingdoms* (1990) as having been cheated of his own culture, "bereft of majesty, besieged and abandoned in a world of disputatious dull dogs, short-changed in the currency of the spirit."[7] The work of historian Manning Clark is saturated with the rhythms and imagery of Christian religion, and especially of the King James Bible, though he professed no religious faith. Dixson's own answer to this problem of the cultural vacancy of identity is to reclaim our Anglo-Celt identity, which she feels has been guiltily expunged by the demands of multiculturalism, and merge it with the newer ethnic cultures. Religion, it seems, is at any rate far too weak a glue to bind society together.

Exile, a sense of truncation from Europe, solitude, denial, the inherited stain of convictism (perhaps the most risible suggestion of any of these)—all have been offered as explanations of the sense of Australian identity. It is curious to note how many Australian novelists, especially those like David Malouf and Liam Davison who are explicitly concerned with the question of identity, have gone back to the past for their fictive material. Three of Peter Carey's novels, including the last two, have been set in the nineteenth century. Thea Astley often deals with specific incidents in the past though she writes about the present too. Tom Keneally is another writer who ransacks the past for material. So did Patrick White. Robert Drewe turned away from the treatment of contemporary issues to write *Our Sunshine* (about Ned Kelly) and *The Drowner,* set in the nineteenth century. Even Frank Moorhouse, who won his reputation with brilliant short dissections of contemporary urban life, has most recently written two long novels about the League of Nations. The contemporary urban life with which Moorhouse dealt is not the subject of much fiction anymore, though there are signs of its return in the so-called grunge literature and the novels of Steven Carroll.

Malouf has also sought to define Australian ideals in comparisons with the United States, which he sees as a model that we can define ourselves against. He wrote:

> Young men would no longer go up to London, as Ben Jonson's Kastril does, "to learn to quarrel," but to learn to be "polite." This was the language Australia inherited. The language of reasonable argument. Of balance. Of compromise. We may envy Americans the line of evangelical idealism that runs, say, from Jonathon Edwards to Jefferson, Emerson, Whitman and on to Martin Luther King, but we are not seduced by it.[8]

Tertiary Education

For a long time, tertiary (university) education was very expensive and remained the prerogative of only a minority. As part of the great rise in public building that accompanied and resulted from the prosperity of the second half of the nineteenth century, Sydney University was founded in 1850 and the University of Melbourne followed closely in 1853. The other colonies eventually followed—Adelaide in 1874, Tasmania (1890), Queensland (1909) and Western Australia (1910).

Secular and state-funded, the universities concentrated on practical areas such as science (geology, chemistry, physics) and engineering, but had room also for law, classics, history and philosophy. Mostly they had small enrollments and were usually led by English and Scottish professors. Only after World War II did the numbers of students begin to rise dramatically.

The number of university students grew rapidly in the 1960s and 1970s, placing the educational system under enormous strain, and federal funding increased accordingly. New universities were established in rapid succession—the University of New South Wales (1958), Monash (1958) and then La Trobe (1964) in Victoria, Macquarie (1963) and Newcastle (1965) in New South Wales, and Flinders (1966) in South Australia.

State aid was granted to private schools in the 1970s and the federal government provided funds distributed on a basis of need to all schools, Catholic, private, and government. The sometimes ambiguous gap between universities on the one hand and the more vocationally oriented institutes of technology and colleges of advanced education began to diminish. Under Labor in the 1980s, the distinction virtually disappeared as universities, colleges, and institutes were amalgamated. Their number dropped from 94 in 1978 to 38 in 1991 and increased government control ensured that economic outcomes became far more imperative.

Under various headings such as "The clever country" and "Knowledge Nation," politicians have attempted in recent times to expand educational opportunities for Australians. In 1901 there were 2,500 students enrolled in higher education; by 1999 the number was 686,300, the most dramatic advances having come mainly in the last two decades.

Until quite recently there were no private universities in Australia, with the state expected to take responsibility for this as well as most other aspects of the welfare of its citizens. Since then, Bond University has been established in Queensland and the Catholic university of Notre Dame in Western Australia, while more recently the University of Melbourne has attempted to establish its own private sector. Australians have always been far more dependent on the State to supply their wants than in the United States, a situation that probably stems from the circumstances of its original colonization where most individuals were virtually powerless to control their own lives and needs.

Society has become atomized in all sorts of ways. A survey from 1995 established that there were one-third fewer Boy Scouts as compared with the 1960s, the number of Freemasons had declined by more than two-thirds since 1945, and membership of the Country Women's Association had fallen from 110,000 in 1954 to 48,000. Although there are still many thriving organizations such as sports clubs (even some of these, especially in rural areas, have come under strain), public activism can only be expected to decline further with the rise of the Internet and the increased popularity of electronic games.

Many commentators fear that Australia is becoming much more of a spectator nation and far less of a participatory one. Even communalism takes electronic forms. Many people have experienced that strange new phenomenon by which people prefer to communicate by e-mail rather than speak over the telephone, let alone write a letter. As a new form of companionship, however, they will share mass jokes or stories with those on a long mailing list.

For older people, especially, the tiny face-to-face encounters with other people that make up much of the routine of their day disappear as banking goes online and conductors disappear from trams and guards from railway stations, to be replaced only by the sudden raids of ticket inspectors.

At the same time, all is not gloom and doom. Perhaps it is the forms of civic participation that have changed, more than the numbers. Institutions are less popular and causes, which one can make selectively, more so. The level of volunteer participation at the Sydney 2000 Olympic games astonished visitors, as did the competence and friendliness of the volunteers (though it was, after all, the International Year of the Volunteer)! The same trait was evident during the bushfires that ravaged Sydney over the Christmas 2001 period and then again two years later. And motorists cannot stop at a major intersection on designated charity days, of which there are a great many in Australia, without having tins rattled in their faces by smiling youths calling for donations to various causes.

A former leader of the Liberal Opposition, Dr. John Hewson, makes a distinction between volunteering and joining. He says, "While Australians are now volunteering in droves, they are not joining. Memberships of clubs and organizations throughout our society are being battered, and it doesn't matter what it is, churches, unions, Liberal and Labor parties, Freemasons, bowling clubs, or whatever, they are suffering right now." He focuses especially on the question of the declining membership of political parties: "In politics, people know they have to vote. Yet they know they don't need to be a member of a political party to exercise that vote."[9]

ISLAM

The turning away of the *Tampa* and the terrorist destruction of the World Trade Center a few weeks later, plus dramatic reports of ethnic-based gang rapes in the western suburbs of Sydney, focused attention as never before in Australia on the Muslim population of the country. Islam is fast approaching Australia's second biggest religion with an estimated Muslim population of 450,000 to 500,000.

It is a multicultural faith, with Muslims from many different countries and cultures resident in Australia. There are Arabs (from Lebanon, Egypt, Syria, Palestine, and other Middle Eastern countries); Turkish; Balkan (Bosnia, Albania); Southern Asian (Pakistan, India, Bangladesh, Sri Lanka); Southeast Asian (Indonesia, Malaysia, Vietnam, Cambodia, Burma, and the Philippines); Russian and those from ex-Russian republics; South African and other African states (Somalia, Sudan, etc.); and Australian. Attention was focused on the latter by the discovery that one or two Australians had traveled to Afghanistan to fight with the Taliban. Most of the Muslims in Australia are of the Sunni denomination though some Shiites (practiced mainly in Iran and Lebanon) live in Sydney and Melbourne.

Each state has at least one Islamic primary school and most have more than one; they are recognized by the Australian government and follow the government curriculum. There are Islamic colleges in most states, and most universities have campus prayer rooms and Muslim student groups. Although the first large-scale migration to Australia took place in 1887 when Afghan camel handlers were invited into the country by the colonial secretary, the largest migration occurred in the post–World War II period, particularly in the 1960s and 1970s. Muslim Aid Australia is a leading aid agency, approved by the Australian government. Sponsored by Muslims Australia, it was created to help the 80 percent of the world's refugees who are Muslim. There are 30 Mosques in Sydney alone and almost 100 across Australia.

Until recently, Muslims were able to live and practice their religion in peace and harmony, despite the fact that their appearance and customs make them much more conspicuously different from the general population and can arouse inchoate suspicion. After the events of the second half of 2000, however, the tensions are much more palpable. Individual Muslims have been attacked and mosques desecrated.

During the federal election of 2001 the government claimed that Afghanistan refugees (predominantly Muslim) had thrown some of their children overboard. The government delayed producing evidence for as long as possible, but after the claims had been specifically denied by naval observers, including an admiral, they produced some indecisive photographs. These eventually turned out to be taken two days after the alleged incidents. The children were in the water, in safety jackets, because the ship had caught on fire and begun to sink. Nevertheless, in a poll conducted by the *Herald Sun* newspaper on December 29, 2001, an astonishing 62 percent of respondents said they still believed the children were tossed overboard and 85 percent said that they approved the decision to turn away the boat people. In a more recent poll, 52.8 percent of those questioned expressed reservations of varying strength about accepting a Muslim into their immediate family. The Muslim cause was not helped by a series of rapes by Lebanese-Australian Muslim youths who targeted non-Muslim Caucasian young women in the west of Sydney. With the arrest and sentencing of the youths the rapes have ceased but the speculation as to their motives has not.

Not surprisingly, the Howard Liberal government's tactics during the election were strongly criticized by its opponents—but also by some of its adherents—on the grounds of its use of misleading or simply false information, its deliberate divisiveness, and the long-term scars it will create. Comparisons were made to Billy Hughes's referendum tactics on conscription during World War I and the lasting sectarianism it created, as well as to the tactics Sir Robert Menzies employed during the referendum to ban the Communist Party.

Buddhism

The appeal of meditation and the idea of spiritual awakening have helped make Buddhism the fastest growing religion in Australia, with the number of its adherents increasing by more than 50 percent to around 210,000 over the last decade. The last census showed there were about 2.5 times as many Buddhists as Jews in Australia, and yet their presence has aroused nothing like as much alarm and accusations that their culture is inimical to Australian values as has that of the Muslims. One expert has made the point that "You will find throughout Melbourne—and often in adjacent streets—a Cambodian temple, a Thai temple, Japanese, Korean, Vietnamese, Sri Lankan, Burmese, Tibetan, Chinese. Australia is one of the few countries on earth where Buddhists of all varieties can encounter each other."[10]

The existence of the religion in Australia goes back as far as the 1850s with the Chinese on the gold fields. There were also indentured Sri Lankan workers on the cane fields of north Queensland and Thursday Island. However, it accelerated a century later with a sprinkling of Australians attracted to the emphasis placed on meditation and strong spirituality, and the establishment of the Buddhist Society of NSW in 1953 and a Victorian branch a year later. In 1974 a Sri Lankan monk established Australia's first Buddhist temple since the gold rushes in the Blue Mountains outside Sydney, and in 1975 Buddhist refugees from Indo-China helped swell the numbers.

Interest was also sparked by successive visits by the Dalai Lama. His fourth visit to Australia in 2002, however, was surrounded by controversy, with the visiting Chinese Foreign Minister Tang Jiaxuan calling for Australian leaders to ignore him, and both the prime minister and the leader of the opposition contriving to be out of the country when he arrived. In addition there was a government ban on a nationally televised address at Parliament House.

Science and Invention

At the other end of the scale, it is perhaps part of the bushman heritage of independence and improvisation that Australia has produced, relatively speaking for its size, a large number of inventions and distinguished scientists, though lack of government support and an absence of the American tradition of private largesse has meant that many of them were forced to leave and pursue their careers overseas. For instance, whereas Australia has produced only one Nobel Prize winner for Literature (Patrick White, 1973), it has six in science, though at least half of them spent much or most of their professional life overseas. The historian Geoffrey Blainey has written particularly well about Australian habits of invention and improvisation, though he also points impartially to the major Australian failures of invention, such as the inactivity of bankers and politicians when confronted with the Depression of the 1890s.

William Lawrence Bragg (1890–1971) was, at 25, the youngest Nobel Laureate ever. He and his English father, Sir William Henry Bragg, won the Nobel Prize for Physics in 1915 for the analysis of crystal structure using X-rays—that is, for creating the new science of X-ray crystallography. A student at Cambridge University, Bragg lived permanently in England. Howard Walter Florey (1898–1968) won fame for his work on penicillin. He and two colleagues were awarded the Prize in Physiology or Medicine in 1945. He lived all his adult life in England, and was closely associated with Oxford University, but he was also an adviser and frequent visitor to the ANU.

Born in rural Victoria, Sir Frank Macfarlane Burnet (1899–1985) was co-winner of the 1960 Nobel Prize in Physiology or Medicine for the discovery of immunological tolerance, an insight vital to organ transplantation. The Walter and Eliza Hall Institute he was associated with in Victoria in 1944 contributed almost 50 percent of the literature on immunology during the late 1950s and 1960s.

Sir John Carew ("Jack") Eccles (1903–97) was the son of a teacher who stimulated his early interest in science. He shared the Nobel Prize in Physiology or Medicine in 1963 with two English researchers for his work at the Australian National University in Canberra on how electrical messages or nerve impulses are communicated or repressed by nerve cells.

John Warcup Cornforth (1917–) developed deafness at the age of 10 and went into a career in chemistry where he felt it would not be such a handicap. He and a fellow scientist received the Nobel Prize in Chemistry in 1975 for their work on the stereochemistry of reactions. The most recent winner is Peter Charles Doherty (1940–); he and a fellow researcher were awarded the Prize in Physiology or Medicine in 1996, the first time it had been awarded to a veterinarian, for their work on understanding of general mechanisms used by the cellular immune system to recognize both foreign microorganisms and self molecules. Residing in the United States, Doherty returned to Australia and has called for an urgent increase in funds available for medical research in his native land.

Later researchers have often worked under the auspices of the Commonwealth Scientific and Industrial Research Organization (CSIRO), originally established in 1926 as the Council for Scientific and Industrial Research. Many of the best Australian scientific minds have worked there at some stage and it has made many notable discoveries. Perhaps its most important achievement was to create the deadly poison, myxomatosis, which for a considerable time cured the plague of rabbits in Australia after they had been introduced from England. However, under the present government, over 1,000 jobs have been shed and a much greater emphasis placed on earning funding as against government assistance. There are fears that this will affect its research capabilities and lower staff morale, with leading young scientists no longer regarding the CSIRO as the most attractive scientific employer.

For perhaps the same reason—invention being the mother of necessity—Australians have been in the forefront of scientific discoveries and breakthroughs in terms of their population, though again the inventors have not always been honored in their own country. Predictably, early breakthroughs occurred on the land as farmers struggled with harsh and unfamiliar conditions. The Stump Jump Plough, developed by Richard Smith in the 1870s, revolutionized plowing, as Hugh Victor McKay's Stripper-Harvester, which stripped, threshed, and cleaned grain, did to the wheat industry after 1884. William Farrer developed the drought-and-rust-resistant Federation wheat variety in 1901, and from the late 1950s mechanical harvesters were introduced into sugar-cane fields, later to be sold to other sugar-producing countries.

More recently we have seen the development, sometimes in conjunction with the CSIRO, of devices such as ultrasound, Gene Shear molecules, the Black Box flight recorder, and the Interscan microwave landing system. At a slightly lower level there are the Victa lawnmower (which figured conspicuously in the Sydney 2000 Olympic celebrations), the totalisator machine, Ben Lexcen's winged-keel, which enabled Australia to wrest the America's Cup from the United States for the first time in 1983, and the wine cask. A major invention by Professor Graeme Clark was the bionic ear. Since Clark first implanted his experimental hearing device into the ear of a road accident victim in 1978, 30,000 deaf people have recovered their hearing through the device. In science at least, Australia's tradition of intellectual thought is very strong.

There are recent signs that the government is keen to recognize Australia's proud history of scientific achievement. At the beginning of 2002, *Australia Post* released its Legends series of stamps. Previously honored had been cricketer Sir Donald Bradman, the Anzacs, famous Olympians, country singer Slim Dusty, and one artist—Arthur Boyd. In that year the series consisted of five distinguished Australian scientists. They were recent Nobel Prize winner Peter Doherty; former Australian of the year, Gustav Nossal, whose lifetime quest is to vaccinate all the children of the Third World; microbiologist Nancy Millis; epidemiologist Fiona Stanley; and cell biologist Donald Metcalf, who after 35 years of research found a hormone that formed the basis of a cancer treatment that has removed the need for bone marrow transplants and has saved numerous lives. At the same time, however, the fact that the CSIRO has been steadily denuded of funds, suffered large staff cuts, and forced to reduce research in favor of more directly moneymaking activities has severely reduced its capacity for objective research.

NOTES

1. Helen Irving, *To Constitute a Nation: A Cultural History of Australia's Constitution* (Cambridge: Cambridge University Press, 1997), pp. 134–35; 166–68.

2. C. H. Pearson, *National Life and Character: A Forecast* (London: Macmillan, 1893). Cited in Geoffrey Partington, *The Australian Nation: Its British and Irish Roots* (New Brunswick, N.J. and London: Transaction, 1997), p. 135.

3. Miriam Dixson, *The Real Matilda* (Melbourne: Penguin, 1984).

4. Donald Horne, "The Australian Bush Is an Urban Myth," *The Age,* 1 September 2001.

5. Wayne Hudson, "Ideas, History of," in Graeme Davison, John Hirst, and Stuart McIntyre, eds., *The Oxford Companion to Australian History* (Melbourne: Oxford University Press, 1998), p. 336.

6. John Docker, *In a Critical Condition* (Melbourne: Penguin 1984), p. 72.

7. Patrick O'Farrel, *Vanished Kingdoms* (Sydney: NSW University Press, 1990), p. xxiii.

8. David Malouf, "American Reading," *The Age,* 20 April 2002.

9. John Hewson, *Australian Financial Review,* 18 January 2002.

10. Gabriel Lafitte, quoted in Larry Schwartz, "Buddhism Finds a New Home Down Under," *The Sunday Age,* 5 May 2002.

3

Marriage, Gender, and Children

In its early years, Australia always had many more men than women, and some feminist critics have suggested that this affected male attitudes toward women and continues to do so even today. As the title of one book on the subject suggests, they were, according to this view, either "Damned Whores or God's Police," the latter a phrase first coined by the noted nineteenth-century reformer Caroline Chisholm. The disparity in numbers between the two sexes was even worse in the outback where conditions were hardly conducive to a civilized life and where women with children were actively discouraged as being useless encumbrances. Their absence gave a new significance to the concept of Australian mateship. Historian Miriam Dixson points with ironical scorn to the fact that Australia's unofficial national anthem, "Waltzing Matilda," does not feature a woman, as the title might lead us to expect; the eponymous Matilda is a bushman's swag, the cloth in which he carried his few possessions, and "waltzing Matilda" means merely "carrying a swag."[1]

Dixson points also to the thesis of Russel Ward in *The Australian Legend* (discussed earlier) and argues that the qualities he describes are "misogynist to the core." It centers around a style of masculinity that "reeks of womanlessness." And the true Australian had a further privilege omitted by Ward: the "privilege of despising not only 'new chums and city folk' but also human beings who were female."[2] Indeed, it is argued, most, if not all, Australian historians until recently largely ignored the role and position of women in Australian society.

Ward and what became known as the radical nationalist tradition have come under fire from other commentators as well, with feminist critics claiming that his theories are male chauvinist, racist, and historically flawed. Feminist historians have also argued recently that the role of women as pioneers along with the men in the nineteenth century, as "creating a nation," in the title of one book, has been seriously undervalued. In contrast to Ward's rugged, solitary individualists, men were increasingly likely to marry and father children in the second half of the century as more women became available and the imbalance between the sexes steadily righted itself. They point out that whereas in 1861 there were 138 white men for every 100 white women, by 1891, with the population now over three million, the ratio had changed to 119 to 100 white women. They go on:

> The increasing likelihood that adult men were married or would marry in the not too distant future gave further substance to the valorization of the respectable, prudent family man fostered in the colonies before 1860. It was a model of masculinity distinctly at variance with the rough-hewn independent white male of the frontier myth, and competed with this representation quite forcefully.[3]

Like the novelist Patrick White, Dixson often casts the Irish and their "primitivity" as villains and frequently suggests they play a central part, one quite out of proportion to their number in the community, in the general demeaning of women in Australia. A whole chapter of her book is devoted to criticism of the Irish. Only secondly comes the formative impact of convictism. She traces it also, more plausibly, to Australian males' sexual misuse of Aboriginal women ("black velvet") and their corresponding guilt. But part of her argument, at least, is flawed by the fact that the discovery of a convict among one's ancestors is more likely to be treated as a badge of honor and distinction by most contemporary Australians than the reverse.

In his stories, written around the turn of the twentieth century, Henry Lawson tends at times to idealize or even sentimentalize women, further subtle if unintentional ways of reducing them to subordinate roles, but his lesser-known contemporary Barbara Baynton, in a small collection of stories gathered together as *Bush Studies* (1902), shows a horrified revulsion at the predicament of women in the Bush. The women in the stories run into an almost barbaric as well as deeply hostile world in which they are alone and vulnerable.

As in comparable countries during the same period, there were always women who fought for the rights of their sisters, even if they saw those rights in terms that might now seem narrow and unduly concerned with protection rather than equality. Usually, they were white, middle-class, well-educated women with a strongly moralistic bent. Temperance was high on their list of priorities, and in 1915 they succeeded in having pubs (hotels) closed down by six o'clock in the evening out of deference to the war effort, leading to the infamous "six o'clock swill" by which men forced themselves to down as much beer as they could in the short time after work before the pubs closed. Introduced as a temporary measure, the law was not repealed until 1954.

Such was the strength of the "wowser" (Puritan) lobby in New South Wales that it also successfully agitated for a referendum on prohibition. The vote, which took place in 1928, was overwhelmingly against (896,752 as opposed to 357,684) but it was not the only occasion on which there were attempts to ban alcohol. The four "serpents," in fact, were seen to be gambling, seduction, whisky, and cruelty.

Notable Feminists

Among leading feminists were the admirable Catherine Helen Spence, also a distinguished novelist, of South Australia; Rosa Scott of New South Wales; and the Victorians Vida Goldstein and Louisa Lawson, mother of the famous writer Henry. Louisa founded and for many years largely wrote the radical feminist journal, *Dawn.* Although their vision was limited in many respects, some of the gains they made were real. Some women moved out of the very limited area of domestic work into still lowly but better paid business and factory jobs: Between 1890 and 1910 the percentage of female workers in manufacturing industry in New South Wales and Victoria rose from about 12 1/2 percent to about 29 percent. During the 1880s many single women moved into the workforce, as opportunities in the Public Service became available. One historian notes that "Four high schools for girls were established in NSW after the passing of the 1882 Public School Act,"[4] providing at least a few opportunities for women.

By the 1890s university education was generally available to women who could afford it. The University of Adelaide permitted women to attend lectures from its foundation in 1874 but did not begin to confer degrees on them until six years later. The University of Sydney delayed admission of female students until 1881, making it the last university in Australia to admit women. In Victoria the struggle took nine years and was finally won in 1881 also. Women's franchise was introduced in South Australia in 1894, but in Victoria not until 1908, and the first Commonwealth Franchise Act was passed in June 1902, extending the vote to all people over the age of 21, "whether male or female," except for the mentally unsound, criminals, traitors, and "aboriginal natives," giving them the right to stand for election. Aboriginal people finally received the vote in 1962.

Vida Goldstein was one of the first women to take advantage of the new law. She was one of four female candidates to contest the 1903 federal election. She stood as an independent on a platform of equal rights and pay and the appointment of women to official posts. She received 51,000 of the 80,000 votes she needed for a Senate seat. She went on to contest another four federal elections—two for the Senate and two for the lower house—but was unsuccessful. No women would be elected to parliament until Dorothy Tangney and Enid Lyons 41 years after the passing of the Act. In addition, Goldstein helped to write the Children's Court Act of 1906 and provided some of the information that led to the basic wage judgment.

At the same time, for a whole host of reasons, the role that women played in Australia and the status they achieved were both much less effective than in other developing settler countries. Only in the 1970s did the lag begin to be reduced. Commentators have spoken of a lack of a community of the kind one finds in the United States, for instance, at the same stage of development; of instilled feelings of horror and disgust held toward convict women by their superior sisters; and of the sense of fear and threat toward black women and the sexual opportunities and rivalry they represented to so-called elite women. Most important of all, so the argument runs, the demeaning way in which men behaved toward women led to the latter internalizing their sense of inferiority and unworthiness. Although these attitudes among males have begun to change, they are coming off a low base.

Desertion of various kinds has always been a key factor in the relationships between men and women in Australia. As some historians point out, "Much has been made of the work patterns and ethos of Australia's 'nomad tribe' in the nineteenth century: the phenomenon of men shifting seasonally in search of work or in response to minimal responsibilities. Little has been said of the obverse side of male mobility: family desertion."[5] They go on:

> Yet the abandonment by men of their families has been one of the most persistent characteristics of Australia's past. The move up-country for jobs in the pastoral industry, the pursuit of whales and seals, the stampede after gold in the 1850s and 1860s, the shearing cycle of the late nineteenth century, the rush to the Western Australian goldfields in the 1890s, the flight to the country in times of depression, the enthusiastic response to the call to arms—all left in their wake varying degrees of destitution.

The Current Situation

The Women's Electoral Lobby was partly responsible for some of the considerable gains over the past 30 years—maternity leave, government funding of child-care centers, and anti-discrimination and affirmative action laws. Recently a few institutions have begun to introduce paid maternity leave.

But women are still discriminated against also by profession. While some professions—nursing and teaching, especially primary teaching—actually favor women, others are much harder to gain access to, and even in those that are available, it is difficult for women to rise to positions of seniority. Of the 42,000 police in Australia, for instance, only 5,000 are women and of these only 2 percent are ranked inspector or above.

Feminists now speak of a "glass ceiling," meaning the invisible barriers that can confront women once they reach a certain level of success. There have now been two female state premiers (though no female prime minister or leader of the federal opposition) but both of them, Joan Kirner in Victoria and Carmel Lawrence in Western Australia, came to power in particularly difficult circumstances; in effect, they accepted a poisoned chalice. Lawrence was almost the only woman who has been spoken of seriously as a potential major Party leader but she resigned from the front bench in protest against the Australian Labor Party's policies on refugees—although the fact that she was elected as the Party's president in 2003 suggests her popularity is greater among the rank and file than with her fellow parliamentarians. The ALP has set a target of 40 percent of women members and has so far succeeded in lifting their numbers to over 30 percent. "Tall poppies," an ironic Australian term indicating high achievers who need to be cut down, is also the title of a book that celebrates the successes and achievements of a number of women in various fields. In it, the author sums up the nine examples of successful women she interviews in terms of three requirements—equality, necessity, and autonomy. Despite calls for improvement, the 2002 Australian Census of Women in Leadership, which covered the top 200 companies, found that women held only 8.2 percent of board positions, while 54 percent of companies had no women at all in executive management roles. Fewer than one in ten women are in senior decision-making roles, while only two companies had female chief executive officers.

Gender and Economics

Although lip service has for a long time been paid to the concept of equal pay for equal work, in practice it is honored in the breach more than the observance. The principle was initially accepted by Mr. Justice Higgins in the Fruitpickers' Case of 1912, but the Court also ruled that women had fewer needs than men, who were assumed to be married with children, and consequently merited less pay.

After the Basic Wage Inquiry of 1949–50, women were allotted 75 percent of the male minimum wage and equal minimum wage rates were not approved until the May 1974 National Wage Case. Even now, the average female earnings rate well below those of men, even in comparable positions; women working full-time earned on average 84.3 percent of male wages in 2001.

In some professions the glass ceiling for women is not quite so thick or so low. In 1990 a majority of students aged 20 to 29 were male; now they are being outnumbered by women. The number of female academics also surged between 1990 and 2000 while the proportion of female students has now risen to 55 percent. The number of female lecturers increased from 37 to 44 percent, while at the next level of senior lecturer the increase is even more striking—from 16 percent to 29. But women still have a long way to go, especially at the highest levels of professor, associate professor, and reader, where their numbers increased from just 9 percent to 16 percent.

In other significant changes, the proportion of full-time students in higher education who were also working part-time increased from 40 percent to 45 percent between 1995 and 2000. More women than men had basic vocational and undergraduate diploma qualifications but more men had skilled vocational qualifications. And Australia's spending on all education institutions was slightly below the OECD (Organisation for Economic and Co-operative Development) average.

The problem may be less one of pure prejudice along the grounds of gender than a slowness to adjust outmoded models of work, a refusal to accommodate women other than within a male model of working, which usually entails actual presence at the office, rather than more flexible arrangements that would allow working mothers time with their children.

Laws have steadily changed over the last quarter of a century so that, for instance, women working in private industry have been granted maternity leave, women work in the army, run government departments, ride as jockeys in the Melbourne Cup and are ordained as priests into the Anglican Church. But the inequalities remain.

On the other hand, conservative women have pointed to what they claim are anomalies of a reverse kind. Surveys have shown that if women are divided into three groups, as roughly, those committed to work and career, those committed to family and raising their children, and those who, as well as family duties, want the option of part-time work, by far the largest group is the second. According to a survey conducted in 2001, 69 percent of Australians believed that being a full-time homemaker was the ideal option for mothers with children under six and 81 percent of women opted for full-time mothering.[6] In the view of these women, the recommendation of the ACTU

(Australian Council of Trade Unions) that Australia introduce a 14-week paid maternity leave might have the ironic effect of forcing women to return to the workforce earlier than they otherwise would have or wished to do. And yet, the results of the survey hardly bear out what is in fact the reality of women combining work with family responsibilities.

A different complaint concerns the Family Court and its alleged bias against men. One commentator has said of the Court: "Among the issues causing resentment have been the failure of the court to enforce child contact orders, false allegations of sexual abuse and violence resulting in men being denied contact with their children, men's lack of access to legal aid, and prejudicial treatment by counsellors and judges."[7] In reply, the Chief Justice of the Court stoutly defended its operations, pointing not only to the enormously complex and emotive nature of the issues the Court dealt with but also the fact that only six percent of parents who apply for parenting orders actually proceed to a defended hearing before a judge. The vast majority of cases are resolved privately, sometimes with the assistance of lawyers or of court or community-based mediation services.

LOVE AND MARRIAGE

Just as marriage as an institution has declined sharply and the percentage of marriages that end in divorce has risen, so the rate of childbirth is equally on the decline. It is a process that began more or less out of necessity during the Depression when children were an unwanted burden but is now prevalent for different reasons. According to recent figures, the rate of Australian fertility is little more than 1.7 per woman, below the replacement level of 2.1, compared with 2.95 30 years ago. The falling rate is believed to have several causes, among them women delaying childbirth until their mid- to late 30s and therefore being unable to have many children, and an increasing number of women choosing to remain childless, even if in a relationship with a male partner, owing to the high cost of rearing children and the implications for their careers. In 1996, 20 percent of Australian women age 45–49 with a bachelor's degree were childless. The overall percentage was 11 percent, clearly indicating that it is far easier for women to gain a higher education if they do not have the burden and responsibility of a family.

Successive surveys by the Australian Institute of Family Studies graphically trace the pattern. The first, in 1971, found that 78 percent of married women under 35 felt that whatever career a woman had was not as important as being a mother. By 1982 the figure had dropped to 46 percent and by 1991 it was down to 26 percent.

Divorce had always been more difficult for women until the passing of the Commonwealth Family Law Act in 1975. Previously, all grounds for divorce had been based on the notion of the fault of one party—usually adultery—but also other faults such as cruelty, bigamy, or desertion. In the nineteenth century males had to prove only adultery; women had to supply an additional ground. In the latter part of the twentieth century the rate of divorce increased considerably, from around four percent to as much as one-third of marriages. There is no doubt that the Family Law Act was partly responsible for this. It removed the concept of fault and announced that the only necessary ground for divorce was the "irretrievable breakdown" of a marriage, testified to by the partners' separation for a period of twelve months or more. Maintenance and custody were also decided on a no-fault basis, with the primary emphasis being placed on the welfare of any children resulting from the marriage. Many divorce proceedings are now initiated by women.

In 2001, 55,300 Australian couples divorced—11 percent more than in 2000 and the highest figure since 1976 when the no-fault divorce law took effect—and more than one in five families with children under 15 are headed by a sole parent. But in response to criticisms, the Family Court Chief Justice argued that "I think it's not necessarily a bad thing that there's been an increase in the break-up of unsatisfactory relationships." While sometimes it was too easy for people to walk away from relationships, "you shouldn't be trying to, for example, nurture violent relationships where one party is a victim of psychological abuse or violence."[8]

One change in procedure has meant that the institution of adoption is dying out as state governments use other legal arrangements to care for unwanted and at-risk children. Guardianship orders are now favored over the traditional process of adoption, in which new birth certificates are issued and all legal ties to biological families severed. The number of adoptions has plummeted from nearly 10,000 in 1971 to a record low of 514 in 2001. There has been a 30 percent decrease in the last three years alone. Fewer children are available for adoption because society no longer stigmatizes unmarried mothers to the same degree, and income support for sole parents makes keeping a child more viable.

One sign of the new secular society that drives some conservatives and Christians to despair is that it is no longer necessary to marry if a couple decides to cohabit. This is so even if they have children. The Australian Bureau of Statistics estimates that de facto couples make up over 10 percent of all couple relationships and that the number is rising as the number of marriages is falling. They are now as much a phenomenon of the educated middle-classes as they are of the working class. It is no longer a mark of shame to live in an unmarried relationship and the old term, *de facto,* has largely been replaced by *partner.*

Every so often there are protests from conservative commentators. In 2002, when highly popular tennis star Pat Rafter was declared Australian of the Year (along with the current Prime Minister John Howard), two journalists in leading Australian newspapers criticized the choice because he was living in an unmarried relationship and he and his partner had announced that they were expecting a baby. They had even spoken of having as many as seven children.

Studies have found that women in de facto relationships are increasingly likely to be career women, like Rafter's partner, Lara, who is a model, and have corresponding status and financial independence. They tend to have particularly high expectations of their relationship. The increasingly fragmented nature of the population was shown up tellingly in the 2001 census. The population overall increased by 6 percent in the past five years, but the number of households rose by 9 percent, with the average occupancy falling dramatically to only 2.6 persons. Australia's population has continued to grow, however, as it is bolstered by the immigration program, a subject of constant debate. The current population is 20.3 million, but by 2050 it is projected to be 27.8 million—at an increase of around 15 percent.

POPULATE OR PERISH?

All this feeds into another furious debate as to what the maximum sustainable population of Australia is. On one side is the business community, also many politicians who fear that a population of only 25-or-so million people would not be a viable entity in a highly competitive global economy, that Australia would lack the means of self-defense, and that its economic prosperity and cultural homogeneity would be threatened. These are, in effect, variations on the arguments that were offered in the 1946 "populate or perish" debate. To them can be added the more contemporary one of fears of Australia becoming a mere branch-office in the global economy.

Against them, environmentalists argue that Australia's fragile and ancient ecosystem, together with the damage that has already been done to the environment, means that the number of people the country can support is very low, with estimates ranging between 18 and 25 million at a maximum. Demographers are fairly even divided on the issue.

Added to this is the further complication that the population is steadily aging, with estimates that the proportion of people over 65 will double during the next 50 years from 12 percent of the population to 24 percent—in other words, fewer and fewer workers supporting more and more retired people. In Victoria, for example, figures from the Australian Bureau of Statistics graphically show the changing demographics. At the time of Federation, children age four or under were 11 percent of the State's population. By 2000, this had dropped to below 7 percent. In 1901 men outnumbered women by a proportion of 101.2 to 100. In 1999 there were 97.8 males for every 100 women.

The Government's most recent statement has suggested that it is attempting to draw a measured line between two groups. The first proposes a policy of zero net overseas migration, which would result in a rapid decline in population from about 20 million today to about 14 million by the end of this century. The second calls for a net overseas gain of 1 percent of population a year, which would result in a population of about 38 million by midcentury and 68 million by 2100. The latter, the Government also claims, would require a considerable lowering of migration entry standards to include lower skilled and unskilled people.

The Government believes that it is undesirable and inappropriate to fix an optimum population target. Based on existing and probable trends in immigration, fertility, and life expectancy, Australia should have a stable population of around 24 to 25 million by the middle of the twenty-first century, though the Minister for Immigration concedes that further research is necessary. The Minister sees the areas of future debate as fourfold: The need to maintain and enhance Australia's competitive advantages in immigration management and in particular to continue to attract young, highly skilled migrants with good English language skills; the need to encourage a higher level of labor force participation, especially by older Australians; research into the fertility rate, and in particular, the causes of fertility decline and how such decline might be avoided; and the need to ensure that the impact on the environment of future population levels is sustainable.

The contribution of, arguably, Australia's most original historian, Professor Geoffrey Blainey, to the land and population debate is as provocative as ever. Blainey argues that our maps make the country look far more attractive to outsiders than it actually is. "Australia's makers of maps and namers of places have unintentionally succeeded in informing the outside world that much of the interior is dotted with large attractive lakes," he says. "Alas, Lake Eyre is not like Lake Victoria in Africa."[9] The slogan "Populate or Perish" has itself perished as environmentalists and demographers have begun to make Australians aware of the limitations of the land. But people in adjacent Asian countries remain largely unaware of the fierce debates that range in Australia concerning the country's desired population limit and ability to sustain itself.

"If you kept a clipping service of what was said in South-East Asian newspapers and even things that were translated and reported in our press and radio," Blainey says, "the number of statements made in the course of a year about Australia's big spaces and relatively small population, by South-East Asian standards, are quite large."

In typically paradoxical fashion, Blainey points to an unexpected source of potential legitimacy for whites' occupation of Australia. With national parks and land rights, the Greens and Aborigines have "huge areas of the Outback ... virtually locked up." In tropical and central Australia, these lands form a "long buffer zone" between populous Australia and southeast Asia. "It is just possible," he argues, "that this new protected zone will help to legitimise, in the eyes of the outside world, Australia's possession of this empty and long-defiant territory."

For some observers, the answer is simple. One commentator, for instance, says boldly that "The fact is that we would be a healthier, safer, and stronger society if: Australians married earlier than they are doing today; we had more children and had them earlier; we stuck together more often, rather than getting divorced; fewer children were brought up by single parents (mostly mothers); and children (especially boys) saw more of their fathers."[10] Just how these desires are to be achieved is not a question he addresses, except to relate the problem to a tax system that discriminates in favor of individuals and against families and to suggest paid maternity leave. But as has been pointed out, virtually all the European countries that provide universal maternity leave have fertility rates equivalent to or lower than that of Australia. Countries with high fertility rates generally have low living standards. For instance, countries with fertility rates above 5 percent include Gabon, Congo, Rwanda, Mali, Uganda, Angola, Somalia, Yemen, and Mozambique.

This suggests very strongly that not having children is a matter of choice where possible, and in recent discussion, women have been openly exhorted to become more fertile, at an earlier age, and bring more children into an already overpopulated world. It is not a new complaint. As far back as 1901 one clergyman complained about the declining birth rate as cutting "deep into the canker which is eating the very heart out of our Australian society," and suggested a regular meeting between the clergy and doctors to deal with "what everyone admits is a growing evil and menace to the State," and such a meeting did in fact take place in New South Wales two years later.[11] In 1919 a Royal Commission came to similar conclusions and expressed similar concerns. A typical recent newspaper headline that attempts to apply moral pressure on women is "Falling fertility tells our children we don't value them."

One recent suggestion, based on newly introduced models in Europe, is to provide a home-care allowance for full-time mothers as payment of their child-care work and as a gesture of public recognition. This, it is argued, would appeal to a wider group of women than maternity leave rights to women who are more likely to go back to work anyway—though it does not preclude the provision of maternity leave as well. The current government has apparently shown keen interest in the idea.

Amongst all this debate, however, with conservative commentators bemoaning the loss of fertility among Australian women, pointing to the even more calamitous example of Italy and raising suggestions as to how fertility can be encouraged, there are few who will consider the obvious solution of increased immigration. If the boat people had been welcomed into the community instead of turned away, demonized, or incarcerated, the problem of an aging Australia would soon disappear. As one commentator noted:

> But the insularity of this debate betrays how we remain biological patriots with an attachment to cultural diversity that is only skin-deep. We want the spicy food, but not the people who make it; the world music, but not the people who play it; the handwoven carpets, but not the people who make them—at least, not in large enough numbers to end the births strike.[12]

Aboriginal Health

The figures quoted above are for the population as a whole. When we turn to figures associated with Aboriginal health, however, the story is different. Statistics in New South Wales and Victoria are so poor that they cannot be trusted or tell us little. However, insofar as national figures can be estimated, they show that from 1997 to 2000, indigenous children under the age of 12 months died at a rate of 14.98 per 1,000 live births compared with the overall Australian rate of 5.29.

Aboriginal life expectancy in general lags 20 years behind the general population, at 56 years for men and 64 for women; more alarmingly still, it has done so for 20 years. While both the government and the opposition pay lip service to the scandalous nature of this situation, in fact, almost nothing has been done to address it.

Despite this, the 2001 Census showed that overall numbers of Aborigines continue to rise, with a 16 percent increase over the five years since the last census, to 410,000 people. It is also much younger than the rest of Australia (about 58 percent under 25), and with a much higher fertility rate. The rise may also be partly due to increased willingness among people following movements toward reconciliation and the stolen generations' inquiry to acknowledge their Aboriginality. Many more Aborigines now live in the major cities rather than in remote outback areas.

Commentators have, in fact, pointed to a phenomenon in Australia that has taken far longer to emerge than in the United States, the rise of an Aboriginal, urban middle class. At the bottom end of the scale there are almost twice as many Aboriginal men in prison as there are at tertiary institutions—4,075 as against 2,482; the comparable figures for Aboriginal women are less horrendous—370 as against 4,646. Against this, of the 29.8 percent of Aborigines who live in cities, one in eight is on the middle-class income of $600–999 per week.[13] But of course, this is still a small minority, and even among these affluent few there is little accumulated wealth from previous generations and often familial obligations that Aboriginal custom dictates are obligatory.

Notes

1. Miriam Dixson, *The Real Matilda* (Melbourne: Penguin, 1984), p. 11.
2. Ibid., p. 24.
3. Patricia Grimshaw, Marilyn Lake, Ann McGrath, and Marian Quartly, *Creating a Nation* (Melbourne: McPhee Gribble, 1994), p. 117.
4. Anne Summers, *Damned Whores and God's Police* (Melbourne: Penguin, 1975), p. 123.
5. Marilyn Lake and Farley Kelly, *Double Time: Women in Victoria—150 Years* (Melbourne: Penguin, 1985), p. xi.
6. Quoted in Moira Eastman, "Can Labor Hear the Women Who Want to Be Full-Time Mothers?" *The Age*, 12 July 2002.
7. Bettina Arndt, "Nicholson's Dark Legacy: A Court That Failed Men," *The Age*, 17 July 2002.
8. Julie Szego, "Divorce Rate Not All Bad: Chief Justice," *The Age*, 3 September 2002.
9. Geoffrey Blainey, "A Land of Dark Greens," *The Age*, 19 November 2001. Professor Blainey gave the Boyer lectures in 2001 and his ideas are enunciated in these.
10. Malcom Turnbull, "The Crisis Is Fertility, Not Ageing," *The Age*, 16 July 2002.
11. Cited in Grimshaw et al., *Creating a Nation*, pp. 193–94.
12. Rosemary Neill, "Short of Young People? Try Mass Immigration," *The Australian*, 21 June 2002.
13. George Megalogenis, "Secret Life of City Blacks," *The Weekend Australian*, 28–29 September 2002.

4

Holidays and Leisure Activities

Work and Leisure

It has always been difficult and is currently becoming even more so to talk about leisure in Australia without talking about work. There is in Australia a tension between the work ethic and the attitude symbolized by what is known as "the long weekend"—the fact that Australia's relatively plentiful public holidays are regularly transferred to Monday so that workers can get away for three successive days (or even four if they can swing it with their boss or doctor). One book by social commentator Ronald Conway even has the reproving title *The Land of the Long Weekend* (1978), which followed his equally tart *The Great Australian Stupor* (1971).

Views of Australians (at least until fairly recently) as lazy, and frequent antagonism between employers and employees, where neither group can recognize any common interests, have been noted regularly. Sometimes they are traced back to the origins of Australian labor—a convict system under which the laborer had no rights at all and could even, at the whim of his master, be sent to Sydney with a letter in his hand demanding that he be whipped. The militancy and, for a long time, popularity of trade unions are ascribed to much the same causes. Sydney and Melbourne workers achieved the eight-hour day as early as 1856—although it should be remembered that they still worked six days a week. Not until well into the twentieth century did unions achieve a half-day off on Saturday, reducing the working week to 44 hours, and later to 40.

Today there is the paradox that although the country has over 6 percent unemployment—more than one-half million people—as well as sizeable underemployment, of those in full-time jobs the average number of hours worked is 44 per week, and more than 45 percent of employees work overtime, much of it unpaid. Only in July 2002 did the Court rule that workers could refuse unreasonable demands from their employers to work overtime, although the concept of "unreasonable" was left carefully undefined.

The picture has become increasing clouded by the rise of modern technology and the closing of the clear lines of demarcation between workplace and place of residence. Many modern devices are both tools and toys. Is that student huddled over a computer working on his assignment or is he playing computer games? Is that smartly dressed woman using her mobile phone to conclude a business deal or call up one of her friends for lunch? What is certainly true is that a great many Australians work longer than the regular forty hours, often without pay. So serious has the problem become that recently there have been arguments that workers' hours should be capped at 48.

The idea that Australians are afraid of hard work is dubious. Even colloquial language pays frequent tribute to the centrality of labor in the Australian consciousness, in terms like "hard yakka" or "hard slog" (hard work); "bullocking," "bludger" (the term for someone who will not work and "bludges" on his mates and perhaps the worst insult you can offer an Australian); "graft" (work, especially manual work); "lurk" (an essentially dishonest scheme for making money); and above all, "dole bludger," a term used contemptuously and often unfairly to denote those who dislike honest labor and prefer to rely on government handouts. Unsurprisingly, it is a claim often leveled against Aboriginal people.

TRAVEL AND TOURISM

Nevertheless, there are genuine forms of leisure available to most Australians and many of these have taken on an almost ritualistic air. The rise of leisure really coincides with the increasing access to automobiles after the war, especially the Australian-designed Holden; the increasing affluence of the postwar period; and later, the sharp reduction in air fares, which meant that far more Australians than ever before could travel overseas.

In 1949 one in eight Australians owned a car; just over a decade later, as prices steadily dropped, the ratio was down to one in five. With the car came the associated culture of motels, or motor hotels as they were originally called. In May 1952 *Walkabout* magazine announced that "Australia needs motels." Eight years later its strident call had been answered; by March 1960 there were 272 of them in Australia. Queensland in particular, narrowly followed by Victoria and New South Wales, led the way, with the Gold

Coast, then as now, one of the supreme icons of Australian tourism, boasting 36 of the state's 59 motels. Motels in turn created a need and clamor for new and better roads. Over the last half century Australian roads have vastly improved, though there are still many so-called black spots or areas marked by frequent accidents. A vast freeway system, with signs and construction modeled exactly on the American original, has spread all over the country, with cars diverted past little towns where they would formerly have stopped.

The first motel in Victoria opened with the proud but unintentionally ambiguous advertising slogan, "Your car in your bedroom," pointing out that you could park your car within a short distance of your bedroom, and even today many motels have as a central feature the close proximity of the car and the room. From primitive beginnings with motels that ignored even the beautiful views just outside the window, the architecture steadily improved, aided by trailblazing designs like Robin Boyd's Black Dolphin at Merimbula on the east coast of New South Wales, which was one of the first motels to adopt a deliberately Australian style, with the building carefully blended in with the landscape of native trees and lawns.

Australians have always been quick to adopt new modes of technology, whether it is cars or television sets or, more recently, computers and mobile phones. The hegemony of the car over public transport was not questioned until comparatively recently as demographers and environmentalists began to appreciate the immensity of the social changes it has wrought—ever-expanding suburbs with the high infrastructure costs involved in servicing them; hugely expensive freeways; air pollution; and large numbers of motorists and pedestrians killed or injured every year.

The lowering of airfares had a similarly spectacular effect on people's leisure activities. Schoolteachers, for instance, can now take off immediately when the summer break begins—from shortly before Christmas to roughly the end of January—and need not be seen until just before school resumes. Students can finish their secondary schooling and take a year off, deferring their university education to explore Australia by backpack or spend 12 months in Europe, mixing tourism with casual labor. Closer to home are popular tourist destinations such as Bali, which can be reached at less expense than many parts of Australia and which is one of the places where ecotourism has rapidly expanded, though the terrorist bombing on October 12, 2002, has been a major setback to tourism.

The actual history of tourism in Australia goes back a lot further than most people would imagine. One study of the phenomenon claims 1871 as the beginning of international tourism in Australia.[1] In that year Thomas Cook & Son put together a program for a round-the-world tour, but received not one booking until Australia was removed from the itinerary. The Tasmanian Tourist Association was established at a public meeting held in 1893 and worked hand in hand with the Thomas Cook travel agency to promote Tasmania as a tourist site. New South Wales created an Intelligence Department in 1907 to publicize the state as widely as possible. The already existing railway tourist bureau was part of this.

Most states soon had tourist bureaus though their budgets were usually miniscule. The Australian National Travel Association (ANTA), with the assistance of the travel industry, opened in Melbourne in 1929, hardly auspicious timing. ANTA established a monthly magazine *Walkabout* in 1934; this attracted widespread advertising support from groups associated with the tourism movement and drew attention to areas and aspects of Australia that most of its citizens would have known little about. ANTA became the Australian Tourism Industry Association in 1985, reflecting its growing industry potential, and then the Tourism Council Australia in 1995, but in early 2001 it was placed in receivership. More important now are the Tourism Task Force, established under the Hawke Labor government in the 1980s, and the Australian Tourist Commission.

Australians, at least until recently, have been more prone to travel overseas than to explore their own country, especially its inland. But this has begun to change over the last few years. Now both local and international tourism is steadily increasing, with an estimated 6 million visitors arriving in 2001, and on current projections, some 20 million by the year 2030. Already, tourism earns Australia six times as much money as does wool.

In the last two decades university courses have developed and journals have been founded that focus specifically on tourism. Tourism has also been included in courses in such subjects as geography, planning, and business. As is often pointed out, tourism is, in fact, less a pure activity in itself than a combination of many industries and services, involving national and international transport carriers, accommodation operators, eating establishments of numerous kinds, travel agents and operators, souvenir manufacturers and suppliers, national parks and galleries, as well as convention centers and entertainment facilities. There is a great deal of integration and synergy among many of the participants, with airlines, for instance, owning island resorts and hotels.

Australia's first casino was not opened until 1973, at Wrest Point in Hobart, Tasmania. Unusually, it was supported by both political parties who acted out of fear that Queensland was destroying the impoverished state's success as a tourist destination. Since then, the number of casinos has grown rapidly, with many of them making special arrangements to catch the overseas dollars of the "high rollers," and poker machines can now be found in numerous places of entertainment, to the point where the concern now is with problem gamblers.

Even zoos have plans to reinvent themselves, in response to the wishes of international visitors. The Melbourne Zoo came up with a proposal to build an onsite hotel, camping ground, and 24-hour shopping center. The proposal argues that "Market research is telling us a new vision of interactive zoos, where people experience a magic moment of connection with an animal, needs to be realised.... Simply displaying animals is not enough."[2]

But tourism remains vulnerable to world events beyond its control, such as the Gulf War crisis of 1990–91 or, more recently, the New York Twin Towers disaster of September 11, 2001, both of which disrupted tourist patterns, especially in regard to air travel.

The Gold Coast and the Sunshine Coast have attracted many tourists in recent years. Here, whole cities have grown up primarily in response to international visitors. The opening of Cairns as an international airport in 1984 was the major catalyst in the tourist growth of the north Queensland region. Among the most popular destinations for tourists are Uluru (formerly Ayers Rock, but now returned to its Aboriginal owners), the Great Barrier Reef, Kakadu National Park, the Daintree Rain Forest, and the Great Ocean Road in Victoria. In the 1960s a mere 5,000 Australians per annum visited Uluru. In the year 2000 it received 271,000 Australian visitors and an even higher total of overseas tourists.

Similarly, another great natural wonder, Lake Eyre, in the northeast corner of South Australia, received its largest number of visitors ever in 2000 when the world's largest saltpan was briefly transformed into a vast sea. When filled to capacity, which is seldom, Lake Eyre holds 34 cubic kilometers of water and covers an area of 9,500 square kilometers. However, it has flooded only four times in the last century. Australia has 13 World Heritage listed sites as well as 3,429 protected areas and other lesser-known outback areas.

Only slowly are Australians beginning to understand what Aboriginal people have known for thousands of years—that a landscape viewed by the first European intruders as scrubby, barren, and impoverished is actually rich and varied in a completely different way from European models. Many areas that are often described as "infertile" are actually rich in native plantlife, birdlife, and insects. Not only does Australia have a great diversity of birds, but also one of the highest percentages of nomadic bird species in the world.

On the Beach

At home the elders have their own rites of leisure. Actor Paul Hogan's famous series of advertisements in America ("Throw another shrimp on the barbie"[barbeque]) testified to the popularity and ubiquity of the barbecue of a Saturday or Sunday afternoon, with its atmosphere of sunshine, good will, never-ending supplies of beer or cheap but eminently quaffable Australian wine, and blackened chops and sausages.

"Australians all let us rejoice,/Our land is girt by sea," goes the national anthem, "Advance Australia Fair," and the beach is an important part of Australia's culture. During the summer months, especially, trips to the beach and beach resorts are almost obligatory. Small beach towns swell to 10 or more times their normal population during the months from December to March as holiday makers descend on them en masse, spending enough money to keep the towns viable for the other eight months of the year. With increasing affluence, many people have bought their own summer homes, which they can retreat to during the hotter months, or visit regularly at weekends, especially long weekends.

In the visits to the beach lies the origin of Australia's outstanding record in swimming and surfing and the growth of its famous life savers at Bondi, in Sydney. The Bondi Surf Bathers' Lifesaving Club was formed in 1906, after laws banning surfing in New South Wales were overturned. Although it has been responsible for saving thousands of struggling swimmers since then, ironically its most famous rescue was its first, that of Charles Kingsford Smith, who lived to become one of Australia's most famous aviators, setting a record for flights from Australia to England in 1929.

Australia's preeminence in surfing began with Bernard "Midge" Farrelly, who won the unofficial world surfboard riding championship at Makaha, Hawaii, in 1963. The following year he went on to win the first official world championship at Manly in Sydney. On the darker side, the beach can be a place of menace, especially to tourists who are unable to read the warning signs on beaches. Between 1992 and 1998 there were 102 reported drownings of overseas residents. Although the likelihood of death from shark attack is reputedly lower than that of being struck by lightning, or even being stung to death by bees, sharks strike the same menacing chord in the Australian consciousness as Peter Benchley's novel *Jaws* suggests they do in the United States. Shark attacks have become both more common and more daring in recent years, prompting fierce debates with environmentalists about how far measures should be taken to protect potential victims from the sharks. A similar debate has raged in the north of Australia over how far man-eating crocodiles should be protected or hunted down.

A less conspicuous but equally deadly predator is the bluebottle jellyfish, with its potentially lethal sting, while less dramatically still, but most dangerously, cancers contracted from the rays of the sun are the biggest killer of all. As the hole in the ozone layer has widened and temperatures have slowly risen, Australians have finally begun to realize the danger of prolonged and unprotected sunbathing. Advertising campaigns encouraging sunbathers to wear hats and use preventative creams ("Slip, slop, slap") have changed the culture of sunbathing as much as drunk-driving campaigns have changed public attitudes to driving under the influence of alcohol, or the appearance of HIV/AIDS has changed sexual practices, but there is still a lot of progress to be made.

A statement by SunSmart, the skin cancer awareness program, reads, "Attitudes towards tanning and sun protection have changed dramatically. Australians have realised the pitfalls of their sun-loving outdoor lifestyle and are taking preventative measures to reduce their risk of skin cancer." But perhaps not dramatically enough as yet. According to SunSmart, more than 800,000 Australian men get sunburned every summer weekend, and more than 1,200 Australians, two-thirds of them male, still die from skin cancer every year.

Writer Robert Drewe argues that the beach is an indispensable part of Australian life and myth, often initiating young Australians into sexual experience and drinking. Gabrielle Carey and Kathy Lette in their best-selling novel *Puberty Blues* (1979) echo the thought, though they also point to the ability of the beach's attractions to outweigh even those of the girls: "The beach was the most sacred place of all. Boys' boards came before everything. It was waves before babes. They were faithful to the sea, and we were faithful to them."[3] The beach's almost mythic quality in the Australian consciousness has been captured by several artists, most often in the black and white photographs of Max Dupain (1911–82). His most famous photograph shows a bather, tanned and glistening wet, lying on his stomach and absorbing the sun, the very epitome of hedonism.

In Perth, nudist beachgoers appear in the "best bum" competition at the Swanbourne Olympics. In stark contrast, arid and landbound Alice Springs in the middle of Australia has its own Henley-on-Todd—where the river consists of a dry bed and the competitors carry their boats instead of rowing them. Darwin in the far north has devised another uniquely Australian competition in which rafts race against one another: all are made of beer cans. Even such parodic events, however, testify to the centrality of the beach in Australian leisure. Diggers at Gallipoli during World War I risked their lives to assert their inalienable right to swim off the beach while Turkish snipers took shots at them. One last attraction of the beach is that, for most of the time, it is still free. One study of tourism points out that "Over 95 percent of the Australian coastline is in public ownership. Only a handful of islands and some pre-1910 subdivisions in NSW are in private ownership, along with perhaps 150 marinas developed around Australia since the 1960s."[4]

Luna Park, a popular Melbourne amusement park. Photo by Michael Hanrahan.

Other Forms of Holidaying

At the same time, ski resorts are available in many parts of Australia. Ski clubs had been organized as early as the 1860s and the first successful skiing expedition to the summit of Mt. Kosciuszko, Australia's tallest mountain, although still miniscule by overseas standards, took place in 1897. Now New South Wales has Thredbo and Perisher Valley while Victoria has Mt. Hotham and the Mt. Buffalo National Park. Australia won its first-ever gold medal at the Olympic Winter Games in Salt Lake City in 2002 and followed it up with a second—in short-track speed skating and freestyle aerials, respectively.

Among the newer forms of entertainment are adventure holidays for the young and young-minded. The rise of four-wheel drive vehicles means that more and more of Australia's most isolated places have become accessible, though they have not displaced the old combination of car and caravan, which forms a kind of subculture of its own. Recreational vehicle drivers automatically hail each other as they pass, and some people, especially couples in retirement, have made their RV a kind of permanent, mobile home. This was one reason why, when the Goods and Services Tax (GST) was introduced, there was enormous protest from RV owners and demands that they be exempted.

There are other, more formalized, modes of entertainment. Building on nineteenth-century festivals such as Proclamation Day in Glenelg, South Australia, and the Easter Fair in Bendigo, Victoria, the major cities now mostly conduct their own celebrations. Melbourne has its Moomba festival in March, with celebrations and displays of various kinds—fireworks, exhibitions on the water, a parade through the city, and so on. Sydney more recently has attracted huge crowds, many of them from overseas, for its Gay and Lesbian Mardi Gras, and the growth of artists' and writers' festivals over the last two decades, not only in the capital cities but even in regional centers, has been astonishing. Centenaries provide further regular occasions for celebration.

Sport

Most countries now accept that sport plays a major part in the fabric of their culture, but there would be few countries in the world where it is more highly regarded than in Australia. This is the only nation that holds a public holiday for the running of a horserace, the Melbourne Cup, which is always held on the first Tuesday of November. The Melbourne Cup in 1901 attracted a crowd of 95,000, or virtually one in five of Melbourne's then population. Even now it commands attendance of over 120,000, and the nation traditionally comes to a halt as the race is shown over television. People who never otherwise bet in their lives take a plunge on the Cup and the Totalizer Agency Board (TAB), the State-run offtrack betting agency, is crowded as lines form from early morning. Many businesses organize their own staff "sweeps" where each participating member pays a small sum to receive the name of a horse, and those who draw the winning names receive a prize after the race is run.

Australians play or watch almost every sport there is, and Australia is one of only a small handful of countries that have competed in every Olympic Games. They have twice hosted the Games—at Melbourne in 1956 when they won 13 Gold Medals, their highest achievement to that point, and in Sydney in 2000 when they won a remarkable 58 medals, 16 of them in swimming alone, and came in fourth in the overall medal tally behind the three superpowers, the United States, Russia, and China, an astonishing achievement in terms of the countries' relative populations. But probably the sports in which they excel most are cricket (played largely among Commonwealth countries), tennis, and swimming—as well, of course, as their own indigenous code of Australian Rules football. Among other widely popular sports are golf, Rugby League, Rugby Union, squash, car and motorbike racing, horseracing, boxing, rowing, cycling, yachting, netball, hockey, soccer, baseball, and basketball.

The rise of American's influence can be seen in the growing popularity of the last two sports. There are even a few teams that play American football at a very low level—just as there are countries overseas, including the United States, which have begun to play cricket and Australian football.

Cricket

One of the most popular summer sports is cricket, originally invented in England but enthusiastically adopted in the colonies Ironically, the first Australian team to tour England, in 1868, was Aboriginal. But since then fewer than a dozen players known to be from indigenous backgrounds have ever played first-class cricket in Australia. Before Jason Gillespie, who has some Aboriginal background and who is a current and highly successful member of the Australian Test team, no indigenous male had represented Australia at international level, or at least no acknowledged one: There have been claims that some cricketers who were Aboriginal concealed their identity out of necessity as they would never have been picked.

The last Aboriginal cricketer to play in England was a woman, Faith Coulthard-Thomas, in 1958. Eddie Gilbert, a fast bowler who played for Queensland in the 1930s, was frozen out of the game when his bowling action was declared to be illegitimate. The accusation that he was a "chucker"—someone who threw the ball rather than bowling it with a straight arm—was believed by many to be a fabrication. The same has been argued about Jack Marsh, who played six matches for New South Wales and was one of the best bowlers in the world until he too was umpired out. Not until 120 years after the inaugural tour did the second tour of England by an Aboriginal cricket team finally take place.

In the meantime, a legendary tradition had grown up between England and Australia in which each series of Test matches (usually five) was fought for "the Ashes," reportedly the ashes of a bail or stump contained in a small terra-cotta urn, and now held permanently at England's famous Lords cricket ground. Rivalry between the two countries was always fanatically keen, even today when Australia has established its dominance over England by winning the last eight series, and some observers argue that sport in general and cricket in particular have played an important part in Australia's growth to maturity and self-confidence. Often cited as a factor in overcoming any sense of inferiority is the frank contempt with which Australian captain Warwick Armstrong treated his English opponents on the successful 1921 tour of England.

Although many great names stand out as representatives of Australia, England, the West Indies, South Africa, New Zealand, India, Pakistan, and the other cricket-playing countries, the one that is supreme is the Australian batsman, Sir Donald Bradman. Bradman played for Australia between 1928 and 1948. His batting feats are legion, but perhaps the best way to sum up his greatness is to cite his lifetime Test batting average of 99.94, or virtually 100 runs per inning. To put it in perspective, no other batsman (hitter) who has played a considerable amount of Test cricket has topped 60, so that Bradman was, in effect, two-thirds more successful as a batsman than anyone else who played.

So successful was he, in fact, that on their 1932–33 tour of Australia, England devised the specific and highly questionable tactic called Bodyline to contain him. It consisted of bowling very fast and straight at the head of the batsman, on one side of the pitch, and gathering most of the fielders around him in catching positions. It was successful in that Bradman's series average was only 56.6, but so unpopular was the tactic, with players being frequently struck savage blows to their bodies, that it came near to destroying relations between England and Australia. Crowds were on the point of rioting on several occasions and discussions were held at the highest political levels before the tactic was quietly abandoned.

But Bradman was more than a great sportsman. For ordinary Australians, growing up or living through the Depression when his greatest feats were achieved, he became, like the racehorse Phar Lap, a rare symbol of hope. He was, in the words of one of the songs written about him, "our Don Bradman." A reserved and highly complex man, he did not easily mix well with his teammates, but his behavior and sportsmanship throughout his life were impeccable. After retiring he became Australia's most influential cricket administrator for many years as well as running his own successful business. When he died, at the age of 92, there was a national outpouring of grief.

Australian women first played cricket in 1874 and international Test cricket in 1954. The Australian Women's Cricket Council, established in 1931, has been responsible for tours to several countries, including England, New Zealand, India, the West Indies, and Ireland, as well as visits here. The current Australian women's cricket team is far and away the best in the world, even more dominant than the men's. The importance of cricket in particular, and sport in general, to the Australian psyche can best be measured by the awe in which even a prime minister can hold it. In 1997 the Prime Minister, John Howard, stated: "I really have regarded being captain of the Australian cricket team as the absolute pinnacle of sporting achievement, and really the pinnacle of human achievement almost, in Australia."[5] That this statement was accepted seriously, with no howls of derision, indicates something of the Australian mania for sport.

Football

Especially in Victoria and the southern states, but growing in popularity in Queensland and New South Wales under the relentless promotion of the Australian Football League (AFl), the indigenous code of Australian Rules football is enormously popular. Further north, the two codes of rugby tend to dominate, though the AFl has steadily and systematically eaten into their territory. Ambrose Pratt commented in *The Centenary History of Victoria* (1934) that the typical Victorian "adulates its football and cricket champions but, until they die or win fame abroad, it accords its statesmen, writers, artists and scientists a deliberately abstemious measure of appreciation."[6]

The origins of Australian Rules football are again somewhat contentious. For a long time it was widely accepted that in 1858 a secretary of the Melbourne Cricket Club, T. W. (Tom) Wills, suggested that cricketers should keep fit in winter by playing football, and the first game was believed to be a match between the two private schools of Melbourne Grammar and Scotch College. More recently, however, it has been argued that the game began with indigenous Australians, a contention given more credibility by the extraordinary skills Aboriginal footballers have displayed over the last two decades as their presence became more common. The Djabwurrung and Jardwadjali clans in the western district of Victoria played a game they called Marn Grook, which resembles modern Australian Rules. Wills was brought up in the western district and played regularly with Aboriginal children, although the connection cannot be established with certainty.

In any case, the game quickly developed its own highly idiosyncratic rules—an oval-shaped and therefore unpredictable ball, huge grounds of varying sizes, no offside rule and encouragement for players to climb on opponents' backs to take spectacular "marks"—or catches. A regular competition had been formed by 1877 and eventually, with the advent of television and the increasing competition with other international sports, the Victorian Football League became the Australian Football League, with one side in Queensland, another in New South Wales, and two each in South Australia and Western Australia.

Motor Racing

Car racing began in 1904 with a meeting in Melbourne on March 12 and has grown spectacularly ever since, with Melbourne annually hosting one of the international Grand Prix, and the country producing its own champion in Jack Brabham in the 1950s. Australia has also been more prominent in motorbike racing, producing world champions in Wayne Gardner and Mick Doohan (five times).

Tennis

Norman Brookes put Australia on the tennis map when he became the first Australian to win Wimbledon in 1907. Since then his feat has been duplicated by many Australian champions, beginning with Gerald Patterson in 1919. Surprisingly little known, Patterson went on to dominate tennis for almost a decade. Australia was especially strong in the 1950s, with champions such as Lew Hoad, Ken Rosewall, Frank Sedgeman, Rod Laver, John Newcombe, and Roy Emerson, but has continued to remain among the world leaders since then. The 1950s were the period of intense and almost monopolistic rivalry between Australia and the United States for the Davis Cup, which Australia has now won 17 times. Rod Laver became the first Australian to win the Grand Slam of titles in 1962. In the same year Margaret Court (née Smith), easily the greatest tennis player the country has produced, won the first of her five U.S. Women's Open titles (she won 24 Grand Slam titles in all). More recent champions include Pat Cash, Pat Rafter, and Lleyton Hewitt. The latter two have won the U.S. Open between them three times in the last five years. Cash won Australia's last Wimbledon title in 1983 before Hewitt won in 2002.

Rugby

Australia's rugby union team, the Wallabies, and rugby league team, the Kangaroos, toured England for the first time in 1908. In 1984 the Wallabies made history when they achieved the grand slam of wins against England, Ireland, Scotland, and Wales. Two years later, the Kangaroos defeated all comers on its British tour. Named after a style of football played at the famous Rugby school in England, the sport quickly caught on in New South Wales and then

Jeff Fenech, boxer, and John Lewis, trainer. Photo by Graham McCarter.

Queensland. Though 1865 is generally thought to be the first year in which it was played on a regular, competitive basis, there are reports of a similar game being played as early as 1829. The Rugby Union Wallabies won a gold medal at the 1908 Olympic Games.

League and Union, similar but not identical codes, eventually divided, largely upon class lines, early in the twentieth century. Rugby has the incomparable advantage over Australian Rules of having international connections and teams tour overseas regularly. Since the collapse of apartheid, South Africa has returned to the rugby-playing community.

Boxing

Among the great—and tragic—names in boxing was Australian heavyweight champion Les Darcy, who knocked out American champion Eddie

McGoorty in 1915. Refusing to enlist in the army, Darcy sailed the following year to the United States in search of a world title but died of an infection in 1917. However, Australia has contributed a number of fine boxers including Lionel Rose, an Aboriginal who became world bantamweight champion in 1968. Most Australian champion boxers—Jimmy Carruthers, Johnny Famechon, Jeff Fenech—have featured in the lighter divisions, such as bantam- or featherweight. With small purses and few bouts most have to regard boxing as a part-time activity, and in the heavier divisions especially it has been very difficult for an outsider to break in to the rich international circuit. More recently, however, Australia has produced two super middleweight champions, Tony Mundine and Danny Green.

Horse Racing

The same fate as Les Darcy was to meet the racehorse, Phar Lap, another of Australia's greatest and most popular sporting icons. Born in New Zealand but brought to Australia as a three-year-old, he won a phenomenal 37 races from 51 starts, including the 1930 Melbourne Cup where he started at 8–11, the shortest-priced favorite in Cup history. Known as Big Red, for his chestnut color and huge fighting heart, Phar Lap was taken to America in 1932. He won the Agua Caliente Handicap in Mexico before dying under mysterious circumstances in the United States, which led to many conspiracy theories.

Horse racing ("the sport of kings") has retained its popularity in modern times, despite the rise of less traditional sporting alternatives. A report commissioned by the Australian Racing Board and released in 2001 noted that, among other things, horse racing is second only to Australian Football ("Aussie Rules") as the nation's most popular sport, and is responsible for the full- or part-time employment of 240,000 people. Per capita, Australia is the world's leading country in ownership of thoroughbred racehorses, and prize-money is third highest in the world. Australia is responsible for 16 percent of the world's foal crop, second only to the United States, and has a racehorse population in excess of 31,000.

Cycling

Among the great Australian names in cycling are Bob ("Long Bob") Spears, who won the world professional spring championship in Antwerp in 1920 and dominated world cycling throughout the 1920s, and Hubert ("Oppy") Opperman, who won the Australian road cycling championship four times, beginning in 1924, as well as France's 24-hour Bol d'Or, held over a distance of 909 km, in 1928. Later, as captain of the Australian team, he won the Tour de France in 1931. Opperman served with distinction in the air force during World War II and later in Federal Parliament and was eventually knighted.

Golf

Great Australian names in golf are few, but among the first and most famous are Norman von Nida and Peter Thomson, who in 1954 became the first Australian to win the British Open Golf Championship. He went on to repeat the feat four times. Since then, the most famous name is that of Greg Norman, affectionately known as the Great White Shark. Though Norman has been near the top among golfers for many years, he was unable to win as many titles as he seemed capable of, often finishing with a place.

Soccer

Given its worldwide status, the enormous amounts of money it is possible to earn, and the widespread television coverage of the sport, it is strange that soccer has not taken off in a bigger way than it has in Australia. This is particularly the case given the number of migrants from soccer-mad countries who have come to the country. But the Socceroos have qualified for the World Cup Finals only once—in 1974—though they came close on several other occasions. Australia has, however, contributed several fine players to international clubs—at the moment more than 150 Australian soccer players are based overseas—just as it is now beginning to produce basketball and baseball players for the United States and even kickers from Australian football to the American football leagues. Among the reasons for soccer not being more popular are bitter rivalries among administrators, ethnic tensions between different clubs, many of which show an intense loyalty to a particular country in Europe, and the intense pressure exerted by other football codes to persuade youths to their game.

The 2002 World Cup, held in South Korea and Japan, and therefore at a time suitable for Australian viewing, confirmed the suspicion that soccer is the sleeping giant of Australian sport. Although Australia failed to qualify, television ratings were huge, and even people who had never watched a soccer match before were pontificating knowledgeably on the sport by the time the Final was shown in front of a record audience. Australia's first defeat of England in a so-called friendly match, 3–1, again drew attention to the mass of hidden talent. It seemed for a time as if Australia might have an easier route to the 2006 World Cup through the so-called Oceania group, but this has now been revoked.

Boys demonstrate their karate skills for a crowd at the Queen Victoria Market, Melbourne. Photo by Anna Clemann.

Yachting

Apart from the Olympics, perhaps Australia's most notable international sporting achievement was the victory of the yacht Australia II in the America's Cup race in 1983, the first time in 132 years of challenges that it had left the shores of the United States. There is also the highly popular Sydney to Hobart yacht race, held over Boxing Day (the day after Christmas Day), which attracts large numbers of entrants. Recently the race became enmeshed in controversy when many boats foundered in huge seas and several sailors were killed, but the rules have now been tightened.

Children and Sports

All this sporting prowess was possible, however, only because of the strong grassroots component of the games, with children encouraged (and until a few years ago sometimes compelled) to play competitive sports. Sixty-one percent of children under 14 play some form of sports in clubs and organizations while 32 percent of Australians older than 15 play regular sports. Sports administrators worry, nevertheless, about the fierce competition for young people's attention that society offers, in the form of computer games, virtual reality, cable television, videos, and DVDs. There is now nothing like the world Russell Drysdale depicted in his classic painting *The Cricketers* (1948)—spindly kids playing cricket up against a wall, with makeshift equipment, to the background of a vast desert waste.

Women and Sports

In all these sports women have been, until quite recently, shockingly discriminated against, even though they have shown that once given a chance they can more than hold their own in international competition. Author Richard Cashman cites a 1913 male criticism of women's hockey: "It was suggested that it produces angularity, hardens sinews, abnormally develops certain parts of the body, causes abrasion and imparts disfigurement."[7] Australia's women's hockey team, the Hockeyroos, topped the world ratings for eight years in a row while its soccer team, the Matildas, has had considerable success.

Australia's first female golfing star was Pamela Stephenson, but more recently Karrie Webb is rated as one of the best three female golfers in the world. Originally female golfers were refused permission to use public links on weekends or public holidays. Even today 20.9 percent of men play golf as against 5.8 percent of women.

The NSW Ladies Amateur Swimming Association was formed in 1906, yet as late as 1980, Surf Life Saving Australia refused to allow female members in. Discrimination persists today in more subtle forms. Unable to attract the kind of sponsorship that successful male teams acquire effortlessly, prominent women's teams have been forced to pose nude for calendars in order to earn even basic expenses for training, equipment, and travel. Statistically, the facts speak for themselves. Between 1948 and 1996, women won 40 percent of Australia's gold medals at the Olympic Games, despite competing in only 25 percent of the total events, and comprising only 24 percent of Australia's representatives. Between 1911 and 1990 women captured 35 percent of Australia's gold medals at the Commonwealth Games, even though they only competed in 31 percent of the events and constituted only 27% of Australian athletes.[8] From the same source,[9] comes the information that in national sporting organizations women comprise only 17 percent of the national coaching directors, 10 percent of the presidents, 12 percent of the national development officers, and 18 percent of the executive directors. The spectacle of even the finest Australian women's teams, such as the Hockeyroos, being coached by a male is the norm, rather than the exception.

Television and More

Although a great many Australians still play sports, many more watch from the comfort of their living rooms. Television first came to Australia in

1956, just in time for the staging of the Melbourne Olympic Games, and was enthusiastically embraced by Australians, so much so, in fact, that critics feared it would decimate other forms of entertainment. By 1960 Australians had purchased 600,000 TV sets. For a time it seemed as if the pessimists might be right, with cinemas, for instance, closing down everywhere and live entertainment such as cabaret, circuses, rodeos, and comedy acts disappearing. A favorite joke of the 1950s has a prospective patron phoning the local cinema and saying, "What time does the movie start?" to which the proprietor replies, "Well, what time can you get here?" But most of them adapted and survived. Australians are once again avid cinemagoers and there has been a huge revival of comedy acts, with several capital cities having their Comedy Festivals and Fringe Festivals.

Television, too, continued to adapt, with color television eventually coming to Australia; cable is offering a far wider range of programs, and most recently digital television is being introduced. Australians are also keen concertgoers and attenders of art exhibitions.

Notes

1. Jim Davidson and Peter Spearritt, *Holiday Business: Tourism in Australia Since 1870* (Melbourne: Miegunyah Press at Melbourne University Press, 2000).
2. Maurice Dunlevy, "Zoo Will Put You Up for the Night," *The Australian,* 20 March 2002.
3. Gabrielle Carey and Kathy Lette, *Puberty Blues* (Melbourne: McPhee Gribble, 1979), p. 29.
4. Davidson and Spearritt, *Holiday Business,* p. 114.
5. "Brylcreemed Heroes," *The Age,* 15 November 2001.
6. Cited in Farah Farouque, "Sport Still Defines the State We're In," *The Age,* 8 March 2001.
7. Richard Cashman, *A Paradise for Sport* (Melbourne: Oxford University Press, Melbourne, 1995), p. 83.
8. Cited in Jim McKay, Geoffrey Lawrence, Toby Miller, and David Rowe, "Gender Equity, Hegemonic Masculinity and the Governmentalisation of Australian Amateur Sport," in *Culture in Australia: Policies, Publics and Programs,* ed. Tony Bennett and David Carter (Cambridge: Cambridge University Press, 2001), p. 238.
9. Ibid., p. 242.

5

Cuisine and Fashion

Up until the 1950s Australian cuisine was largely conspicuous by its absence; indeed, probably many people could not have told you what the word *cuisine* meant. There was a preponderance of meat, usually roasted or grilled and invariably overdone, accompanied by soggy vegetables, especially potatoes, and heavy gravy. I remember sitting down at a pub once to a counter lunch of steak and five differently cooked kinds of potato. Fish was almost unknown except to Roman Catholics, who were obliged to eat it on Fridays in deference to a papal decree banning consumption of meat on that day. Most of them survived on the ubiquitous fish 'n chips, eaten, steaming, out of one end of a bag wrapped in newspapers. The fish was usually the delicious "flake" (actually shark), and the food was both cheap and nutritious.

Even at Christmas, English customs were assiduously followed. In the middle of summer friends would send each other Christmas cards depicting snow, reindeer, and English scenery. Stores would play incessantly such classics as "White Christmas" and "Rudolf the Red-Nosed Reindeer." And on Christmas Day, in temperatures approaching 38 degrees Celsius (100 degrees Fahrenheit), families and friends would sit down to plates of steaming roast meat, followed by plum pudding with lavish servings of brandy custard and cream. Cooking was almost always the province of the woman of the house, the males not deigning to indulge in such domestic concerns, and usually adjourning to the "local" (pub—after pubs were finally opened for Christmas Day) to imbibe a few beers before returning home in time for the prepared lunch, after which followed a healthy nap.

The extent to which this has changed represents almost a seismic shift in Australian culture and it is difficult to do justice to it. As many as 27 percent of males are now the primary or sole cook in a household. While still a minority, it represents a huge shift from a generation ago. Even more importantly, the arrival of emigrants from Europe after World War II slowly but steadily transformed the habits of Australian eaters.

Australian cuisine is now among the most culturally diverse in the world, especially in the major cities, but in many regional areas as well. Restaurants have sprung up specializing in a remarkable variety of national foods: Chinese, French, Greek, Indian, Indonesian, Italian, Japanese, Lebanese, Malaysian, Nepalese, Sri Lankan, Afghanistan, Thai, Vietnamese, and even Swedish, Balinese, and self-styled "Modern British." In the past this would have been as much an oxymoron as "Aussie Gourmet." Chefs are now much more confident and daring; experimentation and cross-fertilization are common, especially among the various Asian restaurants, and many restaurants simply like to call themselves "Modern" or "Mediterranean."

Native Food

At the same time, the growth of interest in cuisine led to a reassessment of local food as well. Since 1993, kangaroo, wallaby, and possum have been legally sold in Victoria, New South Wales, and Queensland. Emu is now cultivated, although there is some concern that the numbers of emu have declined by 50 percent over the past 20 years, and buffalo is a common item at fancier restaurants. Imaginative chefs now create dishes like Wallaby Pie with sheep yogurt, or Wallaby Casserole.

Ironically, however, interest in native foods is much stronger overseas—in the United States, France, Germany, and England—than at home. Suggestions recently that wombat could replace the traditional Aussie lamb roast on Sundays were greeted with derision. Other exotic natives mentioned as possibilities for cultivation have been the bettong, a ratlike miniature kangaroo, the diminutive pademelon, and some of the more common species of wallaby. The British, for instance, consume 10 times more Australian native produce—what is often referred to as "bush tucker"—as Australians themselves do. There is even a factory in Glasgow that processes ingredients such as bush tomato, desert lime, lemon myrtle, mountain pepper, and wattleseed into a range of convenience foods specifically labeled as Australian. Some companies sell as much as 90 percent of their Australian produce overseas.

However, if resistance to indigenous food is still strong on the part of Australian consumers, it is beginning to weaken. In March 2001, Coles, one of Australia's two largest supermarket chains, announced its Taste Australia initiative. This had two aims: to bring to Australian consumers some of the foods and tastes that indigenous Australians lived off for many years before the coming of Europeans, and to assist Aboriginal communities to resume sustainable harvesting and cultivation practices. Foods previously sold only in gourmet stores would now become more freely available. These include Kakadu plum jelly, macadamia oil, wattleseed sauce, pepperberry vinegar, bush tomato sauce, lemon myrtle chili sauce, lemon aspen chili sambal sauce, native plum sauce, ironbark honey, and chili sauce and pepper leaf mustard sauce. Twenty-five cents from each sale would be funneled into an Indigenous Food Fund that would be used to ensure the long-term supply of indigenous ingredients.

Australia has—or used to have—a considerable number and variety of fish, but once consumers turned to fish, they did so with such enthusiasm that some species were almost instantly fished out; the rise and fall of orange roughy, for instance, is a dismal saga in itself. Among the kinds of fish whose numbers are low or uncertain are swordfish, school shark (more commonly known as flake), blue warehou (also known as black trevally, sea bream, and snottynose trevalla), rock ling, orange roughy, and eastern gemfish. Nevertheless, according to the CSIRO's marine division, more than 600 species of finfish and shellfish, both marine and freshwater, are caught and sold in Australia for local and international consumption. In Victoria, at least, the 10 most popular kinds of fish are blue grenadier, flathead, pink ling, blue warehou, gummy shark, blue-eye trevalla, king dory, orange roughy, Atlantic salmon (the basis of Tasmania's booming aquaculture industry), and yellowfin tuna—to which should probably be added rainbow trout, garfish, and King George whiting.

Changes

While much of the increased interest in food can be put down to the arrival of migrants from Europe, it was a change already underway. Veteran food writer Margaret Fulton, whose 20 books have sold four million copies, began a column for *Woman's Day* back in 1960 that encouraged imaginative, fresh food even of a simple kind ("101 ways with mince"), encouraged men to take an interest in cooking, and promoted the concept of dinner parties, which in turn led to more dining out. Other influences can be traced back even further. Some Chinese immigrants abandoned the goldfields to cultivate their market gardens, carrying vegetables through towns once a week and finding a clientele.

The rise of the all-pervasive barbecue in Australia is not so much an innovation as a development of practices adopted by the Aborigines, who frequently cooked larger meats and fish with hot stones or coals, which was continued by the early white settlers. One writer on food has noted, "Campfire cooking, in a sense, never lost its place entirely in the Australian way of life. The climate has always been a big factor in this predilection for the bush, the out-of-doors, camping, and the rough, simple life. But in earlier days for many it was a necessity rather than, or as well as, a pleasure."[1]

Drinking Habits

To the growth of interest in new restaurants comes even more strongly a shift in consumers' drinking habits. Among the greatest success stories of exports in Australia in recent times is Australian wine. In the past 15 years wine grape production in Australia has tripled, while its value has risen from $100 million to $2.3 billion. In 2002 the record harvest was 1.5 million metric tons of grapes. Most of the rise is due to exports, though there has been a marked growth in interest and consumption of wines among Australians. The most recent figures available (those for 2001–02) show that wine exports broke the $2 billion barrier for the first time. In the last four years alone, the value of Australian wine exports has more than doubled and Australia is now the world's fourth-biggest wine exporter, exporting 471 million liters of wine in 2002, an increase of 26 percent over the previous record set in 2001. Australia now sells more wine in the UK than the French, while in 2002, notwithstanding the events of September 11, exports to the United States rose by 64 percent, to $741 million. New Zealand was the third biggest market, followed by Canada and Germany.

The Riverland, along a stretch of the Murray River in South Australia, is the nation's largest wine-growing area. Twelve years ago it had an unemployment rate of over 16 percent; now in some areas it is below 5 percent. But there are numerous other areas known for their outstanding wines. In Western Australia the Margaret River, south of the capital city of Perth, makes outstanding cool climate reds especially. Perhaps because of the influx of German migrants there, South Australia has long been known for its outstanding wine areas, such as the Barossa Valley, McLaren Vale, and the Clare Valley. South Australia is the home of Australia's two most prestigious (and expensive) red wines, Penfold's Grange and Henschke Hill of Grace. The luscious fortified wines of the Rutherglen in northern Victoria are a uniquely Australian product and often commented upon by visitors, while the state also has the Yarra Valley and Mornington Peninsula vineyards. New South Wales is best known for its Hunter Valley whites, which have remarkable longevity, while Tasmania makes fine cool climate wines, including excellent sparkling wines. Wine is even produced in small quantities in subtropical Queensland.

The wine industry estimates that, in addition to the huge employment on vineyards and in wineries, there are another 50,000 small businesses serving the industry and forming virtually the basis of some thriving country towns. Vineyards are also generators of a good deal of tourism, both domestic and overseas.

At the top end of the Australian winemaking business, four companies—Beringer Blass, BRL Hardy, Orlando Wyndham, and Southcorp—produce about 80 percent of Australia's wine. The next 20 companies represent around 15 percent, while something like 1,400 so-called boutique wineries produce about 5 to 6 percent. Boutique winemaking is still a growth industry, despite the well-publicized financial hazards. According to one authority, a new Australian wine producer opens a staggering every 73 hours.[2]

The growth of interest in Australian wine has begun to generate an associated interest in Australian cheese. Although only in its infancy, the gourmet cheese industry received an enormous boost when a Victorian cheese, Jindi Brie, won the overall best cheese at the Wisconsin world championship cheese show for 2002—the so-called Olympics for cheeses—and King Island Dairy won most outstanding cheese product at the New York fancy food fair in July 2000.

FASHION

Climate and perhaps natural inclination dictate that most dressing in Australia is extremely informal. Possibly, too, Australia's early history plays a part in ensuring that formal dress is an exception, rather than the norm. In the early days of settlement, fashion was a nonissue. Needs were so basic and clothes so few that the imperative was to find any kind of clothing at all. One woman is quoted as writing in 1790: "It is now so long since we have heard from home that our clothes are worn threadbare. We begin to think the mother country has entirely forsaken us. As for shoes my stock has been exhausted these six months and I have been obliged since that time to beg and borrow among the gentlemen, for no such article was to be bought."[3] Australia's distance from the important European centers also meant that there tended to be a time gap of a year or more before styles from the northern hemisphere became available.

Within 20 years, however, styles of dress had emerged, which emphasized the differences between the established classes and the convicts and settlers, who often had to be content with government issues or secondhand clothing. Though some clothing was locally made, much was imported, and even the locally made was heavily derivative of models from London and Paris, establishing a trend that lasted for many years. An exaggerated concern for overseas models was not uncommon. One writer on fashion reports: "One newspaper...with an outburst of colonial pride, in describing Christmas holiday-makers wearing 'their brightest and best' went so far as to write that owing to the perspicacity of drapers and mercers novelties reached Melbourne six or eight months before hitting the Paris market!"[4] More realistically, another commentator notes that "The Australian fashion industry was practically built on plagiarism,"[5] with the six-month gap serving local designers well. The huge distance from Europe and tiny size of the market made it unappealing for name designers to take legal action. The same writer notes that ironically now Australian designers themselves suffer from imitation by cheaper competitors, the so-called copyrats.

The overseas dictators of fashion were influential and impervious to local differences. Again, the same commentator writes, "The climate and good food endowed the women of Australia with particularly beautiful hair and it was probable, therefore, that there was no need to resort to the addition of artificial hair, though so irrational can fashion become that Bright and Hitchcocks' buyer in London in the sixties was complaining about the lack of sales of this commodity in the colony."[6] By the end of the century, however, the majority of clothing was made locally and there was an abundance of both drapers and well-stocked clothing shops. As with cuisine, distinctively Australian styles did not begin to emerge until the arrival of migrants on a large scale after World War II.

When this occurred, fashions tended to feature ironic humor, self-deprecating prints, and unusually vivid colors; Australian fashion is now almost as distinctive as Australian films, though some critics have pointed to the limitations of the characteristic qualities of both. Fashion commentator Colin McDowell doubts whether Australia will ever produce a world-class designer. "I like Australian fashion because it's not decadent, bored or over-sophisticated," he observes. "But, dare I say it?—Australians are too healthy (to produce a world class designer). Our culture is too bright-eyed, bushy-tailed, youthful."[7] With the possible exceptions of Collette Dinnigan and Akira Isogawa, there are virtually no fashion designers who are widely known overseas. Australia, the argument goes, is six months behind the rest of the world's ambience and zeitgeist, and it is still imperative, as it was for writers and artists 50 years ago, that budding designers move overseas.

Nevertheless, where buyers and importers once returned to Europe for inspirations, Australian designers and models now pursue their own agendas. One of the first successful Australian designers was Prue Acton. While still only a teenager, she borrowed money from her parents to set up her own label in 1963 and quickly gained popularity for her counterculture clothes. Four years later she set sail for New York.

Her example led to others following. In the 1970s, when the rest of the world was wearing beige corduroy, tan leather coats, paisley caftans, and nylon flares, designers like Jenny Kee and Linda Jackson set about providing an alternative fashion landscape, populated with iconic Australian themes. They employed adventurous prints, bold knits, decorative designs, often accompanied by a range of local wild life and fauna—parrots, fish, snakes, and various native flowers. Akubra hats and Drizabone raincoats have become widely popular in some areas outside Australia.

By 1977, Kee's signature "koala, kooka, and kanga" knits and Jackson's opulent handprinted silks were gaining such international interest that *Italian Vogue* editor Anna Piaggi described their outfits as Australian graffiti—which she later confirmed was a compliment. Interest peaked in the 1980s when a pregnant Diana, Princess of Wales, was widely photographed wearing a Kee koala handknit. Kee said that customers from London, Paris, and New York found the images "very exotic." Most of her customers had never even heard of the plant, banksia, before, let alone seen one abstracted and knitted into a dress using many different colors. Kee's success was reflected in *Italian Vogue*'s decision to devote an enthusiastic double-page spread to the designer, and again when in 1983 Karl Lagerfeld unveiled Jenny Kee's Opal Oz prints to great acclaim in his debut prêt-à-porter collection for Chanel.

Perhaps Australia's most famous designer, and one of the most controversial, is Ken Done, whose iconic images of koalas and the Sydney Opera House are snapped up by tourists while often being derided by locals. The tote bags, tea towels, coffee mugs, coasters, and leisurewear have sold prolifically under the label Done Art and Design for over two decades. Done says that life changed for him in 1967 when he saw a Matisse exhibition in London and immediately began painting at every opportunity he had. By 1969 he was successful enough to be painting full time but his real strength has been in the sale of Australian kitsch.

The 1970s was also the decade when surfing labels, Australia's most popular export niche, began their rise. The dream of endless summer was in effect transformed into clothes on backs. Bobbing along on the increasing casualization of clothes, Billabong, Rip Curl, and Quiksilver set themselves up for mass-market success. In most countries people don't even know the names are Australian; they just think they are like a global surfing label. Surfwear is so popular overseas that Billabong, which is now registered as a public company, records 70 percent of its sales outside Australia.

Beachwear is, not surprisingly, the area in which Australian designers have made a particular impact. When Peter and Stephen Hills' Globe International listed on the stock exchange, the company suddenly found it had a market capitalization of $550 million, making it one of the stock exchange's 150 biggest companies. The float revealed the widening appeal of the action sports industry. The brothers acquired licenses for foreign skating equipment and clothing brands as well as starting their own clothing and footwear labels, including the popular youth labels, Mooks, Gallaz, and Globe. The Globe stable relies heavily on first-rate equipment, designed to withstand the rigors of sports like skateboarding, but also a wide variety of different brands, including female-specific brands like Girlstar (surfwear) and Undergirl (underwear).

Similarly, Quiksilver Europe, the continental arm of the antipodean company, pulls in five times the annual profit of the founding company in Australia. Quiksilver, Rip Curl, and Billabong make up the Big Three in the international action sports industry. Australian companies operating in the surfwear, skatewear, and streetwear market have over the last 25 years or so taken somewhere between 60 and 70 percent market share of an industry worth $20 billion a year worldwide. Latecomer Mambo, founded in 1984, records $55 million in sales worldwide.

Unlike these companies, Australian-born couturier Richard Tyler went for the up-market consumer. During the 1970s the flamboyant designer outfitted such pop luminaries as Rod Stewart and the Electric Light Orchestra. Settling permanently in the United States in 1987, he directed his talents into suits and gowns made from luxurious fabrics such as velvet, taffeta, and silk duchesse, in styles that appealed to the most style-conscious of the Hollywood elite. Tyler has 44 buyers for his collection, all high-end fashion stores.

Swimwear can act as a measure of the changes taking place in society, from the cumbersome, androgynous wool tunic and knickerbockers of the late nineteenth century to the contemporary bikini, or even Rudi Gernreich–style topless bathing suits. Australian swimsuits have passed through a number of transformations—Speedo's high-tech Olympic bodysuits, Max Dupain's iconic sunbaker photographs, Gold Coast meter maids in bikinis, zinc-nosed lifeguards, and Mambo boardshorts.

It was Australian champion swimmer Annette Kellerman's scandalous one-piece costume, worn to compete against men in the Thames and English Channel races in the early years of the twentieth century, that challenged codes of modesty and led to swimsuits women could actually swim in becoming acceptable. In the first half of the twentieth century, Australians and Americans led the way in designing innovative swimwear and sportswear designed for local conditions.

Hailed by a wildly enthusiastic U.S. press as "the world's most perfect woman," Sydney-born Annette Kellerman was a star and Australia's first golden girl. She swam the Seine, performed with Houdini, dived into a tank full of crocodiles, appeared in silent movies, and was even arrested for indecency after wearing a skirtless bathing costume in Boston in 1905. Ironically, she took up swimming as a way of strengthening her legs after suffering childhood polio. A movie of her life, starring Esther Williams, was made in 1952.

Local designers began to use Australian iconography and created casual clothing suitable for local conditions. By the late 1920s and early 1930s the big American swimwear manufacturers such as Jantzen, Catalina, and Cole of California all had bases in Australia, recognizing it as a key market. Australian-born John Orry Kelly worked in set design in Sydney before heading to New York in the 1920s. Orry Kelly became one of the main designers for Warner Brothers.

Like Tyler, many current designers have founded their success on garments made for body-conscious people, but unlike Tyler, there has been no need for them to remove themselves physically from their place of birth. Since the 1996 inception of Australian Fashion Week, it is the buyers who determine the latest fashion debutantes. The concept of Fashion Week has steadily grown over the last few years until it now generates $42 million in wholesale orders and $75 million in media coverage throughout the world. According to Simon Lock of The Lock Group and the man behind the concept, the event now costs $5 million annually for international marketing, infrastructure and production, against $1.4 million in 1996. Lock's eventual plan is to add Australia to the big four—Milan, New York, Paris, and London—though most people are skeptical of his chances.

But the most high-profile fashion exporters of the past decade remain Collette Dinnigan and Akira Isogawa. Dinnigan exports 80 percent of her business to more than 100 of the world's best shops. She designed her first ready-to-wear range in 1994, as an extension of the lingerie and delicate slip dresses that she began making for friends when she was laid low with an injury. By October 1995 she had started to show in Paris. Dinnigan remains the only Australian designer to be admitted to the prestigious *Chambre Syndicale de la Couture*—the official organization that assesses the cream of the legions of fashion designers wishing to show in Paris.

Isogawa, who also shows in Paris, is stocked as well in some of the most prestigious fashion stores worldwide, most recently by top Hong Kong department store Lane Crawford, which is rapidly expanding in Asia. The example of Dinnigan and Isogawa in tackling Paris with just a suitcase or two inspired two young women from Queensland, Pam Easton and Lydia Pearson, to do likewise, with considerable success. They formed Easton Pearson in 1999 and now export much of what they make.

The supreme day for fashion in Australia is Melbourne Cup Day, and, in fact, throughout the so-called Spring Racing Carnival, new outfits are displayed and the most outrageous clothes worn. The appearance of famous English model Jean Shrimpton at the 1965 Melbourne Cup in a tiny sleeveless miniskirt that ended well above her knees and wearing no hat, gloves, or stockings signaled a revolution in fashion design. Women took eagerly to the miniskirt and in general toward casual, comfortable clothes more appropriate to an Australian climate, and have never really changed since then.

Most recently, stylist for the hit TV series *Sex and the City*, Rebecca Weinberg, has expressed her admiration for the quality of Australian fashion. The clothes the characters wear are crucial to the show, which averages 70 outfits an episode. On her first visit to Australia, Weinberg bought clothes from Melbourne designers Scanlan & Theodore and Princess Highway and Sydney's Morrissey and Pigs in Space. The show's star, Sarah Jessica Parker, was so taken by the clothes of Sydney-based denim label Sass & Bide that she bought 90 percent of their collection.

Generally, however, trends in fashion affect only a small percentage of the population. A combination of the temperate climate, historical trends, and personal inclination ensure that most fashion in Australia is highly informal.

Notes

1. Anne Gollan, *The Tradition of Australian Cooking* (Canberra: A.N.U. Press, 1978), p. 42.
2. Michael Major, ed., *Australian & New Zealand Wine Industry Directory,* 20th annual ed. (Adelaide: Wine Titles, 2002).
3. Quoted in M. Barnard Eldershaw, *Phillip of Australia: An Account of the Settlement at Sydney Cove* (London: George C. Harrap, 1938; reprint, Sydney: Angus and Robertson, 1972), p. 169.
4. Marian Fletcher, *Costume in Australia 1788–1901* (Melbourne: Oxford University Press, 1984), p. 122.
5. Janice Breen Burns, "Trapping the Copyrats," *The Age,* 12 January 2003.
6. Ibid., p. 140.
7. Quoted in Janice Breen Burns, "Is Australia a Fashion Backwater?" *The Age,* 5 June 2002.

6

Literature

Australian literature began very early in its colonial history. Perhaps the first figure of literary distinction was a British naval officer named Watkin Tench whose diaries showed an acute and curious eye for detail in the new world he was exploring. His *A Narrative of the Expedition to Botany Bay* (1789) was followed by *A Complete Account of the Settlement at Port Jackson and Norfolk Island* (1793). In 1819 a poet with the remarkable name of Barron Field published the first book of poetry in Australia, *First Fruits of Australian Poetry.* Though his verse was pompous and sometimes not much better than doggerel, it did try quite deliberately to deal with Australian society:

> Kangaroo, Kangaroo!
> Thou Spirit of Australia,
> That redeems from utter failure,
> From perfect desolation,
> And warrants the creation
> Of this fifth part of the Earth,
> Which would seem an after-birth,
> Not conceiv'd in the Beginning
> (For GOD bless'd His work at first,
> And saw that it was good),
> But emerg'd at the first sinning,
> When the ground was therefore curst;—
> And hence this barren wood!

As critics would observe later, this was the first of many uses of the rhyme, "Australia/failure."

Poetry in the Colonial Period

In 1820 William Charles Wentworth (1790–1872) entered for the Chancellor's Medal at Cambridge with a poem "Australasia," which was highly laudatory of the country in which he had been born. Although it won only second prize, three years later Wentworth, who had returned to Australia after completing his education, published a volume of verse, *Australasia,* which became the first book of poetry by an Australian-born writer to be published in England. In it he spoke proudly of Australia, in a phrase that briefly passed into the language, as "a new Britannia." In 1824 he founded a fiercely polemical paper called *The Australian* that pushed the cause of the emancipists. Wentworth's own political beliefs, however, were always ambivalent and he later became a conservative, even advocating a proposal for a colonial peerage, cuttingly dubbed "a bunyip aristocracy" by the radical Daniel Deniehy. He was later the subject of a heavily satirical poem, "The Patriot of Australia—An Heroic Poem in Ten Cantos," by Charles Harpur, the first Australian poet of any consequence.

Harpur (1813–68), the son of emancipist parents, is, in fact, the first of three poets who stand out in the colonial period; the others are Henry Kendall (1839–82) and Adam Lindsay Gordon (1833–70). None of them was a major figure in world terms, but all three were heroic in their pursuit of literature in a society that could hardly have been more indifferent to it, a theme that recurs in the work of Harpur and Kendall especially and is perhaps attested to by the short lives of all three.

The son of a junior naval officer, later a clerk, and a woman of Irish descent, Kendall was the first completely free-born and native Australian poet. Well aware of the preeminent position of Harpur in Australian letters, despite his public neglect, Kendall very soon engaged in correspondence with him, though they did not meet until December 1867, a few months before Harpur died. Toward the end of the correspondence Kendall acted as a virtual Sydney agent for Harpur and did his best to promote him in the eyes of the public. He also came to know Gordon briefly in the months before his death, when they could both dwell on the miserable prospects facing Australian writers.

Kendall himself, in fact, was destined to fall into similar neglect to his mentor. He published three collections in his lifetime—*Poems and Songs* (1862), *Leaves from Australian Forests* (1869), and *Songs from the Mountains* (1880)—but although these were well received critically, the sales were not large. His reputation was primarily as a lyricist, based on frequently anthologized poems like "The Muse of Australia," "Bell Birds," and "September in Australia."

So fiercely determined was he to establish himself as a national poet that he would sign himself "N.A.P."—for Native Australian Poet. But, like Harpur and Gordon, he found it hard to break from English models and influences. A deeply melancholy temperament combined with a mellifluous flow of language and excessive use of alliteration and personification to produce poems that were stronger on melody than meaning.

The nationalistic element is present too in Kendall's attempts to write sympathetically about Aborigines, but good intentions are marred by an element of condescension. It is clear that he thought they were doomed to extinction and in one of his best-known poems, "The Last of His Tribe," he mourns the passing of a warrior:

> Will he go in his sleep from these desolate lands,
> Like a chief, to the rest of his race,
> With the honey-voiced woman who beckons, and stands,
> And gleams like a Dream in his face—
> Like a marvelous Dream in his face?

Fifteen years later, in late poems like "Black Lizzie" and "Black Kate," even this well-meaning patronizing has disappeared to be replaced by outright mockery:

> I never loved a nigger belle—
> My tastes are too aesthetic!
> The perfume from a gin is—well,
> A rather strong emetic.

Toward the end of his life Kendall also wrote some cleverly satirical ballads such as "Bill the Bullock Driver" and "Jim the Splitter," which good humoredly mocked Australian stereotypes and bush icons.

Colonial Fiction

The first novel to be published in Australia is *Quintus Servinton,* which appeared in Hobart in 1831. The author, Henry Savery (1791–1842) was an educated man sent out for forgery. The novel is closely autobiographical, except that it seems to have been written as an act of self-solace with the eponymous Servinton triumphing over circumstances in a way that his creator was never able to do.

The history of colonial literature, especially colonial poetry, like that of colonial pictorial art, is one of writers struggling to come to terms with an environment that is totally alien to them and struggling especially to depict it in a way that did not rely heavily on English literary forms. The early days of Australian fiction are especially marked by two kinds of novels, sometimes the two in one, whose literary ancestors are respectively Daniel Defoe and Sir Walter Scott. The first are what can be called the guidebook novel; the second are novels of adventure and romance. Both were written with an English audience largely or entirely in mind. The guidebook novel aims itself at the prospective male immigrant to Australia and reads rather as Daniel Defoe might have written to Robinson Crusoe had he known he was going to be stranded on a desert island. It is full of practical advice and information.

The novel of adventure and romance is aimed at those readers in England who would be titillated by the exotic and novel aspects of Australian life and whose palate has been jaded by the too familiar adventures of their local writers. With remarkable rapidity, the staple themes of Australian adventure fiction soon emerge: the natural hazards of bushfire or flood, the encounters with savage or (as the writers of the period often called them) "ebony" or "sable" or "sooty" warriors, the child lost in the bush. The characters, too, quickly form their own stereotypes: The magnanimous squatter and his invariably young and beautiful daughter; the likeable but feckless Irishman; the sullen ex-convict; the sometimes loyal, sometimes treacherous Aboriginal serving man and self-sacrificing Aboriginal woman; the decadent gentleman turned bushranger (Captain Moonlight) who never turns on women and who usually redeems himself by a noble death. Very early the characteristic Australian male, discussed previously, emerges: tall, lean, a skilled bushman, not overly intellectual or subtle, but marked by loyalty, straightforwardness, and physical competence.

From this period several notable though far from flawless works emerge. Henry Kingsley (1830–76) had some success with his first novel, *The Recollections of Geoffrey Hamlyn,* published in London in 1859. Kingsley's quintessentially Victorian characters emigrated from England to Australia and by the end have all returned home, but not without having made their fortunes and experienced the classic range of Australian bush dramas. Thomas Alexander Browne (1826–1915), who wrote under the pseudonym of Rolf Boldrewood, was the author of many serialized novels of which by far the most famous was *Robbery Under Arms* (1883), the story of the gentleman bushranger, Captain Starlight, as opposed to the "bad" bushranger Morgan, with his pathological hatred of the police. The story is narrated by the straightforward young Sydneysider Dick Marston and is filled with energetic action and vividly rendered landscapes.

Less well known are *Fifty Years Ago* (1867), by Charles de Boos (1819–1900), a powerful and complex novel that tells the story of a white settler's pursuit of the natives who murdered his wife and three of his four children, and his slow realization of the futility of his quest for vengeance; and the similarly impressive *Moondyne* (1879), by John Boyle O'Reilly (1844–90). This is probably the first Western Australian novel and rare for its time in its sympathetic account of Aborigines.

Arguably the most interesting and gifted writer of the time, Marcus Clarke (1846–81) wrote another Australian classic, *His Natural Life* (1874). Despite his premature death, Clarke was a remarkably prolific writer who experimented in a variety of forms, but is best known for this grim, unsparing account of a man who takes on responsibility for a crime he did not commit and is mercilessly degraded and tortured, flogged, and even crucified, before finally achieving peace of mind as he dies in the arms of the woman he loves, the two floating out to sea in death. It is a deeply pessimistic novel, at times highly melodramatic but filled with magnificent pieces of description.

There were also a number of female writers who received less attention than they deserved at the time. Catherine Helen Spence (1825–1910) in *Clara Morison* (1854) tells the story of the gold rushes from the point of view of a woman, much of it by hearsay, but it is, as she says, "a faithful transcript of life in the Colony." The manuscript of *Handfasted* was submitted to the *Sunday Mail,* which was offering a prize for the best novel of 1879, and was not in fact published until 1984. It is one of the finest and most radical examples of the ubiquitous Australian genre of the Utopian novel and was thought by the competition's judges to be "calculated to loosen the marriage tie... too socialistic, and consequently dangerous."

The wife of a clergyman, Ada Cambridge (1844–1926) wrote a large number of novels, of which the most successful was *A Marked Man* (1890). Among their recurring themes are the situation of women in colonial society, the nature and power of sexual passion and the extremes of behavior to which it can drive people, as well as (what must have been especially painful to someone in her position), a crisis of religious disbelief.

Her contemporary Jessie Couvreur (1848–97), who wrote under the name of "Tasma," was also quite productive. Her novels, the best known of which is *Uncle Piper of Piper's Hill* (1899), often reflect closely the circumstances of her life. Very frequently the central situation is that of a helpless woman who marries early, then discovers the flaws in her husband's character, falls in love with another, much finer man, but is forced to renounce him. The novels of both Cambridge and Tasma both suggest a good deal of buried pain.

The novels of Queensland-born Rosa Praed (1851–1935) often center around a sexual triangle involving a woman and two men, one of them sexually attractive but morally dubious, the other less exciting but a man of true worth. The variations on this theme are almost endless and can be highly ingenious, often involving very complicated plotting. The title of one of her best novels, *The Bond of Wedlock* (1887), could well be applied to a number of others. Though not as agonized as Cambridge in her darkest moments, both of them, as well as Tasma, are clearly aware of and suffer from the restrictions on women in colonial society. Less well known but a powerful and original writer is Catherine Martin (1847–1937), whose novels were not discovered and reprinted until a few years ago.

The *Bulletin* School

The last two decades of the century saw the rise of the Sydney *Bulletin*, a weekly magazine that for a time exercised probably more literary influence than any magazine in Australia has done since. Founded in 1880, the heyday of "The Bushman's Bible" was in the 1890s when, under the editorship of J. F. Archibald and the literary editorship of A. G. Stephens, who ran the famous literary Red Page from 1896 to 1906, it discovered and published some of Australia's most popular and distinguished writers.

Among them were the poets Adam Lindsay Gordon and A(ndrew) B(arton) ("Banjo") Paterson (1864–1941), and the prose writers Henry Lawson (1867–1922) and Joseph Furphy (1843–1912). Gordon came to fame with ballads like "The Sick Stockrider" before committing suicide, while Paterson's ballads, such as "Clancy of the Overflow" and "The Man from Snowy River" made him for a time arguably the most widely read poet in the world in terms of head of population. In the 30 years after the publication of *The Man from Snowy River and Other Verses,* Paterson sold over 100,000 copies in a population of about three-and-a-half million people. His "Waltzing Matilda"—about a tramp who steals a sheep and is hunted to death by squatters and police—was for a long time more or less Australia's unofficial national anthem.

Lawson wrote popular ballads also, but these days is remembered far more for his ironic, terse short stories in which for the first time Australians could hear their own voices. Similarly skeptical in his ironic humor is Joseph Furphy who published his novel *Such Is Life* (1903) under the pseudonym of Tom Collins. Apparently sprawling and anecdotal, it is in fact a subtly structured, complex, and very funny exposition of Furphy's essential view that life is inherently meaningless.

Another writer of the period who has received proper recognition only fairly recently is Barbara Baynton (1857–1929). Her collection of short fiction, gathered together as *Bush Studies,* comprised only six stories (she later added two more), but they present a view of the Bush that is not merely bleak like Lawson's but is one of violent revulsion and with no redeeming humor. Her story "Squeaker's Mate" is a powerful assault on all the male myths of mateship.

Writing under the name of "Steele Rudd," Arthur Hoey Davis (1868–1935) gained enormous popularity around the turn of the century for his stories—both hilariously funny but almost unwittingly tragic as well, of the harsh life of "selectors" (farmers who try to make a living from a small area of ground, or "selection") on the Darling Downs of southeastern Queensland. Though not averse to broad humor and even slapstick, Rudd's stories also reveal the grinding poverty, perennial debt, and primitive conditions of life on a selection. His creation of the immortal characters of Dad and Dave ensured his lasting popularity. *On Our Selection* was adapted for the stage in 1912 and several films, including one of the first major silent pictures in Australia, have been made of his work. The last of these was as recent as 1994, testifying to the durability of Rudd's work and its appeal to a very different Australia. There have also been radio serials, a television series, and even comic strips.

Twentieth-Century Poetry

Australia's first significant poet of the twentieth century is Christopher Brennan (1870–1932), the Sydney-born son of Irish Catholic immigrants and a tragic figure in Australian literature. So intelligent and learned was Brennan that it was said he could have had his choice of four Chairs in the University of Sydney, but in the rather jejune cultural life of Australia around the turn of the century he was, to quote one of his admirers, "a sonorous island in a lonely sea."[1]

Brennan's studies as a young man overseas led to his lifelong fascination with the French symbolist school and especially Mallarme, tastes that were virtually unknown in his native country at the time he returned in 1894. His drinking habits, opposition to the Boer War, and later open cohabitation with a woman who wasn't his wife mitigated against any hope of academic preferment. As a poet he never really lived up to his immense talents. In the words of one critic, his was "a bush of poetry that smoulders and never really burns."[2]

Most of Brennan's best work is contained in the volume *Poems* (1913), which, following Malarme, he conceived of as a *livre compose,* or volume thought of as a whole, but made up of many separate parts. Its theme is the quest, eventually a doomed one, for a paradisal state of bliss. The first section, "Towards the Source," speaks of both the longing for Eden and the sense of its loss. The poems center around the German woman Brennan married but already (only months after his marriage) betraying the poet's doubt and skepticism. The second section, "The Forest of Night," turns inward as the poet explores the terrors and darkness of his own psyche. The third and probably most famous section, "The Wanderer," returns the poet to the material world. Abandoning his quest for Eden, he accepts more or less, with a resignation that Brennan failed to achieve in his own life, the finiteness of the actual world, while acknowledging that there is "no ending of the way, no home, no goal." Anticipation for Brennan was always richer than experience.

John Shaw Neilson (1872–1942) is often mentioned as one of Australia's most charming poets for such works as "Love's Coming," "Song Be Delicate," and, most famously, "The Orange Tree," but the rather reductive view of Neilson as merely a gentle, charming lyricist hardly stands up to analysis. His poetry is darker, more troubled, more socially aware, and more various than many of his critics would suggest. As well as the lyrics for which he is best known, Neilson's work includes poems of protest, especially against war and social injustice, satires of urban life, and a deep hatred of greed and materialism. "The Soldier Is Home" could well have been written by Wilfred Owen, while one of his finest poems, "The Poor Can Feed the Birds," makes pointed contrasts between rich and poor:

> But 'tis the poor who make the loving words.
> Slowly they stoop;
> it is a sacrament:
> The poor can feed the birds.

Having received little formal education, Neilson worked as a laborer in the arid Wimmera and later Mallee country of western Victoria for many years, but found immense consolation in its rich bird and animal life, which features strongly in his poetry. At the same time, he struggled with his mother's harshly repressive religion, finally reconciling his own sense of spirituality with her fiercely punitive God in beautiful lyrics such as, "The Crane Is My Neighbour," and especially "The Gentle Water Bird":

> God was not terrible and thunder-blue:
> It was a gentle water bird I knew.

Another of Australia's finest poets of the period is Kenneth Slessor (1901–71). Slessor published his first poem in *The Bulletin* at the age of 16. A journalist, and later Australia's first official war correspondent, Slessor edited and wrote much of the periodical *Smith's Weekly* for a time, working for it between 1927 and 1940 and rising eventually to the position of editor-in-chief. He was a master of light verse but in his more overtly serious poems he writes thoughtful and plangent meditations on the destructive nature of Time, a subject that haunted and obsessed him. Except for a brief period when he fell under the influence of Norman Lindsay and his false vitality, his work is mature and elegant. It was during the late 1920s and 1930s that he wrote most of his finest poems, including the renowned elegy, "Five Bells," about a friend who drowned in Sydney harbor, and the witty and moving portrait of "Captain Dobbin." Slessor gathered his best work together in 1944 as *One Hundred Poems, 1919–1939,* but after it, Slessor, depressed by his failure to find an audience and no doubt exhausted by his less than satisfactory experiences as a war correspondent, wrote little more, with the exception of "Beach Burial," perhaps his finest poem.

R(obert) D(avid) Fitzgerald (1902–87) had a long and distinguished career, eventually winning almost all the awards that it is possible for an Australian poet to win. Often described as a philosophical poet, a claim that both irritated and amused him and that he consistently denied, Fitzgerald nevertheless dealt in his poetry with serious issues and ideas. Writing often in the stiffly declamatory style of A. D. Hope or in the style of the late William Butler Yeats, Fitzgerald was especially concerned with the problem of the material world with all its transience as against the possibility of its transcendence, or at least renewal, though finally, like Yeats, opting firmly for the physical world.

Fitzgerald's earliest work, only a portion of which he later preserved under the ironically self-deprecatory title "Salvage," is concerned with the stereotypical figure of the alienated artist. It bears the stamp of Christopher Brennan, whom he would have known through his uncle, the writer John le Gay Brereton, and perhaps Norman Lindsay and the poets of the Vision school. Quickly abandoning this mode, he became best known for his long, speculative poems, especially "The Hidden Bole" (which he himself was especially fond of but which is marred by abstraction), "Essay on Memory," "Between Two Tides," and especially the shorter "The Wind at Your Door," a powerful poem based on an historical incident of the flogging of a number of convicts, including one named Maurice Fitzgerald. The surgeon in attendance was Martin Mason, an ancestor on his mother's side. Highly esteemed in his own time, Fitzgerald's reputation has probably suffered more recently but his integrity and ambition are unquestionable.

Judith Wright published her first poem at the age of 10 but made her name with her first volume of verse *The Moving Image,* which appeared in 1946 when the poet was 31. Hers was immediately recognized as a distinctively female voice, with its firm privileging of heart and emotion over reason and technology, and its bold expression of the female experiences of sexuality and childbirth. At the same time, as she has continually demonstrated in both her poetry and her activism in causes such as environmental issues and Aboriginal affairs, she wishes to change the world with her art.

In 1985 she gave up writing poetry, citing a lack of energy and disillusionment with the developments that had taken place in Australian society. She has, however, continued to write and speak about the issues that most concern her and is wryly ironic about her own perceived silences.

Wright has reacted fiercely to critical charges that she has neglected her poetry for activist causes. Nevertheless, there is a notable difference in tone between the early poems and the later ones, where the joyous celebration of "Woman to Man" has given way to the fierce environmental rage of poems like "Australia 1970."

The poet most closely associated with Wright, if only because they seemed to dominate the poetic landscape of the 1950s and 1960s, is A(lec) D(erwent) Hope (1907–2000). Born in Tasmania, the son of a New South Wales Presbyterian minister, Hope established a formidable reputation as a poet, teacher, reviewer, and critic before finally publishing his first book of poems, *The Wandering Islands*, as late as 1955. After that he went on to produce many volumes of verse, criticism, and autobiography.

Hope's poetry, like his criticism, is formal, classical, magisterial in tone, calling attention self-consciously to Harold Bloom's "canon" in the great tradition of European literature. Hope is as much at home with ancient myths, on which he plays innumerable variations, as he is with Augustan poetry and with more contemporary poets such as Akhmatova, Pasternak, and Rilke. His insistence on rhyme and formal meter and his rejection of all the developments of modernism has led him to be criticized as reactionary by some younger Australian poets, who have gone so far as to describe his poetry as being actually versified prose.

In fact, carefully structured forms are employed to lock in passionate feeling. It is in this sense that critics speak of Hope's poetry as being both Classical and Romantic, as influenced by Byron, as well as Pope and Dryden, as both Apollonian and Dionysian. His themes are traditional ones: isolation ("The Wandering Islands," "The Death of a Bird"), the terrible force of sexual desire, often of a destructive kind (present in many poems but famously in "Imperial Adam" and "Chorale"), and the rejuvenating and conquering power of art. The first two themes are often present together, especially in his brilliantly satirical poems such as "The Brides," with its misogynistic view of the young women as new cars rolling down the production line, a vision barely held in check by sexual wit and innuendo: "All she needs is juice," "Room for his knees: a honey of a clutch."

Elegant, austere, the poems of Rosemary Dobson (1920–) sometimes deal with dilemmas of familial relationships, but most often testify earnestly to the final power of art and its possibilities of transcendence, although her poetry is not without moments of humor. Dobson says of her poetry that it is "part of a search for something only fugitively glimpsed; a state of grace which one once knew, or imagined, or from which one was turned away . . . a doomed but urgent wish to express the inexpressible."[3] There is a studied, highly allusive quality to her writing, which is filled with references to artists and mythological figures. Even the titles of many of her poems—"Young Girl at a Window," "Detail from an Annunciation by Crivelli"—suggest their painterly quality. Poems like "In a Café," a tribute to Botticelli, are almost verbal paintings in themselves. The title of one of her smaller collections, *The Continuance of Poetry*, aptly sums up her beliefs. Her *Collected Poems* —over 200 poems, the product of more than 50 years' work—testify to a life of quiet dedication to the art and craft of verse.

Gwen Harwood (1920–95) is another female poet whose long dedication to her craft eventually drew attention to her fine achievement. The fact that she has written under several pseudonyms as well as under her own name, that she was fond of satirical poetry, perhaps above all a famous hoax she played upon *The Bulletin* when they published a poem of hers that proved to contain an obscene message—all these have drawn attention to the playful and witty elements in her poetry. Similarly, she is capable of creating the risible figures of Professor Eisenbart and Professor Krote, who become both targets and agents of satire in her verse. But she is capable of deeply disturbing, more overtly serious, poetry as well. Her most famous, or at least controversial, poem, "In the Park," is on the face of it the bitter lament of a woman who chose to have children over the lover she rejected. As she nurses the youngest of her three children she says to the wind, "They have eaten me alive." Harwood's debt to the writings of Heidegger and Wittgenstein has been frequently recognized—including by herself—and philosophical ideas pervade her poetry, as does her love of music (she trained as a musician) and awareness of poets who have preceded her.

Francis Webb (1925–73) is one of the most enigmatic and least accessible of Australian poets, yet he is regarded as being in the first rank of Australian poets by several of his most noted fellow practitioners, such as David Campbell, Peter Porter, Douglas Stewart, and Bruce Beaver. Webb suffered the first of several mental breakdowns in 1949 and for the rest of his life struggled with little success to overcome what was eventually diagnosed as schizophrenia.

Webb quickly established a critical reputation with "A Drum for Ben Boyd" (1946), a lengthy poem about a Scottish entrepreneur who arrived in New South Wales in the 1840s and whose achievements and character are viewed from a number of different perspectives. His poem "Leichhardt in Theatre," published a year later, showed the same ambivalent stance toward the figure of the hero: Leichhardt was the doomed explorer who was also the subject of Patrick White's novel *Voss.*

Webb's later poetry, heavily influenced by both his illness and his intense Catholic religion, is often less accessible, but he wrote a number of lyric poems and some fine poems about his own mental sufferings, notably the magnificent verse sequence "Ward Two," set in the Paramatta psychiatric hospital.

Twentieth-Century Fiction

In a famous essay "A Prodigal Son," an attempt to explain why he felt compelled reluctantly to return to his native land, Patrick White dismissed the fiction of the first half of the twentieth century as "the dreary, dun-colored offspring of journalistic realism."[4] On the face of it he had a case, though there is a great deal of interesting work in the period. Around the turn of the century, and immediately after it, there arose a generation of writers, predominantly male, who set out to record the day-to-day experiences of ordinary Australia, their domestic as well as their working lives, in sober and straightforward prose and realist forms. Vance Palmer (b. 1885), Frank Dalby Davison (b. 1893), Alan Marshall (b. 1902), John Morrison (b. 1904), E. O. Schlunke (b. 1906), Gavin Casey (b. 1907), Dal Stivens (b. 1911), Judah Waten (b. 1911), George Johnston (b. 1912), and Frank Hardy (b. 1917) had a great deal in common. Mostly left wing or politically committed to varying degrees, some of them Communists, most of them ardent nationalists, they write about what several of them refer to openly as "a man's world." As the original title of his first book, *It's Harder for Girls,* suggests, Gavin Casey was aware of the disparities in male and female relationships, and yet of all these writers, he most marginalizes women and celebrates the concept of mateship and male camaraderie. His fiction is so pervaded with drinking that in his novel *The Wits Are Out* (1948), about a party, the most frequently discussed character is the keg of beer.

Stylistically unadventurous (except perhaps for Stivens's ventures into fantasy), these writers are nevertheless sometimes unfairly denigrated, but they did get a great deal of Australian experience down on record. Casey wrote about the gold mines, Morrison wrote with sensitivity and subtlety about wharfies (stevedores), Schlunke gave delicately humorous, perceptive accounts of farming in the Riverina area of southern New South Wales, and Palmer wrote about fishing.

Patrick White's gloomy assessment of Australian fiction, in any case, ignores many notable writers who remained for years outside the mainstream of Australian society. Chief among them is Henry Handel Richardson (1870–

1946), the pen name of Ethel Florence Lindesay Robertson, who left Australia as a teenager to study music overseas and returned only once for a brief visit, though she never disclaimed her Australian identity. Her first novel, *Maurice Guest* (1908), is based in part on her experiences in the musical world of Leipzig, Germany. *The Getting of Wisdom* (1910) is a fine example of another Australian staple, the *bildungsroman,* or novel of growth and discovery. It is an autobiographical account of the author's growing up in a Melbourne school and discovering that she is a misfit before rejecting the school completely. She also wrote some fine short stories, but the core of her achievement is the massive trilogy known collectively as *The Fortunes of Richard Mahony,* which consists of *Australia Felix* (1917), *The Way Home* (1925), and *Ultima Thule* (1929).

Based on the life of her father, the trilogy takes us from the goldfields of Ballarat through the tragic Mahony's obsessive wanderings back and forth between England and Australia to his ultimate madness and death. Written in an old-fashioned, almost naturalistic style that owes more to nineteenth-century and contemporary European fiction than the rise of modernism, it is a work of massive authority and research. In its ambitiously symphonic structure, in the relentless exhaustiveness of its documentation of both a family and a society, and finally, in those great moments such as the trial scene, several of the death scenes, and homecomings, and the descriptions of the onset of Mahony's madness, it contains some of the finest writing Australian fiction has to offer. It was only with the publication of *Ultima Thule,* however, that its greatness was finally recognized.

Australia's other great female novelist of the period, Christina Stead (1902–83) was similarly an expatriate who returned to her home country only toward the end of her life, after her husband died in 1968. Previously a prolific writer, Stead had fallen silent during the 1950s and 1960s, but her return to Australia as a widow after many years spent in Europe and the United States with her American husband coincidentally followed a sudden resurgence of interest in her work. The early 1960s saw the revival of her early collection of related stories, *The Salzburg Tales* (1934); her first novel *Seven Poor Men of Sydney* (1934), her only novel to be set entirely in Australia; her masterpiece *The Man Who Loved Children* (1940); and its successor, *For Love Alone* (1945).

Then there was a flurry of published new work—*Cotters' England* (1967, but first published in the United States as *Dark Places of the Heart* in 1966); *The Puzzle-Headed Girl* (1967), four novellas written largely during the 1950s and set mostly in the United States; *The Little Hotel* (1973), and *Miss Herbert* (1976). The rest of her work was published posthumously and includes one of her finest novels, *I'm Dying Laughing* (1986), an examination of the brief rise and fall of the American Left and a study, among other things, of the McCarthy period.

The Man Who Loved Children is a closely autobiographical study of a young girl who finally escapes from her madly egotistical father and tormented mother and at the end plans to become an artist. In a remarkable feat of research and imagination, Stead transferred the events of Sydney to Baltimore and Washington, D.C. *For Love Alone* in effect continues the story, even though the characters are different. Before that, her finest novel had been *House of All Nations* (1938), a fascinating study of the operations of a shady French merchant bank. Like Richardson, but even more so, Stead is a materialist to whom the notion of spirituality hardly seems to occur. There is much of her father's scientific bent in her. She examines, analyzes phenomena unjudgingly, with deep fascination, and is keenly aware of the importance of money in the world as well as of the desperate stratagems to which sexual imperatives will drive men and women. Her male figures are often ruthless exploiters of women; her women are as often unabashed gold diggers who use their sex as the only weapon they have.

Among comparable female figures, the most important as well as prolific is Katherine Susannah Prichard (1883–1969), whose lifelong political beliefs can be best summed up in the title of her collection of essays and speeches, *Straight Left* (1982). The subjects of Prichard's carefully researched novels include pioneers, opal miners, circus entertainers, "bullockies" and gold miners. Her best known novel, *Coonardoo* (1929), is the first sustained and intelligent attempt to come to grips with the problem of the relationships, and in particular, the sexual relationships between black and white people in Australia, while her short story "Flight" anticipates, albeit in semicomic form, the phenomenon of what later became known as the "stolen generation," the Aborigines who were forcibly removed from their parents and relocated with white foster parents.

New Zealand-born Jean Devanny (1894–1962) had a similar political commitment to Prichard, as well as a similarly intense interest in sexuality and the forces that drive it that is largely absent in their male contemporaries. Many of her novels are about the unresolvable conflict between the two. Her best-known novel *Sugar Heaven* (1936) is a fascinating documentation of the Queensland sugar strike of 1935 and, like most of Devanny's work, is far ahead of its time in its opposition to racism and its insistence on women's right to express their sexuality.

The early novels of Eleanor Dark (1901–85) are subdued, meditative works written in a style that seems to have been influenced by Virginia Woolf, but she found her feet quite late in her career with the historical trilogy, a form popular amongst Australian novelists, consisting of *The Timeless Land* (1941),

Storm of Time (1948), and *No Barrier* (1953). These novels, which cover the settlement of Australia by whites up until the crossing of the Blue Mountains in 1813, are among the most thoughtful attempts to examine the origin of white Australian society. Dark views with detachment the processes of history and the muddled attempts of the protagonists to master them. Often she works by intelligent juxtaposition, as in the contrasting portraits of Governor Phillip and the Aboriginal he adopts, Bennelong, or the defamiliarizing portraits of whites as seen through Aboriginal eyes and vice versa, reinforcing the inevitability of the eventual breakdown between the two groups. Though sluggishly paced at times, the trilogy is a considerable achievement.

Among the lesser talents of the period but still worthy of note is Miles Franklin (1879–1954). Franklin, known to her family as Stella, had an immediate popular as well as scandalous success with her first, astonishingly precocious novel *My Brilliant Career* (1901), the exuberantly written account of the early life of Sybylla Melvyn, who grows up in the country free from the conventional constraints placed upon women. When she begins to feel them she rails indignantly against the institution of marriage, "the most horribly tied-down and unfair-to-women existence going." Though read eagerly as a classic feminist text, which in part it is, it can be more subtly seen as a study of Sybylla's complex and divided feelings about sexuality.

Franklin continued to write prolifically throughout her life but never quite achieved what she seemed to promise. In many ways, her writing life can be best summed up by the title of her second novel (not published until 1946), *My Career Goes Bung.* She lived overseas for a quarter of a century, and on her return to Australia wrote a sequence of interlinked novels under the pseudonym of Brent of Bin Bin about farming country in the Monaro district of New South Wales from the 1850s to the late 1920s. Apart from these, her most successful novel is *All That Swagger* (1936), about an enlightened pioneer, based on the life of her grandfather. Her name is commemorated in the Miles Franklin Award for Australian fiction, which was established from a bequest from her estate.

Another distinguished expatriate, member of one of Australia's most artistic families, was the novelist Martin Boyd (1893–1972), a figure who, like Richardson's Richard Mahony, seemed at home nowhere and wrote frequently on the condition of what one of his characters called "geographic schizophrenia." An elegant and witty writer, Boyd's early novels are scarcely more than trivia, although they do explore uncertainly themes that were of importance to him later.

His first achievement of substance was *The Montfords* (1928), a history of the Langton family (based on his mother's family) from the mid-nineteenth century up until the outbreak of World War I, but this proved to be merely a rehearsal for the much longer and more ambitious Langton tetralogy—*The Cardboard Crown* (1952), *A Difficult Young Man* (1955), *Outbreak of Love* (1957), and *When Blackbirds Sing* (1962). This, with the fine *Lucinda Brayford* (1946), which postulates a life of total personal integrity as the ideal most worth seeking, represents the crown of his achievement. The tetralogy uses a mode of retrospective narration based on diaries, personal recollection, miscellaneous information garnished from members of the family and frank speculation to retrace, like a detective story in reverse, the checkered history of the family from roughly 1860 until just after the end of World War I. *When Blackbirds Sing* is, with Leonard Mann's *Flesh in Armour*, and especially Frederic Manning's *The Middle Parts of Fortune*, among the finest Australian novels written about World War I.

Kylie Tennant (1912–88) wrote a number of novels as well as other books in various genres but is best known for her 1941 novel, *The Battlers*. The title sums up her interests and sympathies. She writes about the dispossessed and people on the fringes of society and of the communities—often rural, usually poor—in which they live. Her earlier work, especially, is sustained by a tough vitality and humor.

The reputation of Xavier Herbert (1901–84) rests largely on the basis of one book, *Capricornia* (1938), though his huge final work *Poor Fellow My Country* (1975) has attracted a great deal of heated discussion. Controversial circumstances surrounded the editing and publication of *Capricornia*, with a noted intellectual of the time P. R. ("Inky") Stephensen claiming that he worked heavily on the manuscript, knocking it into acceptable form, a claim that Herbert bitterly denied.

On its publication the novel was taken to be a polemic against racism, which in part it is, but critics failed to see the anarchistic yet coherent vision behind it. The novel is the story of Norman Shillingworth, a half-caste growing up in the exuberantly created world of Capricornia (the Northern Territory) in the first part of the twentieth century, but it is also the story of the Territory itself, of the tragic love between Norman and Tocky, of Norman's problematic relationship with his father, and of the relationships between aborigines, whites, and those of mixed color. Herbert makes Capricornia itself both fact and metaphor of the anarchic nature of human affairs. Few Australian writers, if any, have created such an original world and made it so distinctively their own.

After *Capricornia*, Herbert began a series of projects that never came to fruition before a sudden burst of productivity brought forth four books in five years. *Seven Emus* (1959) is a minor yarn in the tradition of the tall story. *Soldiers' Women* (1962) is a long, ambitious, but leadenly written account of relationships between the Americans and Australians in Sydney during World

War II. *Larger Than Life* (1962) is a selection of Herbert's short stories, which were unashamedly written for money; they are conventional for the most part but entertaining. After the author's death, a collection of his earlier stories, often written under pseudonyms, appeared under the title *South of Capricorn* (1990). *Disturbing Element* (1963) is a highly entertaining, well-written, but deeply suspect, account of the author's first 21 years.

In 1975 came Herbert's most contentious and ambitious novel, *Poor Fellow My Country*. With the scars of the alleged editing of *Capricornia* still in his mind, Herbert insisted on its being published with no changes and the result was a mammoth work of 850,000 words, the longest novel ever published in Australia by far. Some critics hailed it as a masterpiece; others, while acknowledging the presence of many outstanding episodes, finally found the novel to be overwritten and marred by the fact that its protagonist, Jeremy Delacy, is a racist, sexist, garrulous bore, and much of the novel is taken up with him. The period the novel deals with—roughly 1936 to 1943—is seen as a crucial one in Australian history, with white Australians failing a test of courage and resolution, symbolized in their panic-stricken flight from what was believed to be the imminent Japanese invasion of Darwin. Herbert contrasts the "mongrelized" culture of the whites against the true culture of the Aboriginals, embodied in the figure of the half-caste, Prindy.

The dominant figure on the Australian literary landscape for much of the second half of the twentieth century, however, is Patrick White (1912–80). Born in England of Australian parents, White wrote three novels before returning reluctantly to Australia at the urging of his Greek partner shortly after World War II. His reasons for doing so, and his deep ambivalence toward his native country, are brilliantly documented in the essay "A Prodigal Son."

White then proceeded to produce an extraordinary body of work—nine more massive novels, many stories and novellas, a large body of plays (theater was his first love), and various other books. He frequently postulates a division between those few characters who have access to some kind of spiritual life and inner wisdom and the vast majority of what he calls in one of his novels the "emotionally commonplace." The binary oppositions are symbolized in the titles of two of his novels, *The Living and the Dead* (1941) and *Riders in the Chariot* (1961), but are present in most of his work. In post-Romantic fashion, White focuses on the outsiders, those who are rejected by mainstream society, what he calls in the title of one of his collections of short stories, "the burnt ones," as the repositories and embodiments of true wisdom. His is also a deeply satirical talent. In many of his short stories and plays and in some of his novels he concentrates on the invented Sydney suburb of Sarsparilla as the focus of his hatred of what he saw as the parochialism and triviality of much of Australian suburban life.

In its deliberate mangling of syntax, its intense physicality, and its bravura flights of rhetoric, White's style seems to represent an almost conscious attempt to grapple with the thinness of Australian culture and wrestle meaning out of it. He himself eloquently described his writing as "a struggle to create completely fresh forms out of the rocks and sticks of words." His greatest novels are arguably *The Tree of Man* (1955), *Voss* (1957), *Riders in the Chariot* (1961), *The Solid Mandala* (1966), *The Eye of the Storm* (1973), and *A Fringe of Leaves* (1976), though he himself expressed a special affection for *The Aunt's Story* (1948). In 1973 White became the first and still only Australian writer to win the Nobel Prize. Out of its earnings he established the Patrick White Award to honor and recompense aging Australian writers whose work had not been sufficiently recognized.

The Later Years in Poetry

Probably Australia's finest two contemporary poets are Peter Porter (1929–) and Les Murray (1938–). Ironically, they are almost totally opposites, a fact that Murray himself noted in writing about Porter. In his essay "On Sitting Back and Thinking About Porter's Boeotia," Murray takes Porter's poem "On First Looking into Chapman's Hesiod" as a starting point for his claim that "the work of Hesiod stands on one side of a rift that runs through the whole of Western culture, a fundamental tension which for convenience we may call the war between Athens and Boeotia"; he goes on to suggest that Porter is "Athens" while he himself is Boeotia, "rural, traditional-minded, predominantly small-holding Boeotia" of which Athens is always in contempt. Though he praises the poem—and Porter—generously, it becomes the occasion for his hope that Australia can become the site for a resolution of splits in the old world of Europe: "It may be preserved for us to bring off the long-needed reconciliation of Athens with Boeotia, and create that lasting organic country where urban and rural no longer imply a conflict, and where one discovers ever more richly what one is and where one stands and how to grow from there without loss or the denial of others."[5]

Not surprisingly, in his reply to Murray, Porter disagreed with some asperity and did not seem to relish having the mantle of Boeotia thrust forcibly upon his shoulders. Born in Queensland in 1929, Porter, like most of his fellow Queensland writers, left the state and in 1951 emigrated to England, where he has lived ever since, however, with frequent trips, especially since the 1980s, back to Australia.

His poems are deeply allusive, packed especially with references to music, which Porter has repeatedly acknowledged is his preferred art, as well as to only a slightly lesser extent literature, photography, and pictorial art, especially portraiture. They are consciously exploratory, as even the titles attest, packed with references to various countries, cities, periods in time, testament to his omnivorous curiosity; the poems are often restless, on the move, in transit from one place to another. Though he can set up various personae in his poems ("Someone must have been telling lies about Porter"), he does not inhabit his poems as Murray does, but stands to the side, mocking and self-deprecatory about whatever self there is in the poem even when he names himself, questioning and tentatively asserting.

Even the jokes of the two poets are different. Porter's slyly allusive title, "Once bitter, twice bitten," is in contrast to Murray's much more aggressive, "Lunch and counter lunch," with its reference to the distinctively Australian institution of hotel meals ("counter lunch"). His humanist atheism is in direct contrast to Murray's deep Catholic faith and intense affinity with the Australian landscape.

Autobiographical, often almost confessional in tone, the verse of Dorothy Hewett (1923–2002) deals uncompromisingly with the tumultuous events of her life, including an attempted suicide when she was young, and frequent, often failed, romantic relationships. Hewett also writes movingly about her children in poems such as "Anniversary." In 1975 her ex-husband sued her for libel on the basis of references she made to the autism of one of their children.

Faye Zwicky (1933–) is a West Australian poet whose work is dominated by her German Jewish background. Her best-known poem, "Kaddish," is an elegy for the death of her father. The holocaust makes its way into even more recent events, such as her lament for the dead students in "Tiananmen Square, June 4, 1989"—"The wolves have come again."

Chris Wallace-Crabbe (1934–) is a poet of humane, ironic intelligence who has written productively for over 40 years. Wallace-Crabbe, who is also a critic and former academic, has spoken of his admiration of W. H. Auden, and this appears in his work, not only in its frequent recourse to humor and satire but in its increasing interest in public and political issues. "The Rebel General," for instance, the title poem of a 1967 collection, is a complex, dispassionate, not entirely unsympathetic portrait of a tyrant. Wallace-Crabbe's cautiously affirmative approach to life is probably best summed up in the title of one of his best poems, "Losses and Recoveries."

In his introduction to his anthology *The New Australian Poetry* (1979), poet John Tranter (1943–) argues vehemently for the cause of modernism, for a poem being simply itself, an artifact made of words, and against both humanist concepts of poetry and what he sees as the academic conservatism of poets like A. D. Hope, his bête noire. Although not everyone would agree, and some critics even argue that Tranter violates his own beliefs at times in his poetic practice, his views have been deeply influential on contemporary Australian poetry. Like other younger poets, Tranter has turned far more to American models than to English, to free verse rather than rhyme, to the dissonance and allusiveness of modernism.

Robert Gray (1945–) was born and grew up on the northern coast of New South Wales, an area he returns to often in his writing. Like Les Murray, he is master of the long line but his celebration is less of the bush than of his birthplace or of Sydney, as in the fine poem "Bondi," about Sydney's famous beach. A poet of considerable versatility, Gray can write sparely, objectively describing natural phenomena as in the haiku of "5 poems " but can also write movingly about his aging mother in "The Dying Light."

John A. Scott (1948–) arrived in Melbourne from the United Kingdom in 1959. He first established a reputation with a long narrative poem, "St. Clair," and has subsequently continued his interest in narrative verse. Quite logically, and like many other Australian poets such as David Malouf and Rodney Hall, Scott turned to fiction with *Blair* (1988), a novella, *What I Have Written* (1993), and two additional novels. However, he has also written some accomplished lyrics.

The poetry of John Forbes (1950–98) contains many of the omens of his short life. "Speed, a pastoral" is about the pleasures of taking the drug, speed, while "Drugs" indicates a preference for alcohol over other drugs. Forbes, like Tranter, was deeply influenced by American models such as Frank O'Hara. His poetry is full of energy and a kind of wry humor and witty, highly self-conscious speculation. In general, the poetry scene in Australia has a rather bleak look about it at the moment. Major Australian publishers such as Angus & Robertson and Oxford University Press have ceased to publish poetry altogether, citing economic imperatives, but in their place smaller, indigenous companies have sprung up, publishing modest editions, and in the major cities, especially, poetry readings in pubs and cafés are flourishing.

Prose—1972 and After

If we focus on the year 1972 as the beginning of a radical series of changes in Australian literature, it is partly for symbolic reasons. In that year the Labor government of Gough Whitlam, with its notably more sympathetic stance to the arts, came to power and though it lasted only three years, it transformed many of the attitudes toward the Australian arts. Local publishing was encouraged and a host of small Australian publishing firms sprang up. Subsidies and grants to writers were increased and a Public Lending Right scheme (by which authors received financial compensation for library use of their works) established. This led to a rapid increase in the quantity of publications of Australian writing, of varying quality. Though Patrick White continued to cast his immense shadow over the literary landscape, it was a much more varied and crowded landscape than before, with far greater scope for literary experimentation, frankness in subject matter, and the exploration of many aspects of Australian life that had so far seemed relatively untouched.

However, probably many of the changes that the 1970s ushered in were on their way beforehand. Some of them can be discerned in retrospect in a highly influential anthology titled *The Most Beautiful Lies* (1977), featuring Murray Bail, Peter Carey, Morris Lurie, Frank Moorhouse, and Michael Wilding. The title is a reference to Mark Twain's description of Australian history—"...like the most beautiful lies...full of surprises, and adventures, and incongruities, and contradictions, and incredibilities..."—and emphasizes the new role that formal experimentation and modes of fantasy and the surreal were beginning to play in Australian literature. It is in pointed contrast to White's accusation of dun-colored realism or to an earlier, rather dour anthology by the same publisher, *An Australian Selection* (1974), which featured Henry Lawson, Vance Palmer, Hal Porter, Patrick White, and Peter Cowan.

All the five writers included in *The Most Beautiful Lies* went on to establish or consolidate considerable reputations for themselves, first, as short story writers and then as novelists. Peter Carey, for instance, published two widely praised collections of stories before writing seven novels over the space of some 20 years: *Bliss* (1981), *Illywhacker* (1985), *Oscar and Lucinda* (1988), *The Tax Inspector* (1991), *The Unusual Life of Tristan Smith* (1994), *Jack Maggs* (1997), and the wildly successful *True History of the Kelly Gang* (2000), the second of his novels to win the Booker Prize. A writer of remarkable inventiveness and imagination, Carey has also managed to remain accessible to a wider audience.

Like Carey, Murray Bail is a highly original and inventive writer who moves constantly toward modes of the surreal and the fantastic. Both of them have been compared to American writers such as the fabulist Donald Barthelme, as well as practitioners of magic realism like Gabriel Garcia Marquez. Bail's first volume was a collection of short stories, *Contemporary Portraits and Other Stories* (1975), which contained no story called "Contemporary Portraits." It was later republished as *The Drover's Wife and Other Stories* (1986), in order to draw attention to Bail's most famous story, a cleverly satirical rewriting of Lawson's masterpiece, based on Russell Drysdale's painting of the same name. Bail has since published three novels, as well as sundry other works. *Homesickness* (1980) is a brilliantly comic account of a group of Australians abroad on a package tour. *Holden's Performance* (1987) rests on a sustained analogy between Australians in general and the country's favorite iconic car, but with

Eucalyptus (1998), Bail finally achieved what is probably his most successful marriage of the absurd and the romantic.

Frank Moorhouse built a considerable reputation as one of Australia's finest short story writers over a number of years with a series of what he cleverly called "discontinuous narratives"—stories that are not so closely coherent that they form a novel, but in which there is nevertheless a constant interplay and series of cross-references, so that, for instance, a minor character in one story might appear as the protagonist of the next. Moorhouse's ambivalent fascination with the United States, one he shares with Carey (who now lives in New York), and Michael Wilding, is captured in the title of his most famous collection, *The Americans, Baby* (1972), and especially with the figure of Becker, the Coca-Cola salesman from Atlanta. More recently, however, Moorhouse has written two long and ambitious novels about the workings of the old League of Nations, *Grand Days* (1993) and *Dark Palace* (2000).

As late as 1975 a critical book could argue that women's writing had been largely neglected by both predominantly male critics and the public they influenced. Whatever the truth of this accusation then, it is patently not the case now. The last quarter of a century has seen the rise of an enormous variety of successful and widely read female authors, and just as women easily outnumber men as book buyers so they probably outnumber them now as writers.

The process began with a group of women who were born within a few years of each other, roughly from 1916 to 1925, and who, with one exception, came to fiction writing or at least publishing, quite late in their lives but then prospered. The exception is Thea Astley (1925–), whose first novel was published in 1958 and who went on to have a long and distinguished career as a novelist, winning the Miles Franklin Award three times. Her novels are noted for their tart wit, anger at social injustice toward the less privileged members of society, and sardonic satire of the parochialism of small towns in the north of Australia.

However, among her near contemporaries, Jessica Anderson (1916–) published her first novel in 1963 and finally achieved widespread recognition with *Tirra Lirra by the River* in 1978. Amy Witting (pen name of Joan Levick [1918–2001]) was a similar late bloomer, publishing her first novel *The Visit* only in 1977 and winning fame with *I for Isobel* in 1989. Her last years were marked by several publications. Even more remarkable is the story of Elizabeth Jolley (1923–), who migrated to Australia from England in 1959 and wrote furiously but did not publish a book until *Five Acre Virgin* (1976), which made an enormous impact. What followed was a steady outpouring of published work—almost 20 novels and collections of short stories at a rate of almost one a year—among which is some of the finest work in Australia of that period. Like Astley, she has won most major Australian literary awards, often more than once. Especially noteworthy are the blackly comic novel *Mr. Scobie's Riddle* (1983) and a trilogy written about her painful experiences growing up in England—*My Father's Moon* (1989), *Cabin Fever* (1990), and *The George's Wife* (1993). Jolley's bleak view of the universe is qualified by moments of people coming together and by her compassionate, unjudging view of human folly.

Better known as a distinguished poet and playwright, Dorothy Hewett also published a novel, *Bobbin Up* (1959), about her experience in a Sydney factory, and late in life produced *The Toucher* (1993) and *Neap Tide* (1999).

Among the newer novelists, almost too numerous to mention, a few stand out. Christopher Koch (1932–) published two novels in London when he was young but then abandoned fiction writing for the exigencies of making a living in the Australian Broadcasting Corporation as an overseas reporter. At the age of 40 he resigned to devote himself full time to fiction, and most of his work has been done in the last quarter of a century. As well as rewriting his early novels, *The Boys in the Island* (1958, 1974) and *Across the Sea Wall* (1965, 1982), Koch has also published four more novels and two works of nonfiction. A slow writer and meticulous craftsman, Koch has drawn heavily on his experiences as a correspondent for his fiction. *The Year of Living Dangerously* (1978) is set in Indonesia during the last days of the Sukarno regime, while *Highways to a War* (1995), which Koch called part of a "diptych" (with *Out of Ireland*) deals in part with the Vietnam war and its aftermath. Koch is a lucid, graceful, and highly intelligent writer.

David Malouf (1934–) began his writing career as a poet, but like many Australian poets, he later turned to prose. His versatility is indicated by the fact that he has written poetry, novels, short stories, memoirs, and autobiography, as well as librettos for opera. Born in Brisbane, of Lebanese and English parents, Malouf has frequently concerned himself in both prose and poetry with reconciling the new world and the old, the northern and southern hemispheres, Australia and Europe. His collection of short stories is called *Antipodes* (1985). Malouf's novels are often consciously poetic and stylized, less concerned with social interaction than with his characters' escape into some timeless, asocial world, often through transcendent death.

Thomas Keneally (1935–) is one of Australia's most prolific, durable, and popular novelists. After abandoning his study for the priesthood at the age of 25, Keneally turned to writing full time and had his first big success with *Bring Larks and Heroes* (1967), which won the Miles Franklin Award. Since then he has gone on to write well over 20 novels, as well as a number of plays and nonfiction works, and has won just about every Australian literary award as well as a good many overseas ones, including the Booker Prize for the novel that established his international reputation, *Schindler's Ark* (1982). Many of his novels explore history—both that of Australia and other countries—and his fictive interests range from Aboriginal and convict history in Australia to Joan of Arc, the American civil war, the World War I armistice, Yugoslav partisans in World War II, and Nazism. Although an uneven writer, at his best Keneally succeeds in straddling the line between popular fiction and work that has earned the respect of critics and reviewers.

Gerald Murnane (1939–) is a highly original novelist who is much admired by his peers. His first two novels were comparatively conventional. *Tamarisk Row* (1974) tells the familiar Australian story of growing up as a Catholic, in this case in country Victoria, while *A Lifetime on Clouds* (1976) has some of the same concerns. But with *The Plains* (1982), Murnane made a decisive break, abandoning the conventions of realism and turning to a mode of fiction—consciously mythic, sometimes surreal—that has seen him compared to writers like Borges, Garcia Marquez, and Calvino. His works become more self-referential, concentrating on inner landscapes rather than outer ones, and yet several of the stories in *Velvet Waters*, for instance, are extremely moving and almost hypnotic in their rhythmic intensity.

Beverley Farmer (1941–) has written several novels but her best work is largely in the form of the short story. Born in Melbourne but married to a Greek man for some years, Farmer deals often with cross-cultural tensions and the predicaments of people (especially women) who are forced to confront societies whose values they find abhorrent or demeaning. The relationships she depicts are strained, even desolate, but she confronts them with an intense honesty and ability to endure pain.

Helen Garner (1942–) gained immediate fame with her first novel *Monkey Grip* (1977), the story of a young woman living in the inner suburbs of Melbourne and her doomed affair with a drug addict. She continued to gain attention and to arouse controversy with her subsequent works of both fiction and nonfiction, as well as turning her hand to script writing. Her highly praised novella *The Children's Bach* (1984) again deals with a carefully circumscribed world but is a beautifully structured work that depicts a small group of people struggling to live according to their own moral code. (It is not for nothing that one of Garner's works is called *Honour*.)

Dislocations (1986) is the significant title of one of the short story collections of Janette Turner Hospital (1942–). Born in Melbourne, she moved at an early age to Queensland, but has spent most of her adult life in India, Canada, and the United States. It is hardly surprising, then, that she is fascinated by people who are at odds with their surroundings. Her protagonists are almost always out of harmony with their world, whether because of national or sexual identity, loss of roots, imprisonment, barriers of language,

age, or even something close to madness, living on the edge. Again, significantly, her best novel is titled *Borderline* (1985). Sometimes Hospital tried to juggle almost more ideas than she can handle, but her writing at its best is sensitive and full of energy.

Former journalist and private investigator, Robert Drewe (1943–) also deals in part with Asia in his second novel, *A Cry in the Jungle Bar* (1979), which is set in the Philippines, but his fiction is more often located in Australia. Drewe examines questions of national identity, as in his novel, *Our Sunshine* (1991), about the Kelly gang, but perhaps even more is concerned with cultural as well as personal dislocations. Beneath the surface calm his characters often lead lives of quiet desperation. Drewe is also a fine short story writer who has published two collections, including the beautifully titled *The Bay of Contented Men* (1989).

David Foster (1944–) is a formidably erudite and intelligent novelist, who comes from a scientific background. His novels are often comic but in a hard-headed, cerebral kind of way that has found more favor with critics than with a wider audience. The most successful of them is perhaps *Moonlite* (1981), an ingenious narrative of the picaresque adventures of Finbar ("Moonbar") MacDuffie, which amount to an allegorical account of the history of immigration to Australia, but Foster also had considerable success with the more recent *The Glade Within the Grove* (1996).

Brian Castro (1950–) is another writer who has received less popular attention than he deserves. Born in Hong Kong but brought up in Australia from an early age, Castro writes in an increasingly complex and intricate way about the phenomenon of displacement. The relative simplicity of his first novel, *Birds of Passage* (1983), which juxtaposes the life of a Chinese man in the gold mines in the 1850s with his mixed-race contemporary descendant Seamus, gives way to novels that employ increasingly complex narrative techniques. His most recent work, *Shanghai Dancing* (2003), is a vastly ambitious account of his family history ranging over several hundred years.

Kate Grenville (1950–) is one of several writers who came to prominence with the assistance of the Vogel/Australian award, conducted jointly for unpublished younger writers by a bread company and one of Australia's leading newspapers. Her novel, *Dreamhouse* (1986), was runner-up in the competition in 1983. However, by the time it appeared, Grenville had already published a collection of short stories, the ambiguously titled *Bearded Ladies* (1985), and the novel that made her reputation, *Lilian's Story* (1985), based on the life of a well-known Sydney eccentric. Grenville returned to much of the same material in her novel *Dark Places* (1994). A strongly feminist writer, Grenville locates many of the misfortunes that befall Lilian directly in male mistreatment and vanity.

Another writer to have profited from the Vogel award is West Australian Tim Winton (1960–) whose precocious talent led him to publish five books of fiction in six years when he was in his early twenties. Winton's early fiction is deeply influenced by Ernest Hemingway, not always for good, but his later work is more assured and ambitious. Winton's three most recent novels, *Cloudstreet* (1991), *The Riders* (1994), and *Dirt Music* (2001) have had enormous critical and popular success.

This necessarily truncated account of the literary landscape has had to ignore highly successful popular writers such as Colleen McCullough, Bryce Courtenay, and many others, as well as the innumerable crime writers, led by the doyen of them all in Jon Cleary. There is also a rich vein of nonfictional prose in Australian literature. Autobiography has always been a favorite and popular form in Australia. There are also many talented writers for children and young adults, while over the last decade or two there has been a notable increase in the number of writers of what could generally be called belles lettres—memoirs, essays, and so on—led by Robert Dessaix, Brian Matthews, Drusilla Modjeska, and others.

Notes

1. A.R. Chisholm, *Quadrant,* I 3 (1957), p. 79.
2. A.G. Stephens, *Chris Brennan* (Sydney: The Bookfellow, 1933), p. 291.
3. Rosemary Dobson, Preface to *Selected Poems* (Sydney: Angus & Robertson, 1980), p. xiii.
4. David Marr, ed., *Patrick White, "A Prodigal Son," Australian Letters* (Milsons Point: Random House, 1958).
5. Les Murray, *The Peasant Mandarin* (St. Lucia: University of Queensland Press, 1978).

7

The Media and Cinema

The media have always exercised considerable power in Australia, partly because a small number of people in a vast geographical space can only be reached by forms of mass media and partly because there are relatively few major players. Politicians in particular display intense nervousness toward the media, whether it is newspaper editorials, television discussion shows, or the "shock jocks" of talk radio (or "talkback radio," as it is known in Australia), aggressive, mostly openly conservative hosts of radio talk shows who command a wide and intensely loyal following in some parts of the community. So loyal is it, in fact, that not even the revelation that some of them took money in order to promote what were essentially advertisements in the form of news items, did anything to destroy their popularity.

Magazines

Australians are avid consumers of magazines. The Australian Bureau of Circulation lists some 70 magazines with large circulations, ranging from about 20,000 to well over half a million; the Australian edition of the weekly *Woman's Day,* for instance, at last count had a circulation of 536,074 while the top-selling *Australian Woman's Weekly* (actually a monthly) sells over 700,000. Like many other Australian magazines, however, especially those aimed at young women, their circulation has been steadily declining, and several magazines have closed since the turn of this century. The causes for this have been variously cited as the newly imposed GST (Goods and Services Tax), the Internet, and increasing ownership of mobile telephones; the theory goes that now young people can talk to each other readily they have less need of magazines for company. In addition, there are simply far more alternative forms of entertainment available to women and far more magazines to choose from. In response to the fall, many of the top women's magazines have gone upmarket, with longer news stories, fiction by well-known writers such as Tim Winton, and a higher quality of journalistic investigation.

Almost every human activity is catered for by the range of magazines: family, house and garden, health, money, women's affairs, politics, sports, and so on. Lifestyle is always a popular issue. The top-selling food magazines, for instance, are *Super Food Ideas* (314,018 readers), *Good Taste* (173,184), *Gourmet Traveller* (87,269), *Table* (80,726), and *Vogue Entertaining* (68,463).

Probably the most famous Australian magazine ever published was *The Bulletin*, a weekly based in Sydney that, in the first 20 years of its existence at the end of the nineteenth century, achieved an astonishingly widespread influence over large numbers of Australians. Although it was not as simplistically nationalistic as it is often portrayed as being—its finest editor, J. F. Archibald, would often boast of his Francophile leanings and alleged origins, saying that his initials stood not for John Feltham but for Jules Francois—it was militantly Australian insofar as that applied to white Australians. Its slogan "Australia for the Australians" was replaced in 1908 by the less ambiguous, "Australia for the White Man," and this was not removed from the cover until the editorship of Donald Horne in the early 1960s. Horne credits himself with opening the magazine to new groups including migrants and women.

In a characteristically Australian way, it managed to combine loyalty to the "mother country" with almost incessant sniping at and ridicule of it—like a clever youth who wants to show off in front of his parents. Most of Australia's then leading writers worked for it at some time or other and it also developed a brilliant group of pictorial artists—"Hop" (Livingstone Hopkins), Norman Lindsay, and his lesser-known brother, Lionel, Will and Ambrose Dyson, and David Low, among others. Its Red Page, the literary page edited by A. G. Stephens, opened up opportunities for many new writers who made their name there, most notably Henry Lawson, "Banjo" Paterson, and "Steele Rudd."

In advocating qualities of brevity, laconicism, and realism among his contributors, Stephens became a profoundly influential editor though it is arguable how far he promoted those qualities or how far he capitalized on what he saw as innately Australian characteristics. Although the magazine became steadily more conservative, it continued to encourage new Australian writing, especially under the editorship of the Red Page by the poet Douglas Stewart over the 1940s and 1950s.

Although *The Bulletin* is still in existence and has a circulation of around 80,000 compared to the 3,000 with which it began, it has nothing like the influence it once exercised. During the 1920s and 1930s, especially, its more radical elements were largely taken over by *Smiths Weekly.* Like *The Bulletin,* a strange mixture of radicalism and reactionary tendencies (it was violently anti-Semitic, for instance), *Smiths Weekly* was irreverent in tone and prided itself on the frequent number of libel actions it was involved in. Like *The Bulletin* it had a number of brilliant black-and-white illustrators such as Stan Cross and George Finey and concentrated heavily also on comic articles. It had its own team of poets, led by Kenneth Slessor, who was already beginning to make a reputation for himself and who wrote superb light verse. Other well-known contributors included artists, cartoonists, and novelists like Ronald McCuaig, Kenneth Mackenzie, and Lenny Lower.

Magazines came and went. *Art in Australia* was founded in 1916 by painter Sydney Ure Smith and Bertram Stevens and for many years played a major role in promoting the arts in Australia. On Stevens's death in 1922, the poet and art lover, Leon Gellert, took his place as coeditor. *Art in Australia* was one of the first magazines to recognize the significance of Aboriginal art and to run a regular section on architecture.

Gellert later became editor of *Home,* a now-forgotten magazine that in its time was quite significant, seeking to encourage Australian arts and letters and promote artistic taste by what was sometimes called a *Vogue*-like approach. *Home* was unusual in being a glossy magazine with a consciously international approach. It carried full-length covers by prominent Australian artists but inside could be found fashion and society notes.

During the generally stagnant 1950s, Australian media life was enlivened by the appearance of two new magazines, *The Observer* and *Nation. The Observer* began as a fortnightly magazine in 1958 under the vigorous editorship of Donald Horne, who was to become a cultural spokesman on Australian issues for almost half a century, and who, with the title of his best-selling book, *The Lucky Country,* introduced a new catch phrase into the Australian vocabulary. Surprisingly it was the conservative publisher Frank Packer who gave him his head. *The Bulletin* by this stage was in a state of complete atrophy, and though Horne was hardly a radical—later he became coeditor of Australia's most conservative cultural magazine, the CIA-funded *Quadrant*—he had read widely, was passionately interested in cultural matters, and introduced what could be described as a "new, alert conservatism."

He was all for debate and the freeing of Australian intellectual life from what he saw as a stiflingly parochial preoccupation with nationalism. Art and book reviews were plentiful, some signed, some not, and it was Horne who gave Robert Hughes his first big break by appointing him as art editor; later Hughes adopted the same role with *Time* news magazine.

Nation appeared seven months later in somewhat unusual circumstances. Its editor was Tom Fitzgerald, the Financial Editor of the *Sydney Morning Herald*. When he told the Board of the newspaper that he intended to launch an independent fortnightly he immediately assumed that he would be relieved of his position, but after consultation with each member of the Board, the Director of Fairfax, in a move of remarkable generosity, said that he could stay on with his job at the SMH provided the new editorship did not interfere with it.

Although it never paid its contributors well and achieved only a modest circulation, the rather more left-leaning *Nation* always had an influence beyond its size, especially, ironically enough, in Melbourne. It was run almost solely by Fitzgerald and George Munster, who not only managed the journal, but was a voluminous contributor on a wide range of topics. It attracted a range of (mostly young) contributors who would later become distinguished intellectuals in various roles. Clive James cut his writing teeth there while Robert Hughes switched from *The Observer*.

But the most important and longest-lasting of Australian magazines had no such intellectual pretensions at all. Founded in 1933, *The Australian Women's Weekly* has consistently been Australia's best-selling magazine as well as what one commentator has called an articulate barometer of female sexual identity in Australia. At its peak of popularity, during the 1950s and 1960s, it was read in one of four Australian homes, making it the highest-circulation women's magazine per head of population in the world. Its founding editor, George Warnecke, instructed his journalists to give it an unswervingly Australian outlook and to try and make everything they wrote, no matter how apparently banal, newsworthy. The secret of the magazine's success was in its constant ability to change and respond to changes in its audience without ever losing contact with it.

Among other magazines are *Woman's Day* and *New Idea*. All three magazines have lost circulation in the 1990s—*Women's Weekly* from around 1 million in 1994 to about 700,000 in 2001; *Woman's Day* from 900,000 to around 550,000 in the same period; and *New Idea* from 800,000 to about half that. According to the magazine industry's representative body, Magazine Publishers of Australia, there are now about 730 consumer magazines in Australia, compared with 417 (excluding imports) in 1990. In such a fiercely competitive climate it was inevitable that some of them would close.

Recent trends suggest that teen, TV, and gossip magazines are losing sales to magazines that promote certain lifestyles or offer practical advice for anything from diet to gardening to cooking. Among recent improvers are *Super Food Ideas* (up 18.85 percent to 361,211, making it Australia's sixth most popular magazine), *Australian Good Taste* (up 5 percent), and *Burke's Backyard,* based on a popular TV program (up 15.46 percent). All this is suggestive of a more interactive approach by readers to the magazines they select. The other area where sales have improved is finance titles, especially magazines devoted to financial planning and personal finance.

There are also a number of small intellectual magazines with influence out of proportion to their often tiny circulations. Although many of these have risen and fallen with notable rapidity, a number have been surprisingly stubborn stayers. They include *Meanjin,* established in Brisbane by Clem Christesen; *Southerly,* now run from the English Department of the University of Sydney; *Quadrant,* established in Sydney in 1956 under the editorship of the distinguished poet James McAuley; *Overland,* a left-wing, strongly socialist magazine; *Westerly;* and the relatively new *Heat.* These provide an opportunity for creative writers to express themselves although the remuneration is poor. There are also a number of more directly literary and scholarly magazines such as *Australian Literary Studies* and *Meridian,* sponsored respectively by the University of Queensland and La Trobe University.

NEWSPAPERS

The first Australian newspaper to appear was the *Sydney Gazette* in 1803. It was followed by other, often short-lived papers, though there are some exceptions, such as the *Sydney Herald,* which was founded in 1831 and is still in existence as the *Sydney Morning Herald.* Similarly, the *Moreton Bay Courier,* founded in Brisbane in 1846, went through several transformations before arriving at its present identity as the *Courier Mail,* while the *West Australian* began as the *Perth Gazette* in 1833. The *Melbourne Argus* was founded by William Kerr in 1846. In June 1849 it became a daily, and a weekend supplement, *The Australasian,* appeared from 1864. Initially, the paper was liberal in its outlook, advocating separatism and anti-transportation, and critical of Governor La Trobe. It soon became more conservative in its outlook and was to the right of its chief rival *The Age* by the 1860s. *The Age* steadily passed it in terms of influence and reputation, though *The Argus* was still home to columnists as distinguished as the novelist Marcus Clarke. After World War II it was acquired by a British press chain, changed to a tabloid, and reverted to its liberal position. It was outsold by its new arrival, *The Sun,* however, and in 1957 ceased publication altogether.

Various social developments operated upon newspapers to force changes in format, function, and influence. Rising literacy opened the way to larger audiences. The extension of the railway system led to improved distribution. Newspaper proprietors were more than willing to exercise influence and sway public opinion by writing vigorously and openly partisan editorials. David

Syme achieved immense influence with his ownership of *The Age*, for example, on such important policies as Protection, and even now politicians are often unwilling to move without considering or even discussing the likely impact of their policies on public opinion as filtered through newspapers.

The arrival of radio, and then television, forced radical changes in the nature of newspapers. They became less concerned with the merely factual recording of news and more involved with background, interpretation, and the presentation of rival opinions in their columns. As the number of independent newspapers has steadily declined and there has been a clear trend toward the centralization of ownership, especially with the huge Murdoch and Packer dynasties, there have been prolonged and fierce debates about the implications of this, as well as cross-ownership of other media, for the health and independence of the Press.

Among other major newspapers Australia currently produces are *The Adelaide Advertiser*, founded in 1858 as the *South Australian Advertiser*. Initially liberal in tone and pro-protectionism, it was eventually acquired by Rupert Murdoch after he gained control of the *Herald & Weekly Times*. He turned it into a tabloid.

The *Melbourne Age* was first published in 1854 was but taken over shortly afterward by the Syme family. *The Age* supported free selection, free secular education, and tariffs, and was one of the most influential newspapers in the country for many years. It remains, with the *Sydney Morning Herald*, its sister newspaper, and *The Australian*, among the most respected newspapers in the country. In 1983 it was taken over by the Fairfax group. *The Australian* is the country's newest and only national paper and was founded by Rupert Murdoch in 1964. It is generally conservative in tone and heavily oriented toward business; it has a range of columnists of varying political persuasions but mostly to the right.

The *Australian Financial Review* was established by the Fairfax Press in 1951 as a weekly but became a biweekly in 1961 and eventually a daily two years later. Though ostensibly confined to business and finance, the paper steadily expanded its horizons and contains a great deal of reading, especially on politics, of general interest. *The Brisbane Courier-Mail*, established as a result of an amalgamation between the *Brisbane Courier* and the *Daily Mail* in 1933, was later sold to the *Herald & Weekly Times* chain under Rupert Murdoch's News Corporation.

The *Daily Telegraph* was a Sydney tabloid founded in 1879. Its most famous editor was the novelist Brian Penton. Mostly conservative in politics and down-market in style, it was taken over by Rupert Murdoch in 1972 and merged with the *Daily Mirror* to form the *Telegraph-Mirror*. *The Examiner*, Tasmania's oldest newspaper, was founded in 1842 as a weekly before eventually appearing daily. Tasmania also has the *Mercury*, which was founded in Hobart in 1854 and taken over by Rupert Murdoch in 1987.

The *Melbourne Sun* (initially the *Sun-News Pictorial*) was established in 1922 as a daily illustrated tabloid. Highly successful for a long time it was eventually amalgamated with the evening *Herald* to become the *Herald Sun*, though it still preserves most of the features of the original.

MEDIA LAWS

Australia's media laws are both complex and controversial. For years governments have spoke about changing or overhauling them but so far nothing has been done. Under existing broadcasting laws, introduced in 1987, joint ownership of a TV station or newspaper, or a radio station and newspaper is prohibited in the same geographic region. The laws also ban common ownership of radio and television stations. Television proprietors cannot own more than 15 percent of a newspaper in the same metropolitan market, and vice versa. Total foreign ownership of a TV station is limited to 20 percent, and for foreign individuals, 15 percent. For metropolitan newspapers, total foreign ownership is limited to 30 percent and to 25 percent for foreign individuals. This has discouraged foreign media kings such as Conrad Black of Hollinger International from entering the market.

But there is a growing feeling that new technological developments have rendered the laws anachronistic. Digital and interactive TV and the use of broadband Internet to deliver information, education, and commercial services all have revolutionary potential, but government policies so far have failed to stimulate their development.

In most countries where enhanced television services are available, they are offered only through pay TV. But Australia's free-to-air networks are hoping that they too can provide services like booking tickets, calling up information, ordering pizzas, and so on; if not, they believe their advertising revenue is seriously at risk. The other issue under debate is how far Australian viewers are likely to actively pursue new services or whether they will simply want to passively enjoy conventional programs. In the United States this has been called the "lean back, lean forward" dilemma.

Groups calling for change include not only newspaper publishers but Internet content groups, computer equipment manufacturers, academics, the Australian Consumers' Association, Australia's largest advertisers, and the group representing all advertising agencies. The 2000 digital TV legislation allowed existing free-to-air networks to provide some new services, but placed such severe restrictions on the types of services allowed to be offered by datacasters that when the Government attempted to sell the excess digital spectrum the datacasters needed to send their services to digital TVs, the auction was a failure.

Most media chiefs, including John Fairfax Holdings, Kerry Packer's Publishing and Broadcasting Ltd., and Rupert Murdoch's News Corporation support a more relaxed regime that would see the laws dramatically remodeled. Fairfax's expansion plans have so far been thwarted by the legislation, which prevents it from moving into television. The government's proposals would keep cross-media and foreign ownership rules, but allow exemptions if merged groups undertake to keep newsrooms and editorial processes separate; foreign owners would need to guarantee minimum levels of locally produced news and current affairs.

So far the government's plans for change have been resisted by the opposition parties, though recently they have shown some signs of wishing to reopen discussion. However, the bottom line, as the federal opposition has pointed out, is that the media in Australia are one of the most monopolistic in the world. The opposition spokesman has said, "The fact remains that the vast bulk of Australians still get the overwhelming majority of information and opinion by a very small number of organisations."[1]

Under legislation currently proposed or at least debated by the government, planned changes would both remove foreign ownership restrictions and offer exemptions on cross-media ownership restrictions, which currently prevent proprietors from owning television stations and newspapers in the same markets. The changes would clear the way for Kerry Packer, for example, to make a move on Fairfax, publisher of the *Melbourne Age*, while retaining ownership of the Nine National Network and his Australian Consolidated Press magazine empire. Rupert Murdoch would be able to increase his publishing and television holdings in major cities if cross-media ownership restrictions were eased. The opposition Labor party has signaled its likely resistance to the changes, while the Australian Democrats, who control the balance of power in the Senate, have stated that they are open to new proposals without so far committing themselves.

The government has scoffed at fears that the changes would vest too much clout in too few hands, claiming that what they call the "imperatives of commercialism" would prevent media giants from using their products to push a particular political line. Any proprietors who did so would risk financial ruin by isolating "the other half" of the consumer market who did not share their views. It pointed to the fact that the *Sydney Morning Herald* had editorially supported the government in the last federal election while its Melbourne Fairfax stablemate, *The Age*, had supported Labor. (It ignored the fact that *The Age* was, in fact, the only major newspaper to do so.) The government has openly supported and encouraged overseas interest in acquiring Australian media. It has conducted lengthy talks with Rupert Murdoch, has mentioned some of America's largest media companies, such as Vivendi, Viacom, AOL, and Disney as possible candidates, and has also noted interest by Pearson of the UK and Conrad Black's Hollinger, as well as the independently owned *Chicago Tribune.* Hollinger International had a 25 percent interest in Fairfax from 1991 but sold out five years later, frustrated by what it saw as the inflexibility of the laws. Labor, on the other hand, argues that the proposed safeguards would be impossible to police or even measure.

Ironically, the government has revealed in an explanatory memorandum to its new media-ownership bill that it believes foreign ownership would actually increase diversity—the reason being that it believes foreign businessmen are less likely to use their media assets to influence political parties and decisions. It says, "It is unlikely that foreign owners would be as inclined to interfere in domestic affairs as domestic owners, and the pool of potential media owners would be considerably increased."

Meanwhile, readership of newspapers continues to hold up reasonably well but afternoon newspapers have all but disappeared. Both the *Melbourne Herald Sun* and Sydney's *Daily Telegraph* have closed their afternoon editions, though circulation of the *Herald Sun* at about 550,000 remains stable, as does that of the *Daily Telegraph* at about 420,000.

The ABC

The Australian Broadcasting Commission Act was passed in 1932, setting up a national network to take over the Australian Broadcasting Company. Closely based on the style of the British Broadcasting Corporation and its founder John Reith, the ABC was an independent corporation, governed by a board of commissioners. Its first leader, Charles Moses, ran it from 1935 to 1964 before giving way; from 1945 to 1961 its chairman was Richard Boyer, after whom the annual Boyer lectures were named. Between them these two men shaped and fashioned a good deal of its identity, with heavy attention being paid to news, music, education, and drama, such as the long-running serial *Blue Hills.* While its role in the cultural life of the country is constantly changing and being contested, many people would argue that it remains the most important single cultural institution in the country.

Among the unique features of the ABC are that it carries entertainment and education into the homes of the people, and reaches even the remotest settlements. Popularly known as "Auntie," the ABC immediately became and remains both a highly popular and deeply controversial institution with successive governments of both persuasions arguing that it displays political bias against them.

In 1936 the ABC established concert orchestras in all state capitals to perform live concerts under the direction of leading conductors such as Malcolm Sargeant, to make radio programs accessible to all Australians, especially those in remote areas. In 1946 it began to broadcast the proceedings of parliament. One of its most successful and long-running shows was *The Argonauts*, a hugely popular radio program for children ages eight to 16, based on the Greek myth of Jason and the Argonauts setting sail on a voyage of discovery. Introduced in 1941, the program lasted until 1972.

The ABC led the way in presenting a program for preschool children, *Kindergarten of the Air*. This began in strange circumstances when kindergartens were closed in Western Australia, because of fears of an invasion after the fall of Singapore to the Japanese in February 1942. The Kindergarten Union approached the ABC to provide a daily broadcast. The eastern states followed with their own version, and by the 1950s *Kindergarten of the Air* was broadcast over more than 50 ABC stations. The ABC's two talk flagships are Radio National and ABC News Radio, but also popular is its National Music Radio, which broadcasts a wide range of music from classical to pop.

Radio Australia is heard by millions of people in 25 Asia-Pacific nations. Programs range over a number of issues from immigration policies to the workings of international money markets, from agricultural programs to sports news. In all, 130 foreign radio stations relay or rebroadcast Radio Australia each week in languages ranging from English to Mandarin, Indonesian, Vietnamese, Khmer, and Tok Pidgin.

The ABC has also moved recently to reestablish its television links with neighboring Asian countries through ABC Asia Pacific, a live Asian news bulletin that reaches viewers from Jakarta to northern China. Similarly, there is Asia Pacific Focus, a magazine program. In 1993 the ABC had set up Australia Television International on a government grant but with firm instructions that it should become self-supporting. When this failed to occur, the service was scrapped by the incoming Liberal Government in 1996. Though subsequently bought by the Seven Television network its content was poor and in 2001 the service was abandoned.

Since its inception, the ABC has run into constant difficulties with whatever government is in power. Unlike the British Broadcasting Corporation, it does not receive automatic funding from the sale of TV licenses, but is dependent on the largesse and good will of the government. The ABC's Quentin Dempster has pointed out that "The BBC gets $2.1 billion of unconditional license-payer funding compared to $474 million operational funding for the ABC, in 1998–99."[2] The ABC has often been accused of a left-wing bias, but Labor governments can be just as hostile to criticism as the conservatives, and former Labor Prime Minister Paul Keating once said of it that it was "the most self-indulgent and self-interested outfit in the country."[3]

Among the perennial issues of concern are whether the ABC should chase ratings or stick to a small, elite audience; how much local content it should insist on as a minimum; how much of what it does should be outsourced as against in-house production; and whether it should court advertisers as a way of making up for insufficient governmental funding, thereby risking the integrity of its programs by allowing insidious commercial influences on, for example, so-called infotainment shows. But despite all the criticism leveled at it, the ABC remains a uniquely popular institution in Australian life. A group called Friends of the ABC has long existed to fight for its independence.

CINEMA

The earliest surviving footage shot in Australia is, appropriately, that of a horserace, the 1896 Melbourne Cup at Flemington race course. Claims have been made for a silent epic, produced by the Salvation Army from their Limelight Studios in Melbourne, called *Soldiers of the Cross* (1900) as being the first Australian film. However, this was essentially an illustrated lecture made up of 15 one-minute films and 220 slides. Nevertheless, the volume of film production in the first decade of the twentieth century is striking, with almost 100 productions listed that might qualify as features.[4] Much of the original celluloid has been lost and often there are only contemporary accounts to go on.

As in the United States, cinema started in disreputable or at best unpretentious places—circuses, vaudeville halls, often the open air—but wherever it went, it was taken up enthusiastically by Australian audiences. One contribution was the traveling picture show: horse-drawn wagons that were used to visit country towns where films were shown in makeshift surroundings. This in fact became the basis of the 1977 film, *The Picture Show Man.*

It has been claimed too that a feature film produced by J. and N. Tait, and directed by their brother Charles, was the longest narrative produced anywhere in the world at that time (1906) and the first feature-length film. *The Story of the Kelly Gang,* of which only a small amount has survived, was immensely successful. It established the bushranger/outlaw genre, roughly comparable to the western in the United States, and led the way to successful industry development until 1914.

Over 50 features were made during the 1914–18 period, many of them, unsurprisingly, set in a wartime context, and another 90 or so features produced in the following decade to 1929. There was also the usual mix of melodramas, bushranger films, and action/adventure movies, the latter including the athletic exploits of Snowy Baker, legendary all-around sportsman and a kind of antipodean Douglas Fairbanks.

A lonely pioneer during this period was Raymond Longford (1878–1959), who directed not only *The Sentimental Bloke* but other stories by the hugely popular Steele Rudd, such as *On Our Selection* (1920), and *Rudd's New Selection* (1921), as well as dramatizing the verse of popular writer C. J. Dennis who created *The Sentimental Bloke.* But Longford's career declined with the premature death of his chief collaborator and lead actress, Lottie Lyell (1895–1935), and eventually he was driven out of business, finishing his working life as a night watchman on the Sydney wharves.

Another of the early heroes of Australian cinema was Charles Chauvel (1897–1959), together with (again) his lesser-known wife and helpmate Elsa May. Chauvel's uncle Harry had been a commanding general of the Light Horse during World War I, and Chauvel was drawn to subjects that displayed Australian heroism and mateship. After making *In the Wake of the Bounty* in 1933, he released his most successful film, *Forty Thousand Horsemen,* a treatment of the Light Horse, in 1940. In 1944 he returned to war and the heroism of the diggers with *The Rats of Tobruk* and dealt with the early pioneers in *Sons of Matthew* (1949). In 1955, Chauvel released *Jedda,* the first film to feature Aborigine actors in lead roles as well as being the first Australian color film.

Ken G. Hall (1901–94), house director for Cinesound Productions, also battled to make films, tapping into Chauvel's rich vein of patriotism with *Smithy,* a 1946 biopic about the aviator Charles Kingsford Smith.

However, in general, the coming of sound in 1929 had brought to the surface all of the problems Australia cinema was struggling to live with. A predominantly local audience in a nation with a small population meant competing with the far greater resources of the American and British industries. Although feature production in the 1930s was a matter of cultural and economic concern to government, with inquiries and legislation arising out of fear for the effects of films on the vulnerable, there was little attempt by government to stimulate local production. The pattern of production up to 1970 would consist of the occasional brave individual attempt, experimental or documentary efforts, and international so-called coproductions.

Director Tim Burstall notes, "In the '60s, the only industry we had were sponsored documentaries and ads, plus the very occasional feature film as made by Chips Rafferty or Charles Chauvel, once every 10 years. Insofar as we had an industry, it was all geared to what I remember as the hideous John Grierson documentary tradition."[5]

Burstall himself had won an award at the Venice Film Festival in 1960 for a short film called *The Prize* and had hoped it would launch his feature film career. But it took him 10 years to raise the money for his first feature, *2000 Weeks*, and when it appeared it was a flop. Nevertheless, the early 1970s saw the revival of the Australian film industry. Burstall was able to make *Stork* (1971), based on David Williamson's play *The Coming of Stork* (1970), and the success of this led to his smash hit *Alvin Purple* (1973), a sex comedy designed to take advantage of the newly introduced *R* certificate. Suddenly he was no longer on his own and the Australian film industry had been reborn.

Later came Italian-born Georgio Mangiamele, who arrived in Australia in 1952, age 26. Mangiamele made four films on a shoestring budget, each examining critically the relationship of Italian migrants to the wider, often bigoted Australian community. Then in 1965 his film *Clay*, shot in 35 mm, became the first Australian film to be selected for the Cannes Film Festival. The government refused his appeals for assistance, and Mangiamele, who had mortgaged his house to make the film, was only able to take it to Cannes when an anonymous woman handed him an envelope containing 55 pounds ($110), and a shipping line agreed to subsidize his trip to Europe. He made only one more film, *Beyond Reason* (1970), and was reportedly working on another when he died in 2001, at age 74.

When films were occasionally made on location in Australia, from Australian material, they featured a preponderance of overseas stars and directors, with perhaps small roles for Australian actors and technicians. *The Sundowners* (1960), based on a novel about an Australian bushman, starred Deborah Kerr and Robert Mitchum and was directed by Fred Zinnemann. *The Summer of the Seventeenth Doll* (1959), based on perhaps the most famous Australian play at that time, starred Ernest Borgnine. *On the Beach* (1959) was directed by Stanley Kramer and starred Gregory Peck, Ava Gardner, Anthony Perkins, and Fred Astaire. Other such films, some made by Ealing Studios and usually based on Australian novels, included *The Overlanders, Eureka Stockade, The Shiralee, Age of Consent,* and *They're a Weird Mob.* The main interest for local audiences in these films was to see the variety of ways in which the actors could mangle Australian accents. Australian actors such as Chips Rafferty would be given only supporting roles.

In a new development of this practice, large studios have been built in Sydney and Melbourne and big-budget American films such as the *Star Wars* and *Matrix* sequels have been filmed in Australia. Other American films have been made on locations around Australia, including Melbourne, Coober Pedy, Alice Springs, and Sydney. Early in 2003 two Australian-made American movies, *Darkness Falls* and *Kangaroo Jack* topped the U.S. box office.

Though many actors traveled abroad, mainly to London, very few of them made it to international status. Notable exceptions were Tasmanian-born Errol Flynn in the 1930s and later Peter Finch and Rod Taylor. A member of a boxing troupe, Errol Flynn was spotted by Charles Chauvel and made his acting debut in his *In the Wake of the Bounty* (1933). The rest is history.

Later came the period of what was to be termed cultural nationalism. Television drama had brought local production into Australian homes and Australian plays were beginning to be performed. In 1969 the then conservative Prime Minister, John Gorton, established a film school, an experimental production fund, and an organization (the Australian Film Development Corporation, later to become the Australian Film Commission) to fund feature productions.

In the 30 years since then, Australian feature films have appeared at the rate of 10 to 15 per year. The forms of government funding have varied—sometimes direct investment, sometimes tax concessions, sometimes expert assistance, or completion guarantees. Among the most successful films of those years a necessarily subjective list would include *Sunday Too Far Away* (1975), *Picnic at Hanging Rock* (1975), *Newsfront* (1978), *My Brilliant Career* (1979), *Mad Max* (1979), *Breaker Morant* (1980), *Lonely Hearts* (1982), *Strictly Ballroom* (1992), *The Piano* (1993), *Muriel's Wedding* (1994), and *Shine* (1996).

The films generated a great deal of talent, much of which has gone overseas. Among the noted directors who have worked in Hollywood, often establishing a permanent career there, are Peter Weir, Gillian Armstrong, Philip Noyce, Bruce Beresford, Jane Campion, Baz Luhrman, and Fred Schepisi. Stars include, most famously, American-born but Australian-trained Mel Gibson, Russell Crowe, and Sam Neill (like Armstrong, New Zealand-born), Paul Hogan, Hugh Jackman, Heath Ledger, Nicole Kidman, Judy Davis, and Geoffrey Rush. The 2001 Golden Globe nominations included 10 Australians, four of whom were successful.

Even film composers have joined in the action, making the notion of globalization a more complex one. Lisa Gerrard did the score for *Ali* (with Pieter Bourke) and the previous year for the Academy Award–winning *Gladiator.* Cezary Skubiszewski has done films like the Australian *Two Hands* and *The Sound of One Hand Clapping.* David Thrussell did the score for *Angst* and David Bride for *The Man Who Sued God,* while Paul Grabowsky scored *Siam Sunset, Last Days of Chez Nous,* and, most recently, Fred Schepisi's *Last Orders.* Burkhard Dallwitz did *Paperback Hero* and *The Truman Show,* David Hirschfelder's *Elizabeth, Sliding Doors,* and *Better than Sex,* while John Clifford White has scored *Romper Stomper, Angel Baby,* and *The Heartbreak Kid.* Oddly, almost all of them live in Victoria; most claim that in a world where technology can put you instantly in contact with someone else the advantages of relative isolation far outweigh the drawbacks.

Australia has also recently established a fine tradition of film photography. It goes back as far as 1943 when the courageous war cameraman, Damien

Parer, won a posthumous Oscar for his wartime documentary *Kokoda Front Line,* and was added to by Perth-born Robert Krasker's 1949 Oscar for *The Third Man.* More recently, there have been three Oscars for photography awarded to Australians: Dean Semler for *Dances with Wolves* (1990), John Seale for *The English Patient* (1996), and Andrew Lesnie for *Lord of the Rings: The Fellowship of the Ring* (2002).

In addition, there have been lesser-known directors who have defied the mainstream to make disturbing and adventurous films that extend the notion of "Australian" identity in the cinema. Ana Kokkinos's *Head On* is concerned with both ethnicity and homosexuality, while Alex Proyas's *Dark City,* also released in 1998, is a sci-fi film that owes nothing to conventional representations of Australian city but far more to German Expressionism of the 1920s.

More recently, the ranks of new cinematic talent have been swelled by a number of Aboriginal directors such as Rachel Perkins, Erica Glynn, Sally Riley and Ivan Sen. Rachel Perkins, the daughter of a famous Aboriginal activist, Charles Perkins, in fact made a documentary, *Freedom Ride,* in 1992 that concerned a legendary freedom ride through western New South Wales in the 1960s, led by her father. Then a university student, Perkins went on to become the nation's first Aboriginal university graduate and eventually one of the country's leading civil servants. The film depicted a busload of students who, inspired by the example of Martin Luther King Jr. in the United States, traveled through small, race-ridden country towns, challenging local rules such as bans on Aborigines swimming in the local town pool.

Perkins probably speaks for most indigenous directors when she says that, without losing her hatred of racism, she wants to tell stories with a universal appeal and without didacticism: "My work is still strongly political, but I want it to be appealing and compelling, because people don't respond to being bashed over the head by something. That's the thing about drama, and it can be the thing about documentary—if you move people emotionally, then you're much more successful. And the way to move people is to affect them and draw them into a story."[6]

After making a number of highly praised short films, Ivan Sen, with his first feature, *Beneath Clouds,* won the Berlin Film Festival's inaugural prize for best feature from a first-time director. The son of an Aboriginal mother and a white father of German-Hungarian descent, Sen is intensely interested in the dilemmas of people of mixed race caught between two cultures.

NOTES

1. Lindsay Tanner, quoted in Annie Lawson, "Is Labor Ready to Re-Write Its Media Policy?" *The Age,* 5 January 2002.

2. Quentin Dempster, interview with Ramona Koval, *Australian Book Review,* December 2000/January 2001, p. 29.

3. Quoted in Ken Inglis, "ABC Shock Crisis Threat," *Media International Australia,* No. 83 (February, 1997), p. 10.

4. Pike Andrew, and Ross Cooper, *Australian Film 1900–1977* (Melbourne: Oxford University Press, 1980).

5. Tim Burstall, quoted in Philippa Hawker, "The Direction of Burstall," *The Age,* 1 June 2001.

6. Rachel Perkins, interviewed by Jennifer Sexton, *The Weekend Australian,* 3–4 November 2001.

8

The Performing Arts

The performing arts can encompass many activities in Australia, from the formality of opera to pop singers or even buskers on a street. Though increasingly these arts seem threatened by various forms of technological entertainment—radio, television, the Internet—somehow they survive. There is, in fact, a long tradition in Australia of most of the performing arts. Circuses, for instance, first appeared in 1847 and Ashton's Circus, founded in 1851 by an ex-convict, is said to be the oldest one in the world. Leading performers in all of the arts visited Australia regularly, especially during the affluent days of the gold rushes, and since then international entertainers from all over the world have continued to make the long and arduous journey to Australia and its enthusiastic audiences.

THEATER

The first performance of a play in Australia is thought to be of George Farquhar's *The Recruiting Officer* as early as 1789; Tom Keneally dramatized this event in his novel *The Playmaker* (1987). Barnett Levey's Theatre Royal was opened in 1833 and was followed by other venues. Amateur performances soon proliferated, with even convicts participating, and most of the bigger cities quickly developed their own theaters, which sometimes doubled during the day as churches and courthouses.

In the second half of the nineteenth century there were attempts to promote a native Australian drama. English-born Alfred Dampier (1843–1908) was an indefatigable supporter of local playwrights as well as collaborating on plays himself. In particular, he worked on successful stage adaptations of classic Australian novels, such as *For the Term of His Natural Life* and *Robbery Under Arms.*

Early in the twentieth century, a Scottish-born writer, Louis Esson (1879–1943), who had traveled widely and been much impressed by Irish poet, W. B. Yeats, and his attempts to build a national Irish theater, worked hard to establish a theater in Australia. With ardently nationalist writer Vance Palmer, Esson formed the Pioneer Players, but his most successful play was titled, perhaps appropriately, *The Time Is Not Yet Ripe* (1912). Esson was a lone voice in a culture that looked fondly back to English plays for its models and its staple theatrical entertainment. The leading theatrical company, J. C. Williamson, steadfastly refused to put on any Australian plays, preferring even the most commonly recycled English and American shows.

After Esson and his valiant attempts to reproduce the kind of resurgence of theater that characterized the Irish National Theatre, there was a long period of virtual silence. *Brumby Innes* (1940), a powerful play by the left-wing novelist, Katharine Susannah Prichard, received little attention at the time of its writing but was rediscovered during the resurgence of Australian theater in the early 1970s.

But the revival of Australian theater probably began with Ray Lawler's *Summer of the Seventeenth Doll* (1955), a hallmark play and a resounding success with audiences who delighted in the recognition of their own idiom on stage for the first time. It is concerned with two cane-cutters who return from Queensland each year to resume their relationship with two women from Melbourne, and the women's deepening disillusion as the relationships slowly stagnate. Its themes of the nature of Australian "mateship" (friendship between men) and male attitudes toward women are staples of the Australian consciousness. Although Lawler continued to write and in fact made *The Doll* the first part of a trilogy, he never achieved such a success again. The play was followed by Richard Beynon's *The Shifting Heart* (1958) and Alan Seymour's *The One Day of the Year* (1962), which bravely challenged the myth of Anzac (Australia and New Zealand) Day, but what promised to be a renaissance of Australian theater petered out until a second revival a decade later, which proved to be more enduring.

This coincided with the rise of independent Australian theater groups such as La Mama and the Australian Performing Group (APG) in Melbourne, and the Nimrod Theatre in Sydney, which gave opportunities to a whole host of gifted writers and performers, and eventually forced the mainstream companies to stage Australian theater. Playwrights to emerge from the APG included David Williamson, Jack Hibberd, Barry Oakley, Alex Buzo, and John Romeril. The most commercially successful of all of them, Williamson came to the fore with two big hits, *Don's Party* (1971), about a group of young people who

Street performer playing folk songs on his accordian, Queen Victoria Market, Melbourne. Photo by Michael Hanrahan.

gather together on the night of the 1969 federal election, and *The Removalists* (1971), a powerful and early treatment of the violence that lies beneath an apparently peaceful society. Williamson has continued to pour out a stream of plays dealing with serious themes, cleverly modified by witty one-liners. He has an almost uncanny awareness of the concerns that engage his audience, and subjects have ranged from the politics of Australian Rules football (*The Club,* 1978) and academia (*The Department,* 1975) to criticism of Australian materialism (*Money & Friends,* 1992). His most recent play, *Up for Grabs* (2000), achieved notoriety during its London premiere simply because it starred singer/actress Madonna in the leading role. She insisted on Williamson internationalizing the play, replacing Brett Whiteley with Jackson Pollock, Sydney with New York, and Australia in general with the United States.

Dorothy Hewett (1923–2002) has a considerable reputation as a poet and also wrote three novels and two autobiographies, but is probably best remembered for her plays, especially *This Old Man Comes Rolling Home* (1966) and *The Chapel Perilous* (1971). A committed left-winger and for a long time member of the Communist Party, as well as an ardent feminist, Hewett was also a deeply romantic writer who explored sexuality in women as a means of both imprisonment and release. Her plays range over a number of modes, from expressionism through a kind of naturalism to Brechtian alienation. There are other female dramatists who have tended to be neglected. Oriel Gray's play *The Torrents* tied with Lawler's *Doll* in a Playwrights' Advisory Board Competition in 1955 while Betty Roland and Dymphna Cusack, better known as a novelist, wrote noteworthy plays. Of the 80 Australian plays performed at Sydney New Theatre, 44 were written or cowritten by women.

As with Australian fiction, much of contemporary and recent theater is almost obsessively concerned with the past and with particular events and characters who seem to delineate Australian identity. There have been several plays devoted to Governor William Bligh, most notably Ray Lawler's *The Man Who Shot the Albatross* (1971; Alexander Buzo wrote a play on *Macquarie* (1971); while there have also been dramatizations of the lives of lesser known figures such as politician King O'Malley (Michael Boddy and Bob Ellis, 1970), Archbishop Daniel Mannix (Barry Oakley, 1971), the eccentric Victorian sex reformer Chidley (Alma de Groen, 1976), the equally eccentric nineteenth-century poet, R. H. Horne (Oakley's *The Ship's Whistle*, 1979), and Ronald Ryan, the last man to be hanged in Australia (Barry Dickins, 1993). The Eureka stockade and Ned Kelly have also been popular subjects while, in an unusual move, *Manning Clark's History of Australia* was presented as a musical in 1988 but failed. Yet playwrights have dealt with more contemporary subjects too, even if not with the systematic thoroughness of Williamson.

Much of Oakley's writing for drama, like his novels, is satiric in its treatment of public figures, but he has also frequently fallen back on comic yet poignant studies of difficult marital relations, as in *Bedfellows* (1975) and *Marsupials* (1981). Alex Buzo first came to critical attention with a controversial one-actor *Norm and Ahmed* (1968) about racial prejudice in Australian society. Buzo was prosecuted for obscenity because of the frankness of the play's colloquial language, something now taken for granted. His second play *Rooted* (1969) landed him in trouble again because of the pun in the title ("rooted" in the Australian vernacular can be a euphemism for sexual intercourse). His later plays, such as *Coralie Lansdown Says No* (1974), *Martello Towers* (1976), and *Makassar Reef* (1978) are witty but serious examinations of their protagonists' search for meaning and fulfillment in a world (often that of Sydney) that seems to deny them this. More recent plays, such as *Big River* (1980) and *The Marginal Farm* (1983) confirm these tendencies. In more recent years, Buzo has turned to writing fiction as well as prose works of miscellaneous kinds, on subjects as varied as sport and popular language and its misuse.

Jack Hibberd (1940–) was part of the explosion of theatrical talent that occurred in Melbourne in the late 1960s and early 1970s and was associated especially with The Australian Performing Group. Hibberd has written poetry and, more recently, several novels but is best known for his satiric, often absurdist theatrical assaults on Australian masculinist conventions. *White with Wire Wheels* (1967) is a satirical account of three car- and girl-obsessed young bachelors who are brought down by a woman who is much tougher than they are. His most popular and successful play, *Dimboola* (1969), is a comic account of a wedding in the eponymous country Victorian town, in which the audience become guests and participate in the ceremony. It is still staged regularly all over Australia. But although Hibberd has written many plays and shorter sketches, he is probably best known for *A Stretch of the Imagination* (1973). In this solo piece an aging man confronts his imminent death and the failures of his life. It has produced some fine virtuoso performances by Australian actors. Although, following his much-admired Bertolt Brecht, Hibberd has frequently asserted his wish to appeal to a wide audience, his language is in fact not easily accessible; it is a unique mixture of the vernacular and the highly stylized, even baroque. Like Buzo, Hibberd has also turned more recently to writing fiction as well has returning to his old love, poetry.

Another product of the APG is John Romeril (1945–). Like Hibberd, with whom he collaborated on *Marvellous Melbourne* (1977), Romeril is a prolific and, if anything, even more deeply political writer, many of whose works are polemics against what he sees as the evils of contemporary Australian society. His finest play is perhaps *The Floating World* (1974), in which a survivor of the Burmese-Thailand railway embarks on a sea cruise to Japan. As the journey continues, Les Harding's mass of prejudices cracks open and he begins to hallucinate, viewing all those around him on the boat as figures from his wartime past.

Alma de Groen (1941–) was born in New Zealand but finally settled in Australia in her thirties; since then she has been highly productive. De Groen experiments constantly with form in order to explore the nature of male/female relationships in what she sees as a patriarchal society. She is also interested in the figure of the artist and the artistic type, and has written about Arthur Cravan, the nephew of Oscar Wilde, and her distinguished fellow expatriate, Katherine Mansfield. Apart from *Chidley* she is probably best known for *The Rivers of China* (1987).

A prolific and versatile playwright as well as novelist and script writer, Louis Nowra (1950–) ranges fearlessly over Australia as well as other locations—Russia, Paraguay, China—but his drama is primarily interiorized, concerned to place characters within historical and social frameworks from which their struggles to free or define themselves can be shown with objective, almost Brechtian detachment. In plays like *Inner Voices* (published 1977) and *The Golden Age* (1985), Nowra explores the relationship between language and meaning. In 1988 he adapted Xavier Herbert's novel, *Capricornia,* for the stage. He is often compared to his contemporary Stephen Sewell (1951–), who is similarly cosmopolitan and political in outlook.

Among the more successful of younger contemporary playwrights is Hanny Rayson (1957–) whose *Life After George,* variously described as "a play about the dangers of privatisation in education" and a eulogy to a womanizing academic, had two successful years in Australia before receiving a West End production in London. Rayson had written several plays before she made a big impact with *Room to Move* (1985) and *Hotel Sorrento* (1990). Her plays typically explore the concerns of women, especially those middle-aged or older, and the dissatisfaction they experience in their relationships with emotionally stunted men. Rayson's most recent play, *Inheritance* (2003), is an impressive and ambitious treatment of the problems global changes have wrought in country towns in Australia and the misery and violence that can often lie beneath the apparently sleepy communities.

Popular Music

As with most of the performing arts in Australia, intellectual debates often arise over questions of foreign and global domination of the local industry. The point has been made that between 85 and 90 percent of trade in recorded music is currently controlled by the subsidiaries of five multinational corporations whose head offices are located elsewhere—in Germany, Britain, Holland, Japan, and the United States. The sixth is controlled by Australian-born U.S. citizen Rupert Murdoch.

Furious battles with the most improbable allies and enemies have been fought for several years on the question of Australian copyright legislation and the importation of foreign music without tariffs. As with books, a similarly contentious area in the 1980s and early 1990s with the passing of the Copyright Act of 1968, some artists argue that the superior power, numbers, and wealth of overseas industries mean that Australian work would be driven out of the local market. Fierce debates have occurred, especially between proponents and opponents of the practice of parallel importing, which allows license holders in an overseas country to sell intellectual goods in another. Compact discs are one of the last sites of debate between protectionists, who argue that the flooding of the local market by cheap and even pirated overseas imports would destroy local culture; and free traders who point to cheaper prices and the abolition of restrictive trade practices that unfairly favor local license holders. The latter also sometimes claim that the local industry has been conspicuous in its lack of recognition of and refusal to support local talent. However, globalization is a two-edged sword. There are signs that popular music has finally emerged from its domination by foreign interests and a number of Australian bands have had international success.

In 1957 Johnny O'Keefe ("the wild one") recorded Australia's first rock record, "You hit the wrong note, Billy goat." It was the first of many O'Keefe songs, including most famously "Shout" and "She's My Baby." His 1958 "Wild One" became one of the first Australian singles to make the popular music charts. However, O'Keefe battled alcoholism and drug addiction for most of his career and died of a heart attack at the age of only 45, in 1978.

In 1965 a group who called themselves The Seekers had their first big hit, "I'll Never Find Another You," which sold more than a million copies worldwide. They followed that in the same year with "The Carnival Is Over," which sold 93,000 copies on its first day of release in England. Over the following five years the group sold 60 million albums worldwide, an Australian record. They also hold the record for attracting the biggest concert crowd in Australia: 200,000 people flocked to see them perform at Melbourne's Myer Music Bowl in 1967.

In the same year a Sydney group called The Easybeats shot to the top of the UK and Australian charts with the release of "Friday on My Mind." Unlike most Australian bands of the 1960s, the group's Harry Vanda and George Young wrote their own songs. Later hits included "She's So Fine," "Wedding Ring," and "For My Woman." Still in 1967 the 18-year-old British-born Johnny Farnham released "Sadie the Cleaning Lady," which went straight to number 1. Thirty-five years later John Farnham retired after a stellar career. The Aboriginal pop group Yothu Yindi became the first indigenous group to hit the top of the charts with "Treaty" in 1981.

The Bee Gees (short for brothers Gibb) were immensely popular in the 1960s and 1970s, to the point where they became colloquially known as the Australian Beatles. Born in Great Britain, they grew up in Brisbane before departing overseas again in search of success. With record sales of more than 110 million, they earn a place in the top five selling acts of all time, behind the Beatles, Elvis Presley, Michael Jackson, and Paul McCartney as soloist. They had six consecutive number-one singles in the United States and four in Brit-

Didgeridoo, an Aboriginal musical instrument used in Aboriginal ceremonies and part of indigenous Australia for more than a thousand years, is sold here for tourists. Photo by Anna Clemann.

ain, and reached the height of their fame as the voices of the best-selling film *Saturday Night Fever* (1977). The first boost to their career was given by Col Joye who, as Col Joye and the Joye Boys, was extremely popular in the 1960s.

Other chart toppers include Skyhooks's "Straight in a Gay World" (1976), Olivia Newton-John's "Physical" (1981), Crowded House's "Temple of Low Men" (1988), and Newcastle group Silverchair's "Tomorrow" (1995). Men at Work's "Down Under" (1982) had American fans inquiring as to what vegemite was as it shot to the top of the charts. "Down Under" was one song that rated among the top 10 popular Australian songs of all time, as judged by the Australasian Performing Right Association in 2001.

Kylie Minogue first came to popular attention in the highly successful TV soap serial *Neighbours*, but in 1989 her debut LP, *Kylie*, featuring a hit single of the same title, sold 12 million copies worldwide. Minogue has managed to continually reinvent herself through the 1990s and into the twenty-first century, finally commanding attention in the United States.

More typical, however, and far harder to export, might be the ironic humor of Slim Dusty's "Pub With No Beer" (1957) with its mournful lyrics that have become almost a part of the nation's psyche, selling over a million copies. Dusty (David Gordon Kirkpatrick, who died in 2003) began his career at the age of 15, broadcasting music on his local radio station in Kempsey. He has since recorded 100 albums and 1,600 songs.

Midnight Oil's "Beds Are Burning" (1978) is an unashamed appeal to return their land to the Aborigines, while the Don Walker-written "Khe Sanh," (1987) performed by Cold Chisel, is a savage commentary on Australia's participation in the Vietnam War. Despite the political consciousness of these songs, it is hard to generalize about the nature of Australian popular culture from them. One commentator observed of a list of most popular Australian songs, "From this we can deduce that we are a nation of thirsty, politically correct Vietnam vets with a sense of irony."[1]

Other bands that have achieved huge success in Australia and sometimes overseas include AC/DC, Nick Cave, The Angels, INXS, Savage Garden, and Paul Kelly, as well as more recent performers such as Tina Arena and Natalie Imbruglia.

Opera and Ballet

Unlike the United States, where there is a strong tradition of private sponsorship, theater and opera companies in Australia are heavily dependent on government patronage and often live with the almost daily possibility of their demise. When the chief executive of Opera Australia was accused of playing safe in programming and not investing enough in new work, he pointed out that in order to sustain the company, Opera Australia had to take more of its income from the box office than any other opera company in the world.

The Elizabethan Theatre Trust was established in 1954 largely at the instigation of H(erbert) C(ole) Coombs (1906–), arguably the most significant, visionary and humane public servant of the post–World War II period. "Nugget" Coombs was not only founder of the Trust but chair during the period 1954–67. It was Coombs, too, who played a large part in the creation of the Australian Council for the Arts, which he chaired from 1967 to 1973 and of the Australia Council (1973–74). Australian Opera (later Opera Australia) was founded in 1956 and the Australia Ballet in 1962.

When the Council was established in 1968, it took over and brought together the responsibilities of a number of bodies associated with assistance for literature, music, and the visual arts. It operates through the Aboriginal and Torres Islander Art Board, the Literature Fund, the Performing Arts Board, and the Community Cultural Development Board. Opera Australia is funded separately. Like the ABC, the various boards of the Australia Council have been criticized at times for alleged bias, often by disgruntled artists who failed to receive a grant, or received fewer than they felt they deserved, while some conservative politicians have questioned the value of artists receiving grants at all.

The Australian Ballet (AB), which is government-funded, was founded partly out of the wreckage of the privately run Borovansky Ballet. Unlike many overseas companies, it employs mostly local talent, though that term is extended to include New Zealanders. Two foreign artists were hired, however, as the leads in the AB's first performance, *Swan Lake,* in Sydney on November 2, 1962, and in other ways the company bowed to international influence. The founding artistic director was Londoner Peggy van Praagh, and a few months later Robert Helpmann, probably Australia's best-known dancer, was brought back from overseas as codirector, but both eventually resigned in 1974. The company had some successes, notably *Romeo and Juliet* and *Onegin,* and in 1964 performed its first all-Australian work, Helpmann's "The Display." This led in turn to its first overseas tour the following year. But it was still often at odds with the Board and its general manager, Peter Bahen, and the frequent disagreements finally led to a disastrous strike in 1981 that followed 29 resignations over a period of 18 months.

Though a system of regular consultation was put in place when the strike ended, there has been continued tension between dancers and management, with many of the former still making highly public exits. Seven noted dancers resigned over nine months during 1993–94 under the directorship of Maina Gielgud, and again seven, including four principals, resigned in 1999–2000 when Ross Stretton was director. For all its good work, the company has never reached the heights of which it has sometimes seemed capable, although it has produced fine artists such as ballerina Marilyn Jones. In an ironic touch, two of Van Praagh's proteges, Ross Stretton and Gailene Stock, went on to become artistic directors of the Royal Ballet and the Royal Ballet School.

Opera was performed in Australia in the first half of the century but became much more widespread after the gold rushes and the wealth they generated. A Melbourne season funded by George Coppin was unsuccessful in 1856, but shortly afterward William Saurin Lyster established an opera company, which between March 1861 and August 1869, performed 42 different operas over 1,459 performances. When Lyster died in 1880, his work was carried on by the J. C. Williamson organization.

Opera Australia feels the responsibility of representing the great works of opera of the last 400 years—Monteverdi, Handel, Mozart, Verdi, Wagner, Puccini, and so on—but that it does not turn its back on the present is testified to by contemporary works, some commissioned, that it has produced over the first two years of this century: *Batavia* (Peter Goldsworthy and Richard Mills), *Lindy* (Moya Henderson and Judith Rodriguez), *Love in the Age of*

Therapy (music by Paul Grabowsky, libretto by Joanna Murray-Smith), and Peter Carey's novel *Bliss* (music by Brett Dean, libretto by Wendy Beckett).

Classical Music

One of the earliest Australian composers, controversial in his own time but relatively little known now, was George Marshall-Hall, who emigrated from England in 1891 to accept the post of Foundation Professor of Music at the University of Melbourne. Marshall-Hall mingled freely with the Heidelberg School of painters, rather than mixing in academic circles, and his E-Flat Symphony and poem, "Hymn to Sydney," are tributes to the Australian landscape. However, his views on such topics as atheism, bohemianism, and German culture embroiled him in constant controversy, and in 1900 the university failed to renew his contract. He remained director of the Melbourne Conservatorium.

It was Marshall-Hall who directed a benefit concert for the then thirteen-year-old Percy Grainger (1882–1961), Australia's best-known composer, whose life and peculiar habits were recently dealt with in film. Though Grainger's professional life was based first in England and then for the majority of his life the United States, he returned to his homeland periodically on concert tours. The Grainger Museum, built according to his own design in 1938 on the site of the University of Melbourne campus, remains a memorial to him. Grainger, who became an American citizen in 1918, but always spoke of himself as an Australian, left behind him more than 600 compositions, settings, arrangements, and editions, some in multiple versions. His music was primarily influenced by English folk songs, but he also wrote some Australian pieces such as *Colonial Song* (1912) and *Gumsucker's March* (1914). He was a vehement opponent of the tyranny of sonata form and his music strongly emphasized the lyrical rather than the dramatic.

Almost contemporary with Marshall-Hall, Alfred Hill (1870–1960) was Australian-born, spent most of his life in Australia and New Zealand, and has claims to be regarded as the father of Australian composition. His 12 symphonies include the Australia Symphony, written as late as 1953, and several concertos, string quartets, and other chamber works.

The next generation of Australian composers included three women, Margaret Sutherland, Peggy Glanville Hicks, and Miriam Hyde, who all fought courageously against the socially imposed restrictions of the time. They were followed by the generation of the mid-to-late twentieth century, among whom were Richard Meale, Peter Sculthorpe, Ross Edwards, Carl Vine, Richard Mills, Nigel Wentlake, Brenton Broadstock, Colin Brumby, and George

Dreyfus. Probably the best known of the more recent composers are Graham Koehe, Brett Deon, and Elan Cats-Cernier.

Australia has had capital city symphony orchestras since early in the twentieth century, initially under the control of the Australian Broadcasting Commission. This had its advantages, in that there were enough opportunities for conductors and soloists to make the long journey from Europe worthwhile. Otto Klemperer, Thomas Beecham, Malcolm Sargent, and Georg Szell were among the many conducting celebrities to make the trip, and the swift development in quality of the six state orchestras during the postwar decades was the result of the impetus provided by distinguished visitors and quality resident conductors. The Melbourne and Sydney orchestras in particular have now achieved international quality. Emerging conductors, however, must still establish themselves by absence from Australia, with Simone Young the latest success story to follow such stars as Sir Charles Mackerras and Richard Bonyng.

While subscription series to the main orchestras form the center of concert-going to classical music, there are, in Melbourne in any given year, subscription series available through Musica Viva (claimed to be the largest chamber music organization in the world), the Australian Chamber Orchestra (highly praised on its regular concert tours to Europe, Asia, and the United States), the Australian Chorale, the Melbourne Musicians, the Australian Pro Arte Orchestra, the Australian String Quartet, the State Orchestra of Victoria, and the Australian Chamber Soloists.

Perhaps Australia's greatest contribution to the classical music world, however, is the number of outstanding singers (especially female singers) it has produced. Its most famous opera singer is Dame Nellie Melba (1861–1931), who is the subject of a biography by Therese Radic and a play by Jack Hibberd, *A Toast to Melba* (1976). Born Helen Mitchell in the Melbourne suburb of Richmond, and educated at Presbyterian Ladies College where Henry Handel Richardson also studied, Melba traveled to Europe to pursue a musical career. Unsuccessful at first, she burst onto the stage in Brussels in 1887, as Gilda in *Rigoletto,* thus beginning a career that lasted in all some 38 years. She sang all over the world but her ambivalent attitude toward her own country is exemplified in two comments she was famously reported to have made: "I put Australia on the map," she told a friend, while also advising a colleague who was about to tour Australia, "Sing 'em muck; it's all they can understand." She did, however, perform frequently for charities and for Australian troops during World War I. She also made an arduous 10,000-mile tour of the country in 1909. "Peach Melba" is a popular dessert named after her. Toward the end of her career she retired and then returned so frequently that the phrase "doing a Melba" became synonymous with making frequent comebacks.

Melba paved the way for other Australian singers to travel overseas, establish a reputation, and perform at Covent Garden before returning in triumph to their homeland. Florence Austral, who like Melba, took a stage name reflective of her birthplace, became one of the leading Wagnerian sopranos during the 1920s and 1930s, and Dame Joan Hammond established herself among the greats over the middle years of the century. Marjorie Lawrence fought against physical disability to make an international career, and Joan Sutherland burst onto the operatic scene with a vocal instrument the like of which the world had rarely heard. The contemporary scene offers Yvonne Kenny, who is solidly based in the leading ranks, and Lista Casteen who, like Austral, is winning renown in Wagnerian soprano roles. Male singers of international stature are harder to find, with the best, like Peter Dawson and Malcolm McEachern, straddling the line between opera and light classical.

On a different level, Gladys Moncrieff achieved a similar place in the hearts of Australians (to whom she was "our Glad," much as Sir Donald Bradman was "our Don Bradman") by her performances in musical comedy and Gilbert and Sullivan operas. Born in Bundaberg, Queensland, Moncrieff quickly came to the attention of J. C. Williamson's and was soon given a contract. She made her debut in the title role of the Williamson production, *The Maid of the Mountains,* thus beginning her 30-year reign as the queen of musical comedy. Her long stage and singing career, interrupted by a serious car accident in 1938, ended only in 1959, by which time she had given numerous concerts to Australian troops in the Pacific during World War II and later in Japan and Korea during the Korean War. Williamson's were also responsible for introducing Nat Phillips and Roy Rene as the duo Stiffy and Mo in the pantomime, *The Bunyip* (1916); Rene would go on to become Australia's greatest bawdy comedian.

Note

1. Iain Shedden, "Friday-Obsessed Barflies Crying over Absent Beers," *The Australian,* 29 May 2001.

9

Painting

The history of Australian high art in the colonial period is essentially, like that of Australian poetry, one of painters attempting to come to terms with a strange and unfamiliar landscape (as well as sometimes its original occupants) and the attempt to translate its strangeness back into terms that would be comprehensible to English audiences. Although there were some interesting painters in the nineteenth century, it was not until 1885 and the formation of the Heidelberg School of (most notably) Tom Roberts, Arthur Streeton, and Fred McCubbin that Australians began to see their landscape in its own right.

Visual representation of Australia actually begins very early. Drawing was part of the formal education of British officers trained at Christ's Hospital or Portsmouth's Royal Naval College and, given the time they must have had on their hands, it is not surprising that officers drew sketches as well as kept diaries. Among the early artists, Samuel Wallis (1728–95) was captain of a voyage that discovered many Pacific Islands and made at least 40 sketches of them. George Tobin (1768–88) was only 11 when he joined the navy but became a student of natural history, painting birds and fish as well as views of Adventure Bay, Tasmania, Torres Strait, and Tahiti. George Raper (1769–97) sailed with the First Fleet and made further voyages, producing many watercolors of flowers, fish, birds, and a series of coastal profiles. Philip Parker King (1791–1856) was a prolific sketcher throughout his highly successful career. Owen Stanley (1811–50) left behind a large collection of watercolors of topographical subjects and ordinary shipboard life, while James Glen

Petroglyphs, Keep River National Park, Northern Territory. Photo by Jennifer Macklin.

Wilson (1827–63) not only produced many notable oil and watercolor landscapes and sketches but also dabbled in photography.

Of Thomas Watling, the first painter who arrived in Australia after being sentenced to 14 years' transportation for forgery, the art critic Robert Hughes notes that he set about "improving" a landscape he found totally devoid of beauty:

> Thus to a bare and dull view over the west side of Sydney Cove . . . Watling added large feathery *repoussoir* trees, which darkle attractively in the foreground and frame the vista. Other additions of poetic, and excisions of prosaic, material helped to produce the picturesque effect he sought

> in the final canvas, *A Direct North General View of Sydney Cove*...It is agreeably moody, *but* its likeness to Australian landscape is small.[1]

This became a common practice among Watling's successors. How far it was a self-induced myopia or how far it was done out of calculation (the careful adjustment of images to English expectations) is a moot point, but the practice was widespread. "Savages" became noble savages. Hughes claims baldly that "Hardly one good painting was produced in Australia between the arrival of the First Fleet and the appearance of Tom Roberts at the end of the nineteenth century,"[2] though he makes brief patronizing concessions to Conrad Martens, John Glover, Louis Buvelot, and S.T. Gill. He completely dismisses landscape painters such as Eugene von Guerard. "No country in the West during the nineteenth century, with the possible exception of Patagonia, was less endowed with talent," says Hughes.[3] A rather more generous view from another is "...the conditions under which art developed in Australia were probably more unfavourable for the growth of art than those existing during the origins of any other country's art in the history of the world."[4] John Glover (1767–1849) in particular is an underestimated artist. Migrating to Australia in 1830, at the height of his fame in England, he painted unusually clear-eyed portraits of Aborigines and native flora and fauna, including such classics as *Australian Landscape with Cattle, View of Mill's Plains,* and *Mount Wellington and Hobart Town from Kangaroo Point.*

Hughes has modified some cavalier views (made when he was very young), and the reputation of von Guerard (1811–1901) in particular has also risen steadily in recent years. Born in Austria, von Guerard spent almost 30 years in Australia, indefatigably painting landscapes, especially of Victoria, in which he attempted to capture with meticulous accuracy the topographical features of the scene before him. Paintings such as *Ferntree Gully in the Dandenong Ranges* (1857) were highly praised by contemporary audiences and critics for their truthfulness to nature. Nicholas Chevalier (1828–1902) contributed some considerable landscape paintings in the 15 years he lived in Australia, notably *Mount Arapiles and the Mitre Rock* (1863), while there is still interest in the work of Louis Buvelot (1814–88), who lived in Australia only toward the end of his life after traveling for many years.

But in the 1880s four painters emerged who had genuine talent. They were Tom Roberts, Arthur Streeton, Charles Conder, and Frederick McCubbin.

The Heidelberg School

Even as a large number of Australian painters were leaving the country for experience overseas during the 1880s, others were returning home. After extensive travel and observation of European paintings, an advantage he held over many of his Australian predecessors, Tom Roberts (1856–1931) returned to Australia in 1885 and set up a painting camp in the then outer Melbourne suburb of Box Hill, determined to paint spontaneously, gathering the impressions of the moment, en pleine air. He was soon joined by his contemporary, McCubbin. Later they in turn were joined by two other young painters, Conder and Streeton. They established other camps at similarly outer suburbs of Eaglemont and Heidelberg. In 1889, Roberts, McCubbin, Streeton, and Conder, together with a number of now obscure figures, staged their famous 9″ × 5″ show, so called because most of the paintings in it were tiny, and done on cigar-box lids. The group became known as the Heidelberg School.

As well as these spontaneous sketches, Roberts's work included larger and what would become traditionally Australian themes, such as *Shearing the Rams* (1890), a classic painting of men at work, *Bailed Up,* a depiction of a bushranger robbing a Cobb and Co. coach, and *The Breakaway,* which shows a stockman racing to cut off a flock of sheep that are heading toward a waterhole. Much as the writers were doing, Roberts was creating an Australian mythology and defining Australian themes. Roberts was also a more than competent portrait painter. His work in this genre culminated in a commission to paint what he called *The Big Picture,* a vast canvas celebrating the opening of Federal Parliament, a painting that, at 3 m high and 5 m long (10 feet by 16 feet, 8 inches), and including sketches of more than 250 dignitaries, took him two and a half years to complete; it remains the largest painting ever executed by an Australian. But it became what Roberts called his *Frankenstein of 17 ft,* sapping his energies, ruining his eyesight, and leaving him largely drained of his creative energies in the later years of his life.

The reputation of Arthur Streeton (1867–1943) is largely based on his landscapes. He was one of the first painters to respond to the sheer vastness and intense light of the Australian landscape and the way in which it rendered human figures irrelevant. Like Roberts, his best work was mostly done in the 1890s, and though he continued painting for many years afterward, much of his painting is repetitive. Among his most notable works are *Still Glides the Stream* (1889), *Fire's On! Lapstone Tunnel* (1894), sparked off by an explosion in the Blue Mountain foothills in which Streeton saw a laborer killed, and *The Purple Noon's Transparent Might* (1896), an enormously popular painting whose worth has been fiercely contested. His most popular and famous painting, however, is *Golden Summer, Eagleton* (1889), which established a record price for an Australian painting each time it was sold, in 1924, 1985, and 1995.

Native-born Frederick McCubbin (1855–1917) perhaps did more than any other Australian painter to celebrate and romanticize the Bush and Bush denizens. *Down on His Luck* (1889), *Bush Burial* (1890), and *The Wallaby Track* (1896) are all contributions to mateship and the myths of the Bush, while *The Pioneers* (1905) is a deeply nationalistic tribute to the early settlers. *Lost* is yet another addition to the many Australian treatments, in both literature and art, of the theme of the lost child in the bush.

Charles Conder (1868–1909) is less known in Australia than the other three painters, but this may be largely because he returned to his native England in 1890 at the age of 21, unable to make a living as an artist in Australia. But in the six years of his brief life that he spent in Australia, he did much better work than the somewhat effete paintings he completed when he returned to England. His best paintings, *The Departure of the S.S. Orient* (1888) and the playful *How We Lost Poor Flossie* (his dog) in the same year, show a remarkably precocious talent that is urbane and highly composed.

The advantages of returning to one's country, as against the ambivalence or often sheer ignorance with which Australians regard expatriate artists can be seen in the curious case of John Peter Russell (1858–1930). A relatively little known (at least until recently) but underrated painter, Russell suffered from both his absence from Australia, and in particular, the ironic fact that the artist friends he made in France—Van Gogh, Monet, Matisse—who genuinely admired his work, achieved reputations that overwhelmed his. Most of his paintings were executed over a 20-year period he spent on the rugged, windy island of Belle-Ile-en-Mer, off the Atlantic coast of France, about halfway between Brest and Nantes. It was there that he met Claude Monet, who was experimenting with a new, darker kind of Impressionism. With the death of his beloved wife (who used to pose for Rodin), much of the vitality went out of Russell's paintings, yet he remains a unique and impressive figure. He did eventually return to Australia in 1921 and painted some fine views of Sydney and its harbor.

A member of one of Australia's most artistically famous and prolific families, Norman Lindsay (1879–1969) possessed a range of talents from fiction through various forms of art, including cartooning, sculpture, etching, and illustrating. Apart from his novels, he wrote in various genres, and his children's novels, *The Magic Pudding* (1918) and to a lesser extent *The Flyaway Highway* (1936), are classics of their kind.

An ardent admirer of Friedrich Nietzsche, Lindsay argued for a kind of vitalism, a living of the moment to the full. Sexual self-expression was a value far above and opposed to the conventional bourgeois values he despised, and the artist was a supreme figure to whom ordinary ethical restraints did not apply. Needless to say, he was frequently in conflict with the censors. He hated religion, which he saw as suppressing the life force. Though somewhat jejune, his ideas influenced many of his contemporaries. Large, fleshy nudes figure prominently in his paintings, but these overendowed women are essentially the material for masturbatory fantasies. However, the Lindsay painting, *Spring's Innocence* was bought by the Australian National Gallery at the end of 2002 for what was easily a record for a Lindsay painting, A$333,900 (about US$250,000).

Many Australian painters traveled abroad in order to acquaint themselves with the canon of European masterpieces, or perhaps meet contemporary artists, and some of them remained expatriates, as was the case throughout the first three quarters, especially, of the twentieth century. The first part of the century saw the rise of the so-called salon painters, who could return to Australia boasting that they had seen the best work of those overseas. The work of Emanuel Phillips Fox, George Lambert, Rupert Bunny, Hugh Ramsay, and Max Meldrum all shows various European influences operating to differing degrees. Of these, the one who has lasted best is perhaps Rupert Bunny (1864–1947). Much admired in France, where he resided, he was ignored in the country of his birth, but stubbornly continued to display his work in Australia and retained his citizenship. In 1933 he returned to Melbourne and lived in a small flat in which he painted Provencale scenes from memory. Just before his death in 1947 his work was beginning to rise in artistic esteem and has continued to do so.

John Longstaff (1862–1941) dabbled briefly in Impressionism under the influence of Russell while overseas, but his innate conservatism reasserted itself when he returned to Australia. He established a reputation with his *Arrival of Burke, Wills and King at Cooper's Creek* (1907) and quickly became known as a fluent and graceful portrait painter, numbering among his subjects King Edward VII and Queen Alexandra, Australia's first Prime Minister Sir Edmund Barton, and the writer Henry Lawson. Longstaff eventually became an official War Artist with the Australian army in France.

POSTIMPRESSIONISM

The early part of the twentieth century also saw the rise of the Postimpressionist movement. The Postimpressionists, often centered around the Sydney studio of A. Dattilo Rubbo, included Norah Simpson, a young Australian expatriate who returned home briefly, as well as Roy de Maistre, Roland Wakelin, and one of Australia's most distinguished female painters, Grace Cossington Smith, among whose finest paintings are those she did of the Sydney Harbor Bridge. *The Sock Knitter* is also widely acclaimed as the first Postimpressionist painting by an Australian and exemplifies her avowed aim of expressing form in color.

The year 1920 saw the return of Margaret Preston from Europe where she had had the opportunity to see and be influenced by contemporary movements. Ridiculed at first by parochial local critics, the Postimpressionists slowly began to be accepted, to be exhibited, and to sell. George Lambert and Thea Proctor invited them to join an exhibition in Sydney with them, and this, a decisive turning point, became an annual event. *Art in Australia* devoted a special issue to Margaret Preston in 1927 and the Art Gallery of New South Wales asked her to present a self-portrait to the collection in 1929. She was one of the first painters to recognize the importance of Aboriginal art and landscape, though the unconsciously patronizing tone in her attitudes still reveals her to some extent as a prisoner of her time. However, she believed emphatically that Aboriginal art was great art and the foundation of a national culture for Australia.

In Melbourne, Postimpressionism took form a few years later under the influence of George Bell, an academic painter and pillar of the establishment who made a complete about-face and started a modern art school. With Australia generally light years behind movements in Europe still, Bell's stance was viewed with alarm by members of the establishment and a move began to establish an Academy of Australian Art, complete with its own Royal Charter, under the auspices of Robert Menzies, the then attorney-general and later longest-serving prime minister.

Opening an exhibition of the Victorian Artists' Society in 1937, Menzies pointedly disowned modern art on the grounds of its incoherence, insisting that great art speaks a language that every intelligent person can understand. In doing so, he perpetuated a division between conservatives and modernists. The kind of artist he might have had in mind was someone like George Lambert (1873–1930), who was much admired in the 1920s and the years immediately after his death, but is now more usually thought of as an academic realist, a talented painter who took no chances but painted portraits in a style that always found him clients.

In the end, the Royal Charter never came and a Contemporary Art society was formed in 1938, but the intergroup wrangles went on. Meanwhile a new set of painters were about to begin shocking Australian society out of its insularity.

The "Angry Decade"

The new names included artists like Albert Tucker, Sidney Nolan, Danila Vassilieff, John Perceval, and Arthur Boyd. Most of them were of working-class background and with only limited education; often they were largely self-taught. They felt themselves outside the mainstream of Australian society, generally treated not merely with indifference but sometimes hostility, which they returned. They had had no experience of Europe and knew European paintings only by their reproductions. They worked closely and developed friendships with writers, and the special issue of the magazine *Angry Penguins* had a cover illustration by Nolan who, with Tucker, Boyd, and Perceval, closely associated himself with the magazine.

A crucial event in all this was the *Melbourne Herald* exhibition in 1939, which introduced for the first time not only to artists but to a bewildered public the work of such artistic giants as Picasso, Braque, Leger, Matisse, Modigliani, Derain, Cezanne, Van Gogh, Utrillo, and Dali. As late as 1931 a newspaper had quoted the Director of the Melbourne Art Gallery, Bernard Hall, as saying that Australian art was free from what he called "the blight of modernism." Something of the parochialism of the times can be seen in the fact that when the collection of European masters was quarantined in Australia because of the outbreak of war, it was confined to the Gallery's cellars while paintings by the trustees themselves were displayed.

At the same time, not unexpectedly, as well as the Expressionists, there were the social realists like Herbert McClintock, Noel Counihan, and Victor O'Connor who followed the Communist Party line and railed against the policy of withholding knowledge from the public. They soon divided into a separate camp—Counihan, O'Connor, Yosl Bergner, and McClintock against Nolan, Tucker, and their friends, John and Sunday Reed and Max Harris. In retrospect, it seems a particularly futile kind of war as Nolan and Tucker simply went their own way, Nolan producing his first Ned Kelly series of paintings in 1947 and Tucker acting out his apocalyptic sense of the moral degradation of the world in his "Images of Modern Evil" series. These are among the most important paintings of the 1940s, and Nolan's Kelly paintings are probably the most celebrated and widely known series of paintings ever done by an Australian artist.

Sidney Nolan (1917–92) was the first of these artists to make an international reputation, and both this and the astonishingly prolific nature of his work have led to denigration and suspicion. Nolan lived as a young man with John and Sunday Reed, rich and generous patrons of the arts who subsidized and encouraged what they saw as his precocious talent for some years until he was drafted into the army in 1942. Locked away in the distant Victorian army base at Dimboola, Nolan painted the landscapes around him as well as violently distorted images of soldiers.

Discharged from the army in 1945, he turned his attention to the Melbourne suburb of St. Kilda where he grew up, which reoccurs startlingly often among Australian painters, and produced strange, artfully naïve, childlike figures—children floating in the upper parts of the canvas, sticklike bathers grotesquely out of proportion. Many of the same techniques were to be employed in his Kelly series.

Nolan constantly reinvented himself, returning to the Kelly paintings, but also creating fine landscapes of Queensland in its shimmering heat and doing further series, such as the studies of Eliza Fraser, a woman who lived with the Aborigines for six months and who is the subject of several other Australian works, most notably Patrick White's novel, *A Fringe of Leaves*. He also did numerous landscapes of the Central Australian Ranges over which he flew, and a series of Explorer paintings in which he dealt with figures such as Burke and Wills. There was also his successful *Leda and the Swan* series and his series on Gallipoli—like the Explorers work, a celebration of Australian failure.

Albert Tucker (1914–99), on the other hand, concentrated on what he saw as the moral squalor embodied in (again) St. Kilda, and painted crude, embittered distortions of women. Even an activity as harmless as sunbathing comes under scrutiny in *Sunbathers* (1945), with the poor bathers shown as headless, mutilated pieces of meat. Tucker left Australia in 1947, disgusted with it, and for a long time led the life of a nomad. He traveled briefly to Japan, then to London, and in 1948 to Paris, before again moving to a village near Frankfurt, Germany, in 1951. His peregrinations continued, with each new place offering him new challenges and new dissatisfactions.

Some critics have argued that Tucker's art lost its potency when his wife, the distinguished painter Joy Hester, left him. There remain, however, the many fine earlier paintings, such as *The Futile City*, one of the central works of Australian surrealism; *Image of Modern Evil: Spring in Fitzroy* (1943), a series based on the wartime serial killer Edward Leonski; and the playful and self-mocking *Self Portrait* (1945). Later, landscape proved a source of inspiration to him in paintings like *Burke and Wills* (1960, now in the Museum of Modern Art, New York), and *Explorer Attacked by Parrots* in the same year, while there were also the occasional successes of his later work, such as *Extinction Press* (1988) and *St. Anthony in Australia* (1987).

Among the other major figures who emerged from the decade was Arthur Boyd (1920–99), like Lindsay, a member of an illustrious artistic family. Beginning as a conventional landscape painter, Boyd moved closer to expressionism and at times almost surrealism. Boyd's Bush paintings are not barren and empty but filled with demonic, mythological creatures, just like his city paintings. Forms of natural life—trees, vegetation—assume a monstrous, grotesque shape of their own. After the war Boyd's paintings of the city took on many of the features of Tucker and of John Perceval, his brother-in-law and closest friend. They share a dark, cruel quality, although with occasional suggestions of redemption. In works such as *The Mining Town* (Casting the money lenders from the temple), he shows a directly religious impulse, common among many members of the Boyd family.

The later paintings are more reflective, deeply concerned with the effects of distance and light. Between 1958 and 1960, however, Boyd did a fine series based on the love, marriage, and eventual death of an aboriginal stockman and his half-caste bride.

John Perceval (1923–2000) came to notice at the age of 20, when several of his paintings were reproduced in an issue of *Angry Penguins.* His *Boy with Cat 2* (1943) is a terrifying evocation of youthful frustration and distress. He stopped painting between 1946 and 1956, and when he resumed, he concentrated particularly on landscapes, painting en plein air at tremendous speed, aiming for effects of spontaneity and vitality. The change from his earlier work was quite extraordinary. Bernard Smith, comparing him with the later Van Gogh, notes that "Perceval's paintings are also visual and optimistic interpretations of the Australian countryside, full of the joy of life."[5]

Hughes argues in conclusion that the so-called Angry Decade was a crucial time in the history of Australian painting because "it laid a common ground of myth, attitude, and symbolic technique on which the younger post-figurative painters...have taken root."[6] But he locates the anger almost entirely in the much more involved painters of Melbourne. Sydney, he argues, more or less ignored the war and its resultant evils, preferring instead to hearken back to European fashions of the 1930s that they had not even experienced at first hand.

The finest work of Sali Herman (1898–1993), a Swiss who arrived in Australia in 1937 close to age 40, lies in his numerous pictures of Sydney houses in inner suburban slums. Unlike his fellow immigrant who came around the same time, the Melbourne social realist Yosl Bergner, Herman is not angry or politically committed but celebrates the communal life of his mundane subjects.

Important among the Sydney painters were William Dobell and Russell Drysdale. Though the early paintings of Dobell (1899–1970) were comparatively conventional, an increasingly satirical note can be detected in them. Dobell eventually became best known for his portraits—often grotesque, vulgar, and deeply challenging. The controversy concerning modernism reached its peak in 1943 with Dobell's portrait of his fellow artist, Joshua Smith, which won the Archibald Prize, Australia's most prestigious award for portraiture. After a fierce argument, seven fellow entrants in the competition issued a writ against the judges of the competition, claiming wrongful award of the prize to a caricature. The judge brought in a verdict for the defendants after some near-farcical testimony, but the artistic effects on the shy, withdrawn Dobell were disastrous, although he did win the Archibald Prize again in

1948, for a mediocre portrait of Margaret Olley. With a few exceptions, his later portraits are lacking in the energy and originality that marked his earlier work. One of the exceptions is his portrait of the Australian poet Dame Mary Gilmore. Another is his *Helena Rubinstein* (1957).

One of the sources of the greatness of Russell Drysdale (1912–81) is the directness and freshness with which he reacted to rural environments. What looks initially like stark realism soon reveals itself as highly stylized—thin, sticklike figures, elongated shapes, an exaggeratedly flat, bare landscape, figures in a landscape so distorted that they seem almost surreal, as in *Landscape with Figures* (1945). But Drysdale, perhaps the most nationalistic painter of the time, who had been born in England, also had a feeling for quintessential Australian themes that brought him a much wider audience than most of his contemporaries. Paintings like *The Drover's Wife* (based on Henry Lawson's famous story) and *The Cricketers* tapped into basic Australian myths and experiences.

It was Drysdale's traveling in the far north of Australia, a huge area about which he writes in lyric vein, that changed him irrevocably. He began to paint indigenous people, who had long disappeared as poetic subjects except as figures of fun, without either degrading or idealizing them, showing the intimacy of their relationship to the land.

The Later Years

Throughout the 1960s and after, the same kind of cross-fertilization, as well as tension, between traveling or living abroad and staying at home that had always marked the Australian art world continued to exist. Some painters stayed outside the quarrels of the art world, like *The Antipodean Manifesto* with its guarded attack on abstract art. This was the work of seven painters, all but one of them from Victoria, and it insisted on the primacy of the image and of controlled purpose, the artist's mastery over his subject, in art. Talented artists arrived from overseas. Others pursued their art with complete indifference to a society, which had begun to show itself far more interested in art than previously and was prepared to spend more money to support it.

In 1959 a number of painters and the leading art critic, Bernard Smith, formed the Antipodean Group in Melbourne, a group specifically formed to combat what they saw as the evils of abstractionism and to celebrate the idea of the image. Among other things, the manifesto said, "As Antipodeans we accept the image as representing some form of acceptance of an involvement in life. For the image has always been concerned with life, whether of the flesh or of the spirit." Among the ironies of this is the fact that abstract art had hardly ever existed in Australia until then. In 1939 some minor cubist

Artist Donald Friend. Photo by Graham McCarter.

and constructivist painters put on the first group show of abstract painting ever displayed in Sydney, Exhibition 1, but the war put an end to the possibility of any sequels.

Donald Friend (1915–89) stands out as a painter who disengaged himself from contemporary society, following his interest in nude forms by journeying to Africa, to Christmas Island off the west coast of Australia, and to Bali. His work is witty, urbane, often romantic, and he developed considerably as a painter during the 1950s. It was Friend who challenged the contemptuous description of him and several of his contemporaries as "the charm school." "Of course we were charming," he was reported to have said, "we were full of charm, we were bloody beautiful. And we had a marvellous bloody time."

Friend was also a writer of some distinction, though possibly his best work, his personal diaries, is only beginning now to be published.

The end of the pastoral tradition of landscape with its Arcadian dream arrives with the interesting figure of Lloyd Rees (1895–1988), whose work contained a strong vein of romantic lyricism, especially after he visited Italy and allowed the colors and contours of Tuscany to seep into his Australian landscapes. His later work suggests what Robert Hughes calls, "the monumental antiquity of Australian landscape, and its feel of arrested organic growth."[7]

Probably the major new painter to emerge in the 1960s was Jeffrey Smart (1921–), whose cold, almost geometric portrayals of urban scenes have an almost surreal quality and have become extremely popular as expressions of urban angst and isolation. Smart has said of himself, "The subject matter is only the hinge that opens the door, the hook on which one hangs the coat.... My main concern is always the geometry, the structure of the painting."[8]

Fred Williams (1927–82) painted superbly etched landscapes, first in Victoria and later of northwest Australia, to which he returned often. Williams always said that he felt at home in the countryside and felt keenly the connections between his art and the environment. The paintings are exquisite in their fine, almost pointillist detail. Less well known are a brilliant series of portraits he executed during the late 1970s until he discovered and became obsessed by the Pilbara region in northwest Australia. His premature death saw him struck down when he was the height of his powers and just beginning to develop a huge reputation.

Clifton Pugh (1924–90) served in the army before moving in 1951 outside Melbourne to the country area of Cottle's Bridge, thus following the example of Streeton and Roberts for much the same reasons—a dislike of the city and a wish to be immediately in contact with nature. His main distinction has been as a portrait painter and as a painter of landscape. He was deeply aware of the fragility of the environment and in a painting such as *A Cat in a Rabbit-trap* (1957) expressed his hatred of predators like feral cats that devastated the natural world.

John Brack (1920–99) took the cool, satirical tone of Smart toward cities and pushed it much further. His most famous painting, *Five O'Clock Collins Street* (1955) shows a crowd of absolutely expressionless, mechanical figures moving in unison; it recalls nothing as much as the Fritz Lang film, *Metropolis.* His loathing for the city and suburbs of Melbourne is intense but expressed with a passionate iciness. In a series of nudes begun in 1957, Brack both paid homage to and subtly undermined the great masters of the nude figure—painters like Boucher, Gauguin, and Monet.

Painter Tony McGillick. Photo by Graham McCarter.

The art of Charles Blackman (1928–) is deeply influenced by Nolan, with whom he formed a close friendship through John and Sunday Reed. He left his job as a Press cartoonist and traveled widely in the outback, painting mainly landscapes. However, his first exhibition in 1953 was a series on the theme of "Schoolgirls"; a second series on the same theme followed in 1954–55. A further group of paintings on the theme of *Alice in Wonderland* followed in 1957, and showed a marked development in technique; paintings of young girls were becoming a staple subject of his work. Their features are somewhat static but are painted tenderly, and it is probable that the paintings were influenced by Blackman's observations of his blind wife. He grew in confidence after a sojourn in London where he held a successful exhibition. In May, 2001, a painting from the series titled "The Madhatter's Tea Party" that he had sold in 1956 for 20 guineas was sold at auction for A$430,500 (US$325,000).

Blackman has explicitly acknowledged his affinity with the lyric poet John Shaw Neilson. Of his schoolgirl pictures, he once said that they had a lot to do with fear: "A lot to do with my isolation as a person and my quite paranoid fears of loneliness. It wasn't until I started painting schoolgirls that Sunday Reed showed me John Shaw Neilson's poetry about schoolgirls; they were full of a kinship, the sort of thing that I was painting fitted in with it perfectly."[9]

Among the painters who have been at least touched by linear abstraction is John Olsen (1928–), whose work has undergone a succession of metamorphoses. The most striking characteristic of the Australian landscape, claims Olsen, is its intense, often brutal light. He believes that there is a distinctive characteristic of Australian light and the way it sharply defines shapes and forms. It is also the characteristic most commonly mentioned by European artists, used to the softer diffusions of light from the north. Much of his best work is set around Sydney Harbor and celebrates the energy, gusto, and vulgarity of city life. The titles of some of his best paintings—*Entrance to the Siren City of the Rat Race*, *Journey into the You Beaut Country*—convey his warmly ironic humor.

Ian Fairweather (1891–1974) became for a time the Grand Old Man of Australian painting. Fairweather did not take up painting until after World War I (in which he had been a prisoner), and then for many years wandered the world before settling on Bribie Island, off the coast of Queensland, north of Brisbane, where from the early 1950s, he lived the life of a recluse. Apart from painting, his primary interest was Chinese culture and he also took a keen interest in Aboriginal myth and art.

Fairweather's paintings are marked by a strong philosophical and sometimes religious base. During the 1950s they became increasingly abstract though there is always a tension in his work between the abstract and the figurative. One sign of the respect with which he was treated by his fellow artists and critics was the remarkable number of them who bought his paintings, despite being poor themselves. The critic Robert Hughes recalls waiting outside a Gallery all night for the Fairweather exhibition to open the next morning and putting his down payment of 50 pounds on the painting *Monsoon*, with another 250 to come later.

Brett Whiteley (1939–92) remained a controversial figure throughout his relatively brief life, partly because—unusual for an Australian artist—he dealt with sex frankly and enthusiastically in his paintings and partly for less artistic reasons such as the chaos of his personal life. His talent was recognized as early as the age of 17 and he quickly sold works overseas. Whiteley said of himself, "It's strange how an addictive personality like myself, born with a gift,

Artist Brett Whiteley. Photo by Graham McCarter.

has this compulsion to test the gift, challenge it, push it to the edge, almost self-murder it, to see if it is still there and you are in control."[10] Whiteley is probably the first Australian painter to deal with women in an uninhibitedly sensual and even erotic style, unless one includes Norman Lindsay. He is often regarded very much as a Sydney painter—spontaneous, effervescent—whereas Williams is the embodiment of the serious, methodical Melbourne school. Similar comparisons between the two cities are frequently and dubiously drawn.

Almost as rare in Australian painting is a consciously religious bent such as that of Leonard French (1928–) who concentrated especially on murals, done in a heavily elaborate, ornate style. The religious symbolism is often quite explicit, and at times he seems to follow almost medieval conventions of humility and worship.

Among contemporary painters, one of the most outstanding is Rick Amor (1948–). After many years of painting, as well as doing drawings and prints, Amor has only fairly recently acquired his considerable reputation, perhaps because throughout his career he has stuck firmly to the figurative tradition defined in the Antipodean Manifesto, though extending it in many ways. In 2000 he was appointed the official war artist in East Timor. Amor is fascinated by the landscapes and buildings of the Melbourne in which he was born, but it is a city viewed in a darkly suggestive manner. As one critic put it, "heavy grey buildings, narrow laneways, a sickly yellow light, oppressive statues, emasculated trees, a furtive figure slinking in shadows . . . the city as ruin."[11] Something of the nature of his art can be suggested by the title of the only full-length work so far devoted to him—the solitary watcher.

Aboriginal Art

In recent times, the market for contemporary art has grown considerably, aided by the rise of independent art galleries from 1956 onward, clustered especially in the capital cities. Corporate art collections, such as that of the Reserve Bank of Australia or those held by large private companies like Orica, BHP, and Elders have assisted the growth and commodification of pictorial art in Australia, as has the proliferation of prizes and competitions, such as the Helena Rubinstein Prize, and the growth of state arts ministries and agencies. Universities have established schools of fine arts and newspapers devote increasing space to the arts. During the 1980s there were further public purchases of contemporary art as new buildings such as the new Parliament House, Canberra, were opened. For the first time, politicians began to speak of an "arts industry" and of art as an encouragement to tourism, and galleries began to export artistic works. These developments were paralleled by similar ones in the other arts. To justify themselves to political parties the arts had to be shown to have economic and cultural benefits.

Among the artists who have benefited most from this are the hitherto neglected Aboriginal painters, whose work, with only one exception, was lost on white Australians until very recently. Ironically an unknown critic, A. Carrol, wrote a series of articles in *The Centennial Magazine* as long ago as 1888 on the aesthetic value of Aboriginal art and its use of myth. The exception is Albert Namatjira (1902–59), whose Aboriginal paintings of the Australian outback became exceptionally popular in the 1950s and 1960s and fetched quite solid prices. So recognized did Namatjira become that the government granted him and his wife honorary citizenship, 10 years before the rest of the

Aboriginal population, which exempted him from its general ban on Aborigines buying alcohol. Unfortunately, however, when Namatjira, in observance of his people's customs, allegedly bought alcohol and gave some to his friends, he was jailed anyway and died the following year.

More recently, however, a large and prosperous market has developed for Aboriginal paintings. Ironically, this led to a decline in the popularity of Namatjira, who was seen to have too much in common with white traditions in painting, though there are signs recently that his reputation is on the rise again. Johnny Warangkula Tjupurrula painted his *Water Dreaming at Kalipinypa* in 1972 and sold it for A$150 (about US$112)—"to get tucker" [food], as he said. Shortly before his death it was sold by Sotheby's auction house in Melbourne for A$486,500 (about US$365,000). Told of this, the artist was said to have shouted from the halls of his nursing home, "I'm very famous, I'm very famous. I'm number one, number one big-time artist." He is far from being the only one. However, the market has become sullied by accusations of indigenous painters, in an ironic echo of Renaissance practice, farming out work to be done by underlings and themselves signing it, and at least one case of a white artist masquerading as an Aborigine painter.

After the pioneering Albert Namatjira, the most famous Aboriginal artists are probably Kumuntjayi Possum Tjapaltjarri, Emily Karm Kngwarreye, Ginger Riley Munduwalawala, and Rover Thomas. After Possum's death in 2002, only Billy Stockman Tjapaltjarri is left from the original Papunya Tula group of artists. A painting of Tjapaltjarri was sold to the Art Gallery of South Australia in 2001 for A$141,175 (about US$105,000). The artist's agent has claimed that he was offered almost A$2 million (about US$1,500,000) for another of Kumuntjayi Tjapaltjarri's paintings, the huge 1977 *Warlugulong,* which contains thirteen stories or "dreamings" running through it, but refused to allow the painting to leave the country. It is one of three such works that the artist painted.

Ginger Riley Munduwalawala (1937?–2002) was considered one of the best artists to emerge during the boom in Aboriginal art, though he had already been painting for many years. Influenced by Namatjira, he employed strong light and color and figurative art naif images in his many works that celebrated New Territory landscapes.

One of the best known of the younger Aboriginal artists is Judy Watson. She won the prestigious Moet & Chandon fellowship in 1995 and her works were shown at the 1997 Venice Biennial with those of fellow Aboriginal artists Yvonne Koolmatrie and Emily Kame Kngwarreye, who died in 1999. A descendant of the Waanyi people, Watson has traveled widely around Australia as well as abroad. She reuses imagery from her mother's homeland and other regions, but has also been inspired by artists as diverse as French-

American abstract sculptor, Louise Bourgeois, and Brisbane-based Aborigine, Gordon Bennett, who is noted for his confronting political art.

Watson's works on canvas are distinctive for their fluid stains and washes, a legacy from her training as a printmaker, which led her to experiment by layering pigments on canvas. Over the past few years she has received commissions for three major public artworks. The first was Sydney's Casula Powerhouse. In 2000 she had back-to-back openings of the Walama forecourt at Sydney's International Airport, and Wurreka, a large wall with zinc panels depicting Victorian Aboriginal culture at Melbourne Museum's new Bunjilaka Aboriginal Center.

An even bigger star is photographer Tracey Moffatt, who is now based in New York, while Perth-born Aboriginal painter Julie Dowling was nominated Australia's Most Collectable Artist for 2002, by 50 of Australia's top art critics, historians, academics, collectors, and advisers. Dowling paints mostly family portraits that tell the story of Australia's colonial past and what it did to four generations of her family, beginning with Melbin, her maternal great-great-grandmother, who was paraded pregnant through polite English society like a colonial trophy by her white husband.

Another Aboriginal painter of interest is Wenten Rubuntja. Born around 1928 at Burt Creek, north of Alice Springs, Rubuntja has been a tireless worker all his life for reconciliation between Aboriginal and white Australians and for the protection of sacred sites. He is also a painter of distinction, whose work rarely filters down south but is represented in the collections of the Pope, the Queen of England, and former prime ministers Malcolm Fraser, Bob Hawke, and Paul Keating. Albert Namatjira was his father's cousin and provided the inspiration for his long artistic career. Rubuntja says of his water color landscapes, "The landscape painting is the country itself, with *Tywerrenge* [sacred things, or Law] himself. That original Dreaming, he came up from the body of the landscape."[12]

Notes

1. Robert Hughes, *The Art of Australia* (Melbourne: Penguin, 1986; first published 1966), p. 31.
2. Hughes, *The Art of Australia,* p. 35.
3. Hughes, *The Art of Australia,* p. 51.
4. Bernard Smith, *Place, Taste and Tradition: A Study of Australian Art Since 1788* (Melbourne: Oxford University Press, 1979), p. 26.
5. Bernard Smith, *Australian Painting* (Melbourne: Oxford University Press, 2001), p. 322.
6. Hughes, *The Art of Australia,* p. 266.

7. Hughes, *The Art of Australia,* p. 92.

8. In Sandra McGrath, "Jeffrey Smart," *Art International,* January–February 1977, p. 17.

9. Charles Blackman, quoted in Geoff Maslen, "Blackman's Wonderland," *The Age,* 15 March 2002.

10. Janet Hawley, *Encounters with Australian Artists* (St. Lucia: University of Queensland Press, 1993), p. 37.

11. Bernard Smith, with Terry Smith and Christopher Heathcote, *Australian Painting: 1788–2000* (Melbourne: Oxford University Press, 2001), p. 585.

12. Quoted in Carol Ruff, "I Sing for My Land," *The Weekend Australian Magazine,* 27–28 April 2002, p. 35.

10

Architecture

Australia's first major architect was Francis Greenway, who was transported from England for forgery in 1814. The timing was fortunate in that Governor Lachlan Macquarie was anxious to expand the city of Sydney and was looking for architectural talent. After Greenway completed his first commission, the lighthouse on South Head, Sydney Harbour, he was emancipated (freed) and went on to design several noteworthy buildings such as the Female Factory at Paramatta, the new Government House, the Supreme Court in Sydney, and several impressive churches. After falling out with Macquarie, Greenway was dismissed as official government architect in 1822. He was ultimately commemorated as a successful emancipist story when his portrait appeared on the first $10 note when decimal coinage was introduced.

The Edifice Complex

Until recently at least, notable architects were not prominent in Australia and the history of Australia's major buildings is often troubled. For instance, work began on the Sydney Harbour Bridge, Sydney's most famous icon (at least until recently), in 1923. It was designed by John J.C. Bradfield, who has been described as a genius. It took eight years and 1,400 workers to build the world's largest steel-arch bridge. After it was completed, New South Wales Premier J.T. Lang refused to have a member of the British royal family open it. On March 19, 1932, he himself was about to perform the ceremony when Captain de Groot, member of the right-wing New Guard, spectacularly rode up on a horse and slashed the ribbon.

Sydney Opera House. Photo by Luna Shepherd.

The Sydney bridge is still one of the most famous landmarks in the world, but more recently has been rivaled by the Sydney Opera House. In 1957, a Dutch architect, Joern Utzon, won the international design competition, which had been funded by a controversial lottery, with a magnificent vision of sails billowing out over the harbor at Bennelong Point. The original idea for the Opera House was that of Sir Eugene Goossens, who was then director of the Sydney Symphony Orchestra, and the competition attracted 233 entries from 32 countries.

The project, however, was dogged by controversy and the small-mindedness of bureaucrats and the state premier at the time, David Hughes, who, between them, ruined the interior. It was finally opened in 1973, by which time Utzon himself had long left the country in disgust.

Often it seemed as if the building might even abandoned, but in 1973, after 14 years in construction, the Sydney Opera House opened with a performance of Prokofiev's opera *War and Peace*. Utzon's bitterness finally ended, however. In 1992 the Royal Australian Institute of Architects bestowed on him a commemorative medal "with an apology," and in 1998 he was awarded Sydney's highest honor—the key to the city—at a ceremony held in a Majorcan café. When plans for developing design guidelines for the next 25 years were announced in 2000, Utzon accepted an invitation to assist Sydney architect Richard Johnson. Too old to leave his native country, he has worked with

Victorian Arts Centre, home of the performing arts in Melbourne. Photo by Anna Clemann.

his son, Jan, to articulate the overall vision and detailed design for the site, the form of the building, and its controversial interior. Politicians seek to commemorate themselves by ordering the construction of imposing buildings —what critics have derisively dubbed "the edifice complex"—but then cannot refrain from interfering with the architect's vision.

One of Melbourne's first major designs, the Shrine of Melbourne (architects P. B. Hudson and J. H. Wardrop) ran into no such trouble; by the nature of its subject it was beyond reproof. However, Victoria's next major project, the Victorian Arts Centre, overlooking the banks of the Yarra river, paled into insignificance beside the Opera House but also had more than its share of problems. Its cost soared to $200 million—twice that of the Opera House

Flinders Street Station, completed in 1910, is the best-known railway station in Australia and one of Melbourne's most recognizable landmarks. Photo by Alice Macklin.

and more than four times the original estimate of A$45 million (US$337 million). More recently cracks were discovered in the spire that dominates it, and it became obvious that the structure would have to be replaced. In 1997 the repaired spire was unveiled, almost 162 feet taller and illuminated by 14,000 incandescent lamps.

Australia's most recent major public architectural project, Melbourne's Federation Square, ran into the same kind of controversy that dogged so many of Australia's biggest plans. It was not completed until nearly two years after the centenary of federation, suffered bureaucratic intervention, and came in at around four times the original (admittedly absurdly low) estimate. However, some architects have argued that the strong public debate, which was part of the reason for the delay resulted in a better, more democratic building. Many of those who were initially hostile to the building with its odd shapes (nothing could be less "square") and crazily colored cobblestones, propped on a concrete and steel deck over 12 railway lines, have become reconciled to it or even proud of it.

In general, and with the exception of Federation Square, Victorian architecture is more traditional and conservative that that of New South Wales. The Royal Exhibition Building in the inner Melbourne suburb of Carlton,

Melbourne's Royal Exhibition buildings. Photo by Anna Clemann.

for instance, stands as one of the great reminders of the prosperous and confident days of Marvelous Melbourne. Built for the international exhibition of 1880, it is one of very few such great exhibition halls left. In 2002 it was nominated to be placed on the World Heritage Register, the only Australian building so far to achieve that honor.

It was designed by Joseph Reed, a prominent Cornish-born Melbourne architect whose other public buildings include the Public Library and the Town Hall in the provincial Victorian city of Geelong; the former Bank of New South Wales building in Collins Street, Melbourne; the former Independent Church, also in Collins Street; and some of Melbourne's oldest and most famous buildings, such as the Menzies Hotel and the original Wilson Hall at Melbourne University, which subsequently burned down. After becoming the University's official architect Reed was responsible, in fact, for most of its nineteenth-century buildings.

Selected ahead of 17 other proposals, the Royal Exhibition Building is a consciously formal and imposing structure, an unabashedly eclectic building in the way it draws on Victorian models, such as the entrance portals that recall the London Exhibition pavilion of 1862, the radial fan lights over the four arched entrances drawn from London's Crystal Palace of 1851, and the mixture of classic and local themes adorning the cornice panels. Its huge dome, with its gilded lantern and fenestrated drum, was based on

Brunelleschi's *Duomo* in Florence. The building has recently been restored to its original appearance after many years of neglect.

The National Capital

The selection of Canberra as the new federal capital provided a series of challenges and opportunities for architects and designers. After Victoria and New South Wales could not agree on where Parliament House should be sited, a compromise was made in 1908 whereby a new national capital was laid out between the two largest cities—though the Constitution ordained that the capital must be within New South Wales and not less than 100 miles from Sydney. The foundation stone was laid at Capital Hill and the capital christened Canberra, an Aboriginal term meaning "meeting place." Federal Parliament moved from Melbourne in 1927, and by 1938 the city had a population of 9,000—plus two million flowers and shrubs.

In 1912 an American architect, Walter Burley Griffin, had won the international competition for the design of the national capital from a field of 72 entries but as later with Joern Utzon, his plans were fatally compromised. He finally resigned in 1921 but what he called "the Plan" was at least in part saved, perhaps by his very departure. The manmade lake named after him, for instance, was finally built. Griffin and his lesser-known wife, Marion Lucy Mahony, were pioneer advocates of environmental architecture. Among other Griffin buildings are Newman College, Melbourne, and Castlecrag on Sydney's Middle Harbour.

Though Canberra languished throughout the 1940s and early 1950s, it began to prosper under Robert Menzies and the British planner, Sir William Holford. With the construction of new buildings such as the Australian National University (1949) and the Russell Hill defense complex (1958), as well as the more or less forced movement of many public servants to the city, it began to assume a recognizable identity.

An architectural competition failed to produce a satisfactory design for the proposed Australian War Memorial in Canberra, but two of the entrants—Sydney architects Emil Sodersteen and John Crust—were invited to submit a joint design incorporating Sodersteen's vision for the building and Crust's concept of cloisters to house the Roll of Honor. The design was eventually accepted and the building was completed in 1941.

The filling of Griffin Lake and the construction of additional major buildings—the National Library (1968), High Court (1980), and the National Gallery (1982) reached its climax in the new and massively expensive Parliament House on Capital Hill in 1988. Disastrous bushfires at the beginning of 2003 encroached upon the city and destroyed many homes, but residents have expressed the belief and hope that out of the tragedy will come a stronger sense of communal identity for the city.

The Suburban Dream

In contrast to the great dreams of commemorative buildings are the habits of ordinary Australians. Australia is one of the most urbanized countries in the world and this is reflected in its architecture. Throughout the last century there was a constant pattern of movement toward the capital cities and away from the country. In 1911, 43 percent of the population lived in country areas. By 1996, this had fallen to about 13 percent and the sense country people had that their interests were no longer looked after, that they were the

Architecture in the central business district of Melbourne. Photo by Michael Hanrahan.

neglected Australians, manifested itself in shock election results and a bitter turning against what were seen as city-oriented governments.

With few natural obstacles to stop them and with the dream of a house and a quarter-acre block driving them, the capital cities steadily expanded with mile after mile of suburbs. Architect Robin Boyd, the author of books like *Australia's Home* (1952) and *The Australian Ugliness* (1960) (a phrase that has passed into the language), was one of the first and most trenchant of its critics. "Australia is the small house," he said, castigating the quarter-acre block as an aesthetic calamity and material triumph. His views were echoed by many others but did not impinge upon ordinary Australian couples, who continued their love affair with the quarter-acre block, at least until recently. It was Robin Boyd who famously coined the term "Austerica" to signify the slavish adoption by Australians of American styles and fashions of architecture. Its use was sometimes expanded to other areas of life, such as foreign policy, where intellectuals felt there was a similar subservience. Fashionable in the 1950s, it has been less often used since then.

Other architects and social commentators, on the other hand, have defended the suburban house on the basis of its adaptability and affordability (at least until recently) and the range of activities it affords families, such as gardening, pets, treehouses, and even a swimming pool and a barbecue if the owner wants and can afford them.

The houses were relatively cheap and easy to build. Developers could put them up without having recourse to architects. It is estimated that less than 6 percent of Australia's housing stock is architect-designed. Any aesthetic deficiencies could be more than made up for by Australians' passionate love affair with their gardens.

In recent years the ideological tide has turned to some extent in favor of the notion that homes can be mass-produced and affordably priced, yet still exhibit architectural merit. When Gabriel Poole was awarded the Royal Australian Institute of Architects' Gold Medal, the local industry's highest accolade, a few years ago, he made a passionate speech criticizing his own profession and its concentration on a small elite as against the vast majority of aspiring homeowners. "As architects, I consider we have really failed our masters, the population of what could be this great country," he said. "We have as a profession neglected what I see as the most important aspect of our purpose to house the people."[1] Poole at that stage was involved in a project called Capricorn 151, from which he eventually withdrew in disillusion. The houses were designed to compete with the great majority of project houses but contained a number of Poole's characteristic signature traits: walls punctuated with tall, slim, vertical vents to catch passing breezes and improve inflow, thus virtually eliminating the need for powered cooling systems, and rooms designed as broad breezeways, their exterior all but disappearing when retracted. More recently he has become involved with Small House Series, basic designs with innumerable variations that could be easily applied by small-scale builders. Clients can purchase plans only or decide to have the structural elements of their chosen design delivered in kit form.

Throughout the late 1970s into most of the 1990s, most mass-market housing was undertaken by huge developers who were more responsive to the commercial influence of mass producers of building materials than they were to architect designs. Houses were often inefficiently built and had an awful sameness about them. But others involved in the trade, such as NSW government architect Chris Johnson, are determined both to attract architects into the building procedures and keep the price down. Johnson's idea is to take the concepts of architect-designed housing and apply them to an affordable and efficient production-line system marketed via the Internet. He rejects the idea of elevating architects as supreme artists: "There is a role for that, but my belief is that if you're asking how you can nurture and look after the built environment, then you can't have individual people sculpting every bit of every building.... Architects need to get down off that high horse of wanting sculptural control of the object as a one-off and get more involved in building systems."[2]

Kerstin Thompson of Kerstin Thompson Architects is another who sees architecture in a holistic kind of way. Her company has been working with a developer trying to bridge mass-produced housing and the ideals of contemporary architecture, this time within middle-class suburbs. Thompson says, "Architecture isn't just about visual things... It's about understanding how even the smallest building is part of a much larger system of relationships, including a landscape."[3]

Similarly Peter Elliott, who redesigned RMIT (Royal Melbourne Institute of Technology) University's central Melbourne campus, does not design huge buildings or huge commercial projects but instead concentrates on what one architecture professor called "urban fragments." In the words of another commentator, "He is the architect of small things."[4] So successful has Elliott been that in 1987 he was awarded the Order of Australia and his changes and designs are all over the city—in the new Spencer Street footbridge across the Yarra River linking the World Trade Center and the Exhibition Center; redesigning the Carlton Baths; reshaping some of the public spaces around the Arts Center; designing the Observatory Gate, and next working on Melbourne's Collins Street as it is extended into the Docklands on the western side of the city. Elliott describes his work as a shift from twentieth-century architecture's obsession with the heroic new building to a concern with the total built environment.

There is, however, a good deal of argument about how "green" one can make a building, or even of what constitutes "greenness." What is most important—being recyclable, passive comfort through cross-ventilation, or economy of energy? Glenn Murcutt, the winner of world architecture's highest honor in 2002, the Pritzker prize, goes so far as to question the concept of green architecture in general. "Building is one of the most un-green things you can do," he says. He adds, "It's no good building an ugly box and making it perform ecologically—we need to design appropriately to the unique climatic conditions that each place requires."[5]

Some of the most interesting houses, like Victorian terraces, are found in the inner suburban areas, but until fairly recently these tended to be rundown; they were often occupied by newly arrived migrants. In the last quarter of the twentieth century, especially, middle-class couples moved back into the inner suburbs and renovated the houses while the newly prosperous migrants moved out into more distant and expansive suburbs and grabbed their share of the Australian dream. The prices of inner-city houses skyrocketed to an astonishing extent.

In this and other ways, the pattern over the last generation or so has changed considerably. An aging population, the tendency to have smaller or no families among professional people especially, the collapse of the nuclear family, and the realization of the huge costs of both transport and infrastructure have led to increasingly dense building patterns in the inner suburbs, with flats (apartments) and townhouses proliferating. Warehouses have been redesigned as modish apartment buildings.

As well as the rise in high-density housing, an important related trend has been the residential movement back to the major cities themselves. In the 1950s cities were places to work and shop in before you went home to the suburbs; and after five o'clock cities became deserted. This was especially the case during the period of six o'clock closing of hotels, introduced during World War I as an emergency measure but not repealed until many years later. Of course, the cities had theaters, cinemas, and restaurants as well, but almost no actual residents. In recent years a great many townhouses have sprung up, often with a view of the central river, and ideal for retired couples or childless professionals.

Occasionally a beautiful architect-designed house will be built. Austrian-born Harry Seidler's Rose Seidler House in Turramurra, Sydney (1948), for instance, is a masterpiece of European modernism, but mostly architects have to confine their work to public buildings. Seidler arrived in Australia in 1948, at the age of 25, having studied under Walter Gropius and Marcel Breuer at Harvard University, and immediately began a revolution in Australian architecture. The first house he built—at Wahroonga in Sydney for his mother—won the prestigious Sulman Award in 1951 and attracted so much interest from the general public that his mother could hardly step outside for the four-deep crowds peering in through the windows. His modernist designs invariably ran into trouble from local councils who would refuse him, for instance, the right to build a house with the roof sloping inward. He once commented to his friend, the photographer Max Dupain, "In those days, modern architecture was illegal!" But he was quite disarmed by the readiness with which ordinary clients embraced his radical designs and demanded something similar. It would never have happened in New York, he insisted, where even Breuer had trouble finding clients.

Plants and Gardens

At the time of Federation, each colony had internationally renowned botanic gardens, which acted as both great scientific institutions and hearts for the cities. When ideas for the new national capital were called for, one architectural expert aroused comment when he suggested that the nation's headquarters be a garden city.

In 1903 Burnley College made the controversial decision to accept female students in the yearlong course in landscaping for the first time. The women who graduated from Burnley during that time were the first in a line of women who have been a strong force in Australian landscape gardening, design, and architecture. Edna Walling was gardening editor of *Australian Home Beautiful* magazine in the 1930s and 1940s, and another graduate, Emily Gibson, returned to the college after study in the UK to teach and inspire a generation of people to study landscape architecture.

But it was not until after World War II that native plants began to be widely used in exterior design. The nation's first significant native landscaped park was Bruce McKenzie's Peacock Point on Sydney Harbour, created in 1969. Now the use of native landscaping is the norm, rather than the exception, though Japanese tourists are said to be confused by signs outside nurseries that say "Natives for sale."

Contemporary Architecture

A related development is the rise of landscape architecture, the profession concerned with integrating buildings and the landscape. For instance, the acclaimed Archery Park at Homebush Bay is a balance of art, environment, and utility, with complex channels and ponds to recycle water, a forest of telegraph poles, and thick native grasses illustrating the land.

Something of the range and innovative thinking going on in contemporary architecture can be gathered from the winners of the annual Royal Australian Institute of Architects' National Architecture awards. The Walter Burley Griffin Award for Urban Design was won by a group of five students for their Mine of Lode Memorial, Broken Hill. The project is a memorial and visitor center commemorating the many hundreds of miners, some of them only youths, who died while working on Australia's best-known mining town in the heart of the desert in western New South Wales. One of the judges, Dimity Reed, said of the Memorial: "An extraordinary metaphysical relationship between it and the town and people seems tangibly in the air. It has established a relationship with the town akin to that of Sydney with its Opera House."[6] The Robin Boyd Award for Residential Buildings was won by Donovan Hill Architects for D House in Brisbane. Delivered within the tiny budget of $160,000, the house is a masterpiece of subtle planning. "The spaces are so carefully crafted," writes Reed, "that each one merges into the next in a beautiful solution to the challenges that face our cities of getting people to live closer together." But she adds that the battles with bureaucracy are still far from over: the house took two years to struggle through the planning permit stage because it was not imitating an old Queensland house. Other winners were Melbourne's Museum and the Karijini National Park Visitors Centre in the northern part of Western Australia.

Some critics have argued that modernism, under the influence of its original founders in Mies van der Rohe, Le Corbusier, and Marcel Breuer, has made a vigorous return to Australian architecture. The reason, they argue, lies in the greater value Australians place in their home as a form of self-expression; homes are becoming the vehicle of personal expression that clothes and cars have long been. Moreover, the return to relatively confined urban living, rather than the Hills Hoist and quarter-acre block dream of another generation, places more emphasis on careful and imaginative design for confined living spaces.

Some demographers and planners, in fact, argue that the quarter-acre blocks in the suburbs are in danger of becoming white elephants as aging couples move toward both smaller houses and families as well as toward the coast. Of the 15 top-growing towns and cities, 14 are on the coast. Queensland's Gold Coast area is now the seventh largest city in Australia and is likely to overtake Newcastle in New South Wales before too much longer. Yet at the same time, Australians continue to expand their houses as an alternative to selling and buying something bigger. In 1985–86 the average size of a new house was 176 square meters. Five years later this had grown to 2,475 square feet.

Glenn Murcutt's architecture is born entirely of late twentieth-century technology, with its modernist roots in the innovative steel and glass architecture of Ludwig Mies van der Rohe, the finely crafted brick, timber, glass, and concrete work of Finnish architect, Alvar Aalto, and the old iron Australian shearing shed.

One of the Pritzker jurors, the revered Ada Louise Huxtable, said: "Glenn Murcutt has become a living legend, an architect totally focused on shelter and the environment, with skills drawn from nature and the most sophisticated design traditions of the modern movement."[7] Jury chairman, J. Carter Brown observed, "He is an innovative architectural technician who is capable of turning his sensitivity to the environment and to locality into forthright, totally honest, non-showy works of art."[8] Implicit in this, perhaps, is a muted criticism of the so-called celebrity architects (derisively dubbed the "starchitects")—those who create not just art but marketability and money for developers.

Murcutt has designed dozens of relatively small-scale houses, museums, and education and interpretive centers through all Australian climate zones. One of his most internationally celebrated recent projects is the Arthur and Yvonne Boyd Education Centre at Riversdale (1996–99) near Nowra, on the NSW south coast, which he designed in conjunction with architects Wendy Lewin (his wife) and Reg Lark. In 2000 the Riversdale project won the Royal Australian Institute of Architects' top national award, the Sir Zelman Cowen Award for Public Buildings.

Among his many award-winning houses are the dramatically placed Magney House (1982–84) at Bingie Bingie, on the NSW south coast, and the low, long Marie Short Farmhouse (1974–75) at Kempsey on the NSW north coast. The nearby Museum of Local History and tourist office (1981–82) at Kempsey is another of his highly regarded public buildings. Notable inner-city houses include the Magney House (1986–90) in Paddington, Sydney, while at the other end of the scale there is Marika-Alterton House (1991–94) in the Yirrkala Community at Gove, Northern Territory. A landmark work of remote community architecture, it was constructed in parts in Sydney and shipped to Arnhem Land to be fitted together onsite.

Murcutt's credo is that houses should "touch the earth lightly" and disturb the fragile environment minimally. He seeks materials that consume as little energy as possible in manufacture and operation, and designs that respond passively but efficiently to all manner of climatic conditions. Deep shading, metal and glass louvres, fully opening walls, controlled sunlight and air movement, and carefully devised ventilation are all basic strategies. Corrugated iron, steel, timber framing and timber internal cladding, and occasionally off-form concrete are significant elements in his work.

Norwegian national and Queensland resident, Brit Andresen, on the other hand, designs what have been called timber "temples of breezes," airy, climate-responsive designs like Rosebury House in Highgate Hill, Brisbane, which earned her the Royal Australian Institute of Architects Gold Medallion for 2002. She is the first woman to win Australia's most distinguished architectural award. The citation mentions the "exquisite architectural projects of high quality" that she designed in collaboration with her husband Peter O'Gorman, who died just before the award was announced. Andresen was also honored for her skilful use of natural surroundings and attention to light and shade, moonlight and darkness. One of her admirers, Michael Keniger, has noted of her, "She's extremely disciplined, extremely principled. With the intellectual discipline is a sensibility for the sensuality of place."[9] After Joern Utzon, Andresen, who remains a Norwegian national though she has lived in Australia for 25 years, is the second architect from that country to make a major contribution to Australian architecture.

There is at least an implicit awareness in designs like these of the importance of adapting to the environment and in particular attempting to cut greenhouse emissions. The Australian Greenhouse Office, described as "the world's first government agency dedicated to cutting greenhouse gas emissions," has done much to encourage the concept of the "green house" or "house with no bills," a sustainable, energy-efficient house that goes as far as possible to being an energy-neutral house.

Notes

1. Gabriel Poole, quoted in an interview with Julia Richardson, *The Weekend Australian Magazine,* 29–30 September 2001.
2. Chris Johnson, Ibid.
3. Kerstin Thompson, quoted in an interview with Helen Elliott, *The Weekend Australian,* 24–25 November 2001.
4. James Button, "The Architect of Small Things," *The Age,* 16 November 2001.
5. Luke Slattery, "How Green Is Our Building," *The Australian,* 13 December 2002.
6. Dimity Reed, "Architects Add to Our Heritage with a Modern Vision Splendid," *The Age,* 17 November 2001.
7. Quoted in Peter Wilmoth, "The Tin Man," *The Sunday Age,* 12 May 2002.
8. Ibid.
9. Michael Keniger, quoted in Anna King Murdoch, "Light Discipline," *The Age,* 22 June 2002.

Bibliography

Alexander, Stephanie. *The Cook's Companion.* Melbourne: Penguin Books, 1996.

Allen, Traudi. *Cross-Currents in Contemporary Australian Art.* St. Leonards: Craftsman House, 2001.

d'Alpuget, Blanche. *Mediator. A Biography of Sir Richard Kirby.* Melbourne: Melbourne University Press, 1977.

Anderson, Warwick. *The Cultivation of Whiteness: Science, Health and Racial Destiny in Australia.* Carlton; Melbourne: Melbourne University Press, 2002.

Arrow, Michelle. *Upstaged: Australian Women Dramatists in the Limelight at Last.* Sydney: Currency Press, 2003.

Baume, Michelle. *The Sydney Opera House Affair.* Melbourne: Nelson, 1967.

Bennett, Tony, and David Carter, eds., *Culture in Australia. Policies, Publics and Programs.* Melbourne: Cambridge University Press, 2001.

Blainey, Geoffrey. *A Game of Our Own.* Melbourne: Information, 1990.

———. *The Great Seesaw.* Basingstoke: Macmillan, 1988.

———. *A Shorter History of Australia.* Melborne: William Heinemann, 1994.

Brisbane, Katharine, ed. *Entertaining Australia.* Sydney: Currency Press, 1991.

Bunning, Walter, *Homes in the Sun.* Sydney: W. J. Nesbit, 1945.

Burn, Ian. *National Life & Landscapes: Australian Painting 1900–1940.* Sydney: Bay Books, 1990.

Carey, Gabrielle, and Kathy Lette. *Puberty Blues.* Melbourne: McPhee Gribble, 1979.

Carter, Paul. *The Road to Botany Bay: An Exploration of Landscape History and an Essay in Spatial History.* London: Faber & Faber; New York: Knopf, 1988.

Cashman, Richard. *A Paradise of Sport: The Rise of Organised Sport in Australia.* Melbourne, Oxford University Press, 1995.

Cathcart, Michael, ed. *Manning Clarke's History of Australia.* Melbourne: Melbourne University Press, 1997.

Cherikoff, Vic. *Uniquely Australian: The Beginnings of an Australian Bushfood Cuisine—The Bushfood Handbook.* Boronia Park, Australia: Bush Tucker Supply Australia, 1992.

Clancy, Laurie. *A Reader's Guide to Australian Fiction.* Melbourne: Oxford University Press, 1992.

Collins, Diane. *Hollywood Down Under.* North Hyde, Australia: Angus & Robertson, 1987.

Collis, Brad. *Fields of Discovery: Australia's CSIRO.* Sydney: Allen & Unwin, 2002.

Cox, Leonard B. *The National Gallery of Victoria 1861 to 1968: A Search for a Collection.* Melbourne: National Gallery of Australia, 1971.

Crowley, F. K., ed. *A New History of Australia.* Melbourne: Heinemann Press, 1974.

Davidson, Jim, and Peter Spearritt. *Holiday Business: Tourism in Australia Since 1870.* Melbourne: Miegunyah Press at Melbourne University Press, 2000.

Davison, Graeme, John Hirst, and Stuart McIntyre, eds. *The Oxford Companion to Australian History.* Melbourne: Oxford University Press, 1998.

Dixson, Miriam. *The Imaginary Australian.* Sydney: University of New South Wales Press, 1999.

———. *The Real Matilda.* Melbourne: Penguin, 1984.

Dobson, Rosemary. *Selected Poems,* Sydney: Angus & Robertson, 1980

Docker, John. *In a Critical Condition.* Melbourne: Penguin, 1984.

Dutton, Geoffrey. *The Innovators.* Melbourne: Macmillan, 1986.

———. *White on Black.* South Melbourne: Macmillan of Australia, in association with the Art Gallery Board of South Australia, 1974.

Eagle, Mary. *Australian Modern Painting Between the Wars 1914–1939.* Sydney: Bay Books, 1990.

Ebury, Sue. *Weary. A Life of Sir Edward Dunlop.* Melbourne: Penguin, 2001.

Eldershaw, M. Barnard. *Phillip of Australia: An Account of the Settlement at Sydney Cove.* London: George C. Harrap, 1938. Reprint, Sydney: Angus and Robertson, 1972.

Fitzgerald, Ross, and Mark Hearn. *Bligh, Macarthur and the Rum Rebellion.* Sydney: Kangaroo Press, 1988.

Flannery, Tim. *The Future Eaters.* Melbourne: Reed Books, 1997.

Fletcher, Marian. *Costume in Australia 1788–1901,* Melbourne: Oxford University Press, 1984.

Flower, Cedric. *Clothes in Australia: A Pictorial History 1788–1980s.* Kenthurst, New South Wales: Kangaroo Press, 1984.

Galbally, Ann. *Charles Conder: The Last Bohemian.* Melbourne: Melbourne University Press, 2002.

Gerster, Robin. *Big-Noting: The Heroic Theme in Australian War Writing.* Melbourne: Melbourne University Press, 1987.

Gollan, Anne. *The Tradition of Australian Cooking.* Canberra: A.N.U. Press, 1978.

Griffiths, Tom. *Forests of Ash: An Environmental History.* Melbourne: Cambridge University Press, 2002.

Grimshaw, Patricia, Marilyn Lake, Ann McGrath, and Marian Quartly. *Creating a Nation.* Melbourne: McPhee Gribble, 1994.

Haese, Richard. *Rebels and Precursors: The Revolutionary Years of Australian Art.* Melbourne: Penguin, 1981.

Hart, Kevin. *A. D. Hope.* Melbourne: Oxford University Press, 1992.

Hawley, Janet. *Encounters with Australian Artists.* St. Lucia, Australia: University of Queensland Press, 1993.

Heathcote, Christopher. *A Quiet Revolution. The Rise of Australian Art 1946–68.* Melbourne: Text Publishing, 1995.

Hope, A. D. *Judith Wright.* Melbourne: Oxford University Press, 1975.

Hughes, Robert. *The Art of Australia.* Melbourne: Penguin, 1986.

———. *The Fatal Shore.* New York: Knopf; distributed by Random House, 1987.

———. *The Shock of the New: Art and the Century of Change.* London: British Broadcasting Corporation, 1980.

Irving, Helen. *To Constitute a Nation: A Cultural History of Australia's Constitution.* Cambridge: Cambridge University Press, 1997.

Joel, Alexandra. *Parade: Two Hundred Years of Fashion in Australia.* Sydney: Collins, 1984.

Lafitte, Gabriel, and Alison Ribush. *Happiness in a Material World.* Melbourne: Lothian Press, 2002.

Lake, Marilyn, and Farley Kelly. *Double Time: Women in Victoria—150 Years.* Melbourne: Penguin, 1985.

Langton, Marcia. *Burning Questions.* Darwin: Centre for Indigenous & Cultural Resource Management, Northern Territory University, 1998.

Marr, David. *Patrick White: A Life.* Sydney: Random House, 1991.

Martin, Richard, and Harold Koda. *Splash! A History of Swimwear.* New York: Rizzoli, 1990.

Matthews, Brian. *Louisa.* Melbourne: McPhee Gribble, 1987.

McFarlane, Brian. *Martin Boyd's Langton Novels.* Melbourne: Edward Arnold (Australia) Pty. Ltd, 1980.

McQueen, Humphrey. *Black Swan of Trespass: The Emergence of Modernist Painting in Australia to 1944.* Sydney: Alternative Publishing, 1979.

Mitchell, Susan. *Tall Poppies.* Melbourne: Penguin, 1994.

Murgatroyd, Sarah. *The Dig Tree: The Story of Burke and Wills.* Melbourne: Text Publishing, 2002.

Murray, Les. *The Peasant Mandarin: Prose Pieces.* St. Lucia: University of Queensland Press, 1978.

Neill, Rosemary. *White Out: How Politics Is Killing Black Australia.* Sydney: Allen & Unwin, 2002.

O'Farrell, Patrick. *Vanished Kingdoms.* Sydney: NSW University Press, 1990.

Partington, Geoffrey. *The Australian Nation: Its British and Irish Roots.* New Brunswick, N.J. and London: Transaction, 1997.

Pike, Andrew, and Ross Cooper. *Australian Film 1900–1977.* Melbourne: Oxford University Press, 1980.

Roe, Michael. *Nine Australian Progressives: Vitalism in Bourgeois Social Thought 1890–1960.* St. Lucia: University of Queensland Press, 1984.

Rowe, David, and Geoffrey Lawrence. *Tourism, Leisure, Sport: Critical Perspectives.* Melbourne: Cambridge University Press,1998.

Ryan, Peter. *Fear Drive My Feet.* Sydney: Duffy & Snellgrove, 2001.

Santich, Barbara. *What the Doctor Ordered.* Melbourne: Hyland House, 1995.

Sheridan, Susan. *Who Was that Woman? The Australian Women's Weekly in the Postwar Years.* Sydney: University of NSW Press, 2001.

Smith, Bernard. *Australian Painting, 1788–1960.* London: Oxford University Press, 1962.

———. *The Death of the Artist as Hero: Essays in History and Culture.* Melbourne: Oxford University Press, 1988.

———. *European Vision and the South Pacific.* Sydney: Harper & Row, 1985.

———. *Place, Taste and Tradition.* Melbourne: Oxford University Press, 1979.

Smith, Bernard, Terry Smith, and Christopher Heathcote. *Australian Painting.* 1788–2000. Melbourne: Oxford University Press, 2001.

Steele, Peter. *Peter Porter.* Melbourne: Oxford University Press, 1992.

Stephens, A. G. *Chris Brennan.* Sydney: The Bookfellow, 1933.

Strauss, Jennifer. *Judith Wright.* Melbourne: Oxford University Press, 1995.

Stretton, Hugh. *Ideas for Australian Cities.* Melbourne: Georgian House, 1970.

Summers, Anne. *Damned Whores and God's Police.* Melbourne: Penguin, 1975.

Symons, Michael. *One Continuous Picnic.* Adelaide, Australia: Duck Press, 1982.

Trigg, Stephanie. *Gwen Harwood.* Melbourne: Oxford University Press, 1994.

Turner, Ian, and Turner Sandercock. *Up Where Cazaly? The Great Australian Game.* London: Granada, 1981.

Walker, Robin, and Dave Roberts. *From Scarcity to Surfeit: A History of Diet and Nutrition in New South Wales.* Kensington, N.S.W.: NSWUP, 1988.

Ward, Russel. *Australia Since the Coming of Man.* Melbourne: Macmillan, 1987

———. *The Australian Legend.* Melbourne: Oxford University Press, 1958.

Waterhouse, Richard. *Private Pleasures, Public Leisure: A History of Australian Popular Culture Since 1788,* South Melbourne: Longman Australia, 1995.

White, Richard. *Inventing Australia. Images and identity 1688–1980.* Sydney: George Allen & Unwin, 1981.

Wilcox, Craig. *For Hearths and Homes: Citizen Soldiering in Australia, 1854–1945.* St. Leonards, N.S.W.: Allen & Unwin, 1998.

Wilkes, G.A. *R. D. Fitzgerald.* Melbourne: Oxford University Press, 1981.

Williams, John F. *The Quarantined Culture. Australian Reactions to Modernism, 1913–1939.* Melbourne: Cambridge University Press, 1995.

Windschuttle, Keith. *The Fabrication of Aboriginal History.* Paddington, N.S.W.: Macleay Press, 2002.

Index

About the Author

LAURIE CLANCY is an Australian novelist now teaching creative writing at the Royal Melbourne Institute of Technology, Melbourne, Victoria, Australia.